THE ROYAL JEWELS

THE ROYAL JEWELS

Suzy Menkes

REVISED EDITION

GUILD PUBLISHING LONDON

For my husband, David, whose support
while I have been writing this book
has been far above rubies

Published 1985 by
Book Club Associates
by arrangement with
Grafton Books
Reprinted 1986
Revised 1986

Photoset by Rowland Phototypesetting Ltd
Bury St Edmunds, Suffolk
Printed in Great Britain by
William Clowes Limited
Beccles and London

Contents

Preface

The inspiration for this book was the Princess of Wales. She appeared at a diplomatic banquet, the drop pearls on her tiara trembling above a sparkling choker; a duck egg sapphire on one shoulder; jewelled family orders studding her dress. The jewels spelt majesty. The people's Princess had suddenly developed a royal aura as tangible as that of the majestic Queen Mary and as charismatic as that of the Queen herself.

The jewels also looked familiar. I studied the history books. There was Queen Mary in the same bow knot tiara. Was that Queen Victoria's sapphire brooch on Princess Diana's shoulder? The necklace had been worn just one month before by the Queen.

From my researches – and no one has ever before looked so seriously at the royal jewel collection – I realised that the major pieces could be traced back for three, four, five generations. And that the different ways that the jewels were worn, and how the collection was added to and altered, revealed the character of successive sovereigns and consorts.

I started with Queen Victoria, because she built up a collection of jewels, just as her dissolute Hanoverian uncles had dispersed theirs. In a London museum I found a ledger kept by Garrard, the Crown Jewellers, for the 60-year span of Queen Victoria's reign. In it were the jewels – the Koh-i-noor, the diamond collet, the Indian regal tiara – that the royal family wears today, including the original cost, the weight of the individual stones and the style of the settings.

I could also see revealed in these crabby Victorian entries the character of Victoria herself: her sense of the majesty of monarchy; her pleasure in personalised family jewels; her passion for commemoration; the 'poisonous enchantment', as Elizabeth Longford described it, of mourning Prince Albert. The thrifty, sober Queen Victoria of legend took a sensuous pleasure in jewels and spent an enormous sum of money on them to form the basis of the present royal collection.

Queen Alexandra was a puzzle. How did the Danish princess, 'The sea King's daughter from over the sea', who was brought up in simple surroundings become such a vision of grandeur – a queen swagged in jewels, from the choker clasping her swan-like neck to the stomacher dropping to her waist?

I was turning over pages in a book at the India Office Library when I suddenly saw the image of Queen Alexandra – the same wide dog-collar choker, the same festoons and loops of pearls, the same fluttering aigrette, the same overwhelming opulence of jewels. It was a picture of an Indian maharajah, and a few pages further on I began to realise what a torrent of jewels had poured into the royal collection from the Indian Empire, especially on the tour of India undertaken by the Prince of Wales, later Edward VII, in 1875–6.

These are the lost jewels. My efforts to thread these Indian gems through the royal collection have been actively discouraged, apparently by instructions from Buckingham Palace. Most have, I am sure, been used as a gem mine for later generations and less exotic tastes. In the archives of Cartier in Paris, I found records of commissions for Edward VII and Queen Alexandra which record the transformation of historic Indian jewellery into Edwardian splendour.

As royalty has lost its place at the epicentre of political and social life, we like to think of the royal family as god-like figures, or at least as better people than ourselves.

Queen Mary had 'Olympian' majesty. She also had feet of clay when it came to her passion for jewels. Rigid, regal Queen Mary, whose relationship with her husband George V and her five children was undemonstrative, expressed herself emotionally through her collecting. That excuses, or at least explains, her avaricious acquisition of jewels, even *after* she had received the glittering cleavings of the Cullinan diamond which the royal family still call to this day 'Granny's chips'.

The Delhi Durbar of 1911 was a banquet of jewels. The extraordinary Imperial tributes — from pigeon's eggs of rubies to a great lucent green umbrella carved out of a single piece of emerald — are hidden from the public eye, recorded only in the memory of a dying generation and in the unpublished testimony of the Crown Jeweller of the time.

Hidden too, probably from her own husband George V in his last years, were the purchases that Queen Mary made of the Romanov jewels from the exiled Russian royal relatives. One major scandal that came to light only in 1968 was hushed up by Queen Mary's granddaughter the Queen.

The question I have been asked most often during my research has been about the Duchess of Windsor: what did she 'get away with'? I hope that this book will lay to rest some of the myths surrounding the Abdication and the rumours that followed the theft of the Duchess of Windsor's jewellery in 1946. It has been claimed that this robbery was 'master-minded' by the royal family in a bid to get back the 'Alexandra emeralds'.

After careful research, I can publish the complete list of the gems stolen from the Duchess in the robbery of October 1946 and trace some of the jewellery to source. I can also scotch the theory that Queen Alexandra brought emeralds as a dowry on her marriage. The only important emeralds unaccounted for in the royal collection today are those presented by the Indian maharajahs.

I now believe that the fascination of the public with the Duchess of Windsor's jewels has a symbolic explanation. I also know that the fabulous collection of 1930s and 1940s jewellery which the Duke of Windsor bought for his wife, when it was intact, was more aesthetically and historically important, and more valuable, than the heirlooms supposedly 'stolen' from the royal collection.

This book is not an exposé. It started from my own enthusiasm for beautiful jewels and from a fashion editor's knowledge that people express themselves in what they wear. Apart from christening robes, jewels are the only articles of adornment which are passed down from one generation of the royal family to the next.

The jewellery that Princess Diana is heir to is of enormous historical interest as well as of incalculable value. She will ultimately inherit all the Crown Jewellery and some personal pieces collected during a long life by Queen Elizabeth, the Queen Mother. Queen Mary's magnificent personal jewels, which she left to her granddaughter the Queen, will all be passed on to the Princess of Wales.

Or will they?

The conundrum at the heart of *The Royal Jewels* is this: which is the jewellery 'belonging to the Crown and to be worn by all future queens in right of it' and what is personal and private property?

Most of Queen Mary's collection she herself designated as personal, and willed to the Queen. As those jewels skipped a generation, the public's intuition that familiar royal jewels had 'disappeared' when George VI and his wife Elizabeth were crowned in 1937 helped to support the story that the Duchess of Windsor had made off with the royal inheritance.

The Crown Jewels in the Tower of London and the Crown Jewellery – the pieces given by successive monarchs to the Crown – are the responsibility of the Lord Chamberlain. They are cared for and looked after by Garrard and its Crown Jeweller William Summers, who masterminds the fabulous collection from an inventory book originally made at the death of Queen Victoria in 1901.

The first thing I asked for when I undertook this book was a list of the Crown Jewellery from both the Lord Chamberlain's office and from the Crown Jeweller. It is the last thing I found out, after three years' research, after working in the royal archives at Windsor and from studying research papers lodged at the Goldsmith's Hall by a previous jewellery historian a quarter of a century ago.

The trickle and stream and torrent and flood of presents that have been given to the Queen during her 30-year reign is a subject that is totally taboo. If any of these gifts has been made over to the Crown, I have not been able to find out who holds this information.

The Queen's personal and favourite jewellery is under the eye and key of her dresser and companion-servant of 50 years, Bobo MacDonald. But probably only Her Majesty comprehends the vastness of the royal jewel collection and its uncharted shores.

I hope that this book will stimulate interest in the royal jewels. I should also like to think that there might one day be an exhibition of some of the emotive historic pieces – the Timur ruby known as 'the light of the world'; the extraordinary girdle of carved emeralds that once saddled a maharajah's stallion; even the Queen's own favourite pieces such as Queen Victoria's Jubilee necklace and Queen Mary's diamond circle tiara – once the property of the exotic Grand-Duchess Vladimir, and smuggled romantically out of Russia under the nose of the Bolsheviks in two battered Gladstone bags.

Above all, I hope that *The Royal Jewels* will illuminate the least-known part of our royal heritage in all its glittering glory.

The now and future Queens. The Queen wears her most stately jewels: the pearl and diamond Russian tiara inherited from Queen Mary and Queen Victoria's Jubilee necklace. The lovers' knot diamond brooch can be seen among Princess May's wedding presents on page 61. *Below* The Princess of Wales in the bow-knot tiara given to her by the Queen – part of the fabulous inheritance of 'granny', Queen Mary.

Diana's glamorous way with the royal jewels. *Above* the Queen Mother's wedding gift to the Princess of Wales was this ink-blue sapphire brooch set in diamonds. Diana had it mounted on a pearl choker. *Left* Diana added the cabochon emerald drop to her diamond Prince of Wales feather pendant, recalling the style of Princess Alexandra (colour plates between pp.44-5).

Sarah Ferguson's taste mirrors her friend Diana's style.
Above: Sloane Ranger cheeky gold G.B. on a chain. *Below:* The oval ruby, set cluster-style with ten drop diamonds in 18-carat yellow and white gold. Designed by Prince Andrew and made by Garrard the Crown Jewellers. *Right:* The new regal style: £50,000 diamond necklace set with sapphires, on loan from a jeweller.

Diana's squaw headband using Queen Mary's heirloom emerald necklace which the Queen gave her daughter-in-law as a wedding present. *Below* Queen Mary wears the cabochon emerald necklace presented by the Ladies of India at the Delhi Durbar in 1911.

Acknowledgements

My grateful thanks to
HM THE QUEEN
For gracious permission to reproduce material from the royal archives and to publish pictures from the royal collection
HM QUEEN ELIZABETH THE QUEEN MOTHER
For permission to reproduce pictures from her collection, and for the opportunity to view her Norman Hartnell dresses at Clarence House for an article in *The Times*
HRH The Duke and HRH The Duchess of Gloucester

The Marchioness of Cambridge

The Lord Chamberlain

GARRARD, the Crown Jewellers: William Summers, MVO

With warmest gratitude also to the following:
DE BEERS: Susan Farmer, Anne Marie Reeves
BRITISH EMBASSY, PARIS: Lady Fretwell, M. James Viane
CARTIER: Mme Bety Jaïs, Mme Gilberte Gautier, Paris; Monique Boye-Möller, London
CHRISTIES, GENEVA: Hans Nadelhoffer
COURT DRESS COLLECTION, Kensington Palace: Nigel Arch, Joanna Marschner
THE GOLDSMITH'S COMPANY: Rosemary Ransome Wallis, Curator; Susan Hare, Librarian, for permission to study the Twining Papers
ILLUSTRATED LONDON NEWS: Elizabeth Moore
INDIA OFFICE LIBRARY
THE LONDON LIBRARY
THE LORD CHAMBERLAIN'S OFFICE: Marcus Bishop, Alison Taylor
MUSEUM OF LONDON: Valerie Cumming, Amanda Herries
NATIONAL PORTRAIT GALLERY: Judith Prendergast
ROYAL LIBRARY, WINDSOR: Oliver Everett, Jane Langton, Frances Diamond

THE TIMES: the staff of the reference and picture libraries for their patience

VICTORIA AND ALBERT MUSEUM: Shirley Bury, Jane Stancliffe

WARTSKI LTD: Kenneth Snowman, Geoffrey Munn

Hardy Amies, Murray Arbeid, Michael Bloch, Maître Blum, Joe Bryan III, Lady Diana Cooper, Freddie Fox, Lady Hyacinth Gough, Jessica and Charles Douglas-Home, Mrs Edward Hulton, Tikhon Koulikovsky, Maître Lecuyer, Lady Longford, Lady Pamela Mountbatten, Michael Nash, Princess de Polignac, Wendy Ramshaw, Kenneth Rose, David Sassoon, Lord Snowdon, Ginette Spanier, Sir Roy Strong, David Thomas, Diana Vreeland, Leo de Vroomen

And to all those people, closely connected to the royal family, who for reasons of discretion do not wish to be named

My gratitude also to Richard Johnson, Marianne Taylor and Rosamund Saunders at Grafton Books; to Mike Shaw at Curtis Brown; to Christine Painell at *The Times* and to Moira Storie at home. Also to my eldest son Gideon for his help with word processing and to Joshua and Samson for their tolerance.

THE ROYAL
JEWELS

Victoria:
Private and Public

'Et la Reine me montra le portrait du prince, en miniature, fixé sur un
bracelet. "Il ne me quitte jamais," ajouta-t-elle. – Je vis combien elle
amait tendrement son mari.'

'And the Queen showed me the portrait of the prince, in miniature,
attached to her bracelet. "I never take it off," she added. – I realised
how tenderly she loved her husband.'

Le Maréchal Canrobert
of Queen Victoria in 1855

On 18 August 1855, Queen Victoria, 36 years old, mother of eight, ruler of
Great Britain and its Dominions, drove under a sultry sky in an open landau
through the streets of Paris with her husband Prince Albert beside her. The
route was lined with people, flags, torches, welcome banners and (this being
Paris) a lifesize effigy of herself in multi-coloured pieces of hair made to show
off the art of a local wig-maker.

The tiny Queen Victoria, under five foot tall, was dressed in white, engulfed
by a large white silk hat trembling with marabou feathers. In one hand was an
acid green parasol; in the other a capacious holdall gaudily embroidered with
a gilded poodle. On every finger, including her thumbs, were the rings that had
exasperated even Lord Melbourne, the young Queen's first Prime Minister
and indulgent father figure.

Queen Victoria's perpetual parade of rings included two that meant as
much to her as the mighty symbols of state: the emerald serpent engagement
ring she wore above her wedding ring, and the narrow enamel band with a tiny
diamond in the centre that Prince Albert had given his rosy-cheeked cousin in
1836 when they were both 17 and their betrothal was a secret.

The other memento that Queen Victoria prized above her burgeoning stock
of diamonds was her bracelet containing a gold miniature of Prince Albert.
That night at the grand dinner in the Château of St Cloud hosted by Emperor
Napoleon III and his elegant wife Eugénie, Queen Victoria wore a low-cut
white dress smothered with embroidered geraniums (it had been designed by
Prince Albert himself), a diamond tiara, her fistful of rings including an
enormous blood-red ruby, and Albert's bracelet. She showed it proudly to the
dapper General Canrobert, fresh from his victory in the Crimean War. The

*Sixty years a Queen. Queen Victoria
on her diamond jubilee in 1897
refused to swap her widow's cap for
a crown, but scattered the lace with
diamonds. She wears the Crown
diamonds, her charm bracelet and
Albert's portrait bracelet that never
left her wrist.*

suave Frenchman, like the rest of the Parisians, was bewildered by Queen Victoria's odd wardrobe and he recorded his astonishment in his memoirs. (Eighty years later French society was surprised and ultimately captivated by the Victorian-style 'Winterhalter' crinolines created for Queen Elizabeth, wife of George VI.)

General Canrobert was touched by Queen Victoria's transparent and tender love for her husband as she pointed out Prince Albert's bright green Saxon uniform with boots and spurs in the portrait. 'I never take off the bracelet,' she told him.

A few nights later General Canrobert watched a quite different Queen Victoria sweep into the Hall of Mirrors at Versailles, in heavy white satin embroidered with gold and sashed with the Garter, on her head the glittering diadem made for her in 1853 and set with the fabulous Koh-i-noor. With a nice sense of the dramatic, Prince Albert was beside her in a coal black uniform.

The Empress Eugénie and her elegant Parisian court floated through the formal gardens at Versailles with their '*coiffures champêtres*': bacchanalian wreaths sprinkled with grapes and dew drops of diamonds. The Empress had just had the French Crown Jewels reset in Paris to re-create the decorative jewels of the eighteenth-century Queen Marie Antoinette – a style taken up by Queen Victoria's future daughter-in-law Princess Alexandra. Beside Empress

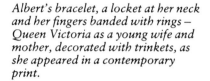

Albert's bracelet, a locket at her neck and her fingers banded with rings – Queen Victoria as a young wife and mother, decorated with trinkets, as she appeared in a contemporary print.

Eugénie's ethereal jewels, Queen Victoria's massive diadem looked solid and stately. The contrast was symbolic, for many of those jewels which Queen Victoria took to Paris have survived, like the British monarchy itself, for four more generations. By 1870, the Second Empire in France had ended, the Empress's jewels had been auctioned off, and Queen Victoria's eldest son Bertie, later Edward VII, was to come face-to-face with the French jewels festooned round the fabulously wealthy Maharajah of Patiala on the quayside in Calcutta in 1876 (Chapter 2).

Queen Victoria's combination of glittering state pieces and domestic trinkets – diamond diadem and Albert's portrait bracelet – is absolutely revealing of her character and of the collection of jewellery that she amassed during her 60-year reign. The wonder was that in 1855, just 18 years after she had taken over a discredited monarchy and its dissipated resources, Queen Victoria had consolidated the Crown and expressed its new pride and prosperity in her jewels.

The first intimation of her destiny had come to Princess Victoria with a jewel, in 1823. Her birthday present from 'Uncle King', as she called George IV, when she was a chubby four-year-old, was his miniature set in diamonds; she wore it to her first state dinner, pinning up the sleeve of her white frock. (The gift of a miniature is still significant to the royal family; Princess Diana wore the Queen's miniature with pride, plus a necklace and a brooch borrowed from her royal mother-in-law, when she attended the banquet at Hampton Court given by Queen Beatrix of the Netherlands in 1982.)

Princess Victoria owed her existence to the tragic and premature death of another Princess of Wales – Princess Charlotte, George IV's daughter and the only legitimate surviving heir of the 15 children of King George III. Princess Charlotte and her stillborn son died together on a grey November morning in 1817, leaving behind her distraught young husband the German Prince Leopold of Saxe-Coburg. To ensure the royal succession, the elderly sons of George III embarked on a royal baby marathon not to be equalled until Queen Elizabeth II and her relations produced a new baby boom in 1964.

Victoria's father, Edward, Duke of Kent, was the fourth son of George III and, like his brothers, pursued his personal pleasures outside the royal circle. On Princess Charlotte's death, he abandoned his long-term mistress and married Princess Victoria of Saxe-Coburg, the sister of the bereaved Prince Leopold and herself a widow with two children. In the undignified marriage scramble, the Duke of Kent and his elder brother William were married in a joint ceremony to German princesses who could scarcely follow the English service and both muttered '*Ich will*'.

William became King William IV and his wife Queen Adelaide, but their two baby daughters both died. The Duchess of Kent struggled back from Germany in the last stages of pregnancy in a run-down carriage that showed her husband's impoverished circumstances. On 24 May 1819, she gave birth to a lusty daughter at Kensington Palace where, 18 years later, the Archbishop of Canterbury and the Lord Chamberlain galloped to tell Princess Victoria that she had become Queen of England.

Baby 'Drina', as she was called by her family, was christened Alexandrina, after her godfather Czar Alexander I of Russia, and Victoria, after her mother: names that caused a series of squabbles with her quarrelsome Hanoverian relations. In less than a year, Princess Victoria's father had died of pneumonia in a Devon resort on 3 January 1820, extinguishing the hopes of producing a male heir for the old and unstable George III, who died the same year.

Princess Victoria's upbringing was less social and less connected to the royal circle than the childhood of Lady Diana Spencer, who lived at Park House on the Sandringham Estate and played with the young princes. The Duchess of Kent was determined to keep her daughter away from the scandal and decadence surrounding the court of the dissolute George IV, and indeed the Princess's only encounter with royal jewellery fulfilled her mother's worst fears. When 'Drina' was summoned to the Royal Lodge at Windsor to see her 'Uncle King', George IV allowed the diamond miniature to be pinned on to the little Princess by his mistress, Lady Coyningham, with whom he was living in a brazen *ménage à trois*.

In Kensington Palace, the Duchess of Kent, Princess Victoria, her half-sister and -brother, Feodore and Charles, lived as poor relations, camping in a few interconnecting state rooms. Princess Victoria may have had a toy crib with a crown on the top to put her dolls to sleep, but she shared a bedroom with her mother and had no trappings of grandeur. Without the help of Princess Charlotte's widower, her uncle Leopold, the Kents would have been even more impoverished and isolated. As well as giving the family emotional support, inviting them to his home at Claremont and ultimately acting as the young Queen Victoria's political adviser, he gave the Duchess of Kent an allowance of £2,000 (later £3,000) a year. When Queen Victoria acceded to the throne and was voted a civil list of £385,000 a year, she paid back £50,000 to settle her father's debts. King Leopold of the Belgians, as her uncle became, was her substitute father. 'My own dearest, kindest father – for as such I have ever loved you,' she wrote to him on the death of her husband Prince Albert in 1861.

This threadbare upbringing was at odds with life at other European courts, such as that of Donna Maria da Gloria of Portugal, who came on a state visit to England in 1830 when both girls were ten. The acerbic and entertaining diarist of the period, Charles Greville, was captivated by the child Queen of Portugal when she appeared at a ball in a crimson velvet dress blazing with jewels. He described Victoria dismissively as 'our little princess' in her simple white frock, 'a short vulgar-looking child and not near so good-looking as the Portuguese'.

In three years' time, Princess Victoria started to write a diary of her own, the first of the exercise books, half-bound in morocco and now preserved in the Royal Library at Windsor Castle, which were to give historians such insight into the character of Princess and Queen. In the years before her accession she recorded her impressions of the trips round the country with her mother each autumn. ('Royal progresses' her uncle King William IV called them irritably.) Her simple routine at home with her mother and her German governess Baroness Lehzen, seemed an extraordinary contrast with the grand life she saw on these visits. 'The breakfast room is magnificent,' wrote Victoria at Lord Grosvenor's stately Eaton Hall in October 1832. The fair-haired child who

Princess Victoria with her mother the Duchess of Kent. 'She was dressed to receive me in white muslin with a coral necklet,' wrote her governess Baroness Lehzen in 1831.

inherited nothing but her father's debts and a direct line to the British throne was impressed by the massive eagle-shaped gold chandelier suspended above her head. She was even more overwhelmed by the breakfast, 'served in handsome tea and coffee pots: a crown of gold with precious stones contained the bread'.

Sixty years later, the mighty Queen Victoria, Regina et Imperatrix, would sit at breakfast in Windsor Castle eating a boiled egg with a gold spoon from a solid gold egg cup, with a kilted Scots retainer at the door and two Indian servants in scarlet and gold behind her chair.

Princess Victoria's journal records the presents she received from her family for birthdays and festivities: 'From DEAR Mamma I received a lovely enamel bracelet with her hair,' she wrote on her sixteenth birthday. 'At 3 came the Duke of Sussex who gave me a gold bracelet with turquoises . . . At 4 came the Duchess of Cambridge, who brought me a lovely turquoise bracelet from Uncle Cambridge.'

The ceremony of present-giving at Christmas is vividly described in 1836, on the eve of Princess Victoria's eighteenth birthday and of her Accession. The family – Mamma, Victoria's governess 'dearest Lehzen', Lady Conroy, the wife of her mother's comptroller Sir John Conroy (whom Victoria hated with passion and outsiders suggested was more than just a friend to the Duchess of Kent) – were accompanied by their King Charles spaniel Dash – a name that the Queen has given today to one of her newest corgis. They were staying with Uncle Leopold at Claremont, where the presents were laid out on separate tables under a tree sparkling with lights and laden with sugar ornaments. Our royal family celebrate in just the same way today; Group Captain Peter Townsend, the equerry to George VI who fell in love with Princess Margaret, described post-war Christmas in the 'tinsel hung ballroom' at Sandringham, a ritual established by the genial Edward VII.

Princess Victoria, who was especially fond of Prince Leopold's stylish new wife, her elegant French-born Aunt Louise, recorded her Christmas gifts with innocent surprise and pleasure: 'From my dear Mamma I received a beautiful massive gold buckle in the shape of two serpents; a lovely delicate gold chain with a turquoise clasp; a lovely coloured sketch of dearest Aunt Louise by Partridge . . . and so like her . . . From my dear Uncle Leopold, a beautiful turquoise ring; from the Queen a fine piece of Indian gold tissue and from Sir J. Conroy a print.'

The trinkets of turquoise and lockets of hair remained the kind of personal jewels she was attached to throughout her life. One of her earliest presents to Aunt Louise was a bracelet made of her own hair, with a clasp of coloured jewels, which was later inherited by Queen Victoria's youngest daughter Beatrice and put on display in an exhibition of royal and historic treasures a century later in 1939.

The dramatic moment when Princess Victoria came of age, became Queen, moved her bed out of her mother's room and presented her much loved governess Lehzen with a brooch containing a lock of hair, marked the end of her girlhood. Queen Victoria acceded to the throne of England in the early hours of the morning of 20 June 1837 at 'an age at which a girl can hardly be trusted to choose a bonnet for herself', as the historian Thomas Carlyle put it.

The eighteen-year-old Queen chose a crown from the Court Jewellers Rundell, Bridge and Rundell on the edge of the City of London. They had handled a lucrative trade in crowns during the Hanoverian era, when they hired out suitably magnificent gems to the impecunious monarchs, then stripped the crowns bare and left them as skeletal frames between each coronation. George IV had paid them the enormous sum of £6,525 for the loan of precious stones for his crowning.

Queen Victoria bucked that tradition by ordering her own permanent gem-set crown, an early symbol of the new solidity and prosperity in her reign. She was soon to change jewellers too, to Messrs Garrard and Company, then sited in the Haymarket. Rundell, Bridge and Rundell's last service to the Crown was to make Queen Victoria's new ruby Coronation ring. ('I had the greatest difficulty to take it off again, – which at last I did with great pain,' she complained in her Journal.)

The diamond diadem, decorated with shamrock and thistle. It was made for George IV with rented gems. The new Queen symbolically soldered in her jewels.

The surrounding crowd swept off all hats in salute to the maiden Queen Victoria as the state coach and its eight cream-coloured ponies proceeded ceremonially towards Westminster Abbey. It was the people's mirror image of the grandiose moment when coronets flashed on to the heads of the peers of the realm as the Queen was crowned. 'The loveliest moment of all' a later diarist, Sir Henry 'Chips' Channon wrote of the peeresses whom he saw 'as a thousand white arms, sparkling with jewels, lifting their tiny coronets' at the Coronation of George VI, Queen Victoria's great-grandson.

The crown that the Archbishop of Canterbury placed on the Queen's bowed head ('as thou dost this day set a crown of pure gold upon her head, so enrich her royal heart . . . and crown her with all princely virtues') was made of light hoops of gold over a royal blue velvet cap and set with the Black Prince's ruby and St Edward's sapphire – the two most ancient and mystical of royal jewels. It was ultimately broken up, but it was the model for the Imperial State Crown made for the Queen in 1953.

From Whitehall to Whitechapel the jewelled crown became the symbol of hope and homage for a new reign and its young Queen. *The Times* listed the Coronation decorations that illuminated the streets: a large imperial crown 'beautifully jewelled with emerald and ruby coloured lamps' in Whitehall; the Royal arms in flaming gas lamps over a bookseller in Regent Street; a crown in gold lamps in St James's; and the most enormous crown studded with gem-stone lights outside the St James's Square home of Lord Lichfield, whose descendant was to record in the flash-bulb of his camera the royal wedding of 1981.

On a more prosaic note, 'resetting the diamonds and precious stones from the Old Crown of England into a new Imperial Crown with the addition of Brilliants, Pearls and a fine sapphire' cost £1,000, according to the Lord Chamberlain's accounts.

This was nothing compared to the sums which Queen Victoria started to spend with Garrard, her new Crown Jeweller, which had always had close connections with the royal family since its foundation in 1721, but took on its official title – which it still holds today – in 1843.

Realising that jewels are the outward and visible symbols of kingship, Victoria invested not only in crowns state and imperial but also in magnificent suites of sapphires, diamonds and her own favourite blood red rubies. Over the 60-year span of her reign, she spent with Garrard £158,887, a fraction of which was for state gifts, a proportion on family presents and the vast bulk of which provided an incalculable collection of royal jewellery. This sum, averaged out over the reign and translated into twentieth-century terms, puts the equivalent figure for Queen Victoria's expenditure on jewellery and silver at £8 million.

The ledger of her transactions with Garrard, covering almost the entire length of her reign, from 1843 to her death in 1901, has been discovered in the Victoria and Albert Museum in London, where it was sent and then mislaid 30 years ago when Garrard moved premises from Albemarle Street to its present site in Regent Street.

The crumbling mustard-leather-bound volume with its brass clasp and marbled endpapers throws as revealing a light on Queen Victoria's taste and character, her preoccupation with family and passion for commemoration, as do her published diaries and letters. The detailed entries not only reinforce the judgements made by historians about the Queen, they also give a fascinating insight into the development of the taste in jewellery and decoration that we have come to describe as 'Victorian'.

Through the ledger, the jewellery expert can trace the changing fashions in stones: the constancy of the diamond, usually brilliant cut, from Coronation

Queen Victoria wore the diamond diadem in a miniature in this presentation bracelet she had made in 1840.

7

to Jubilee; the arrival of emeralds from the Empire; the craze for turquoise, topaz and amethyst; the unwavering red line of the Queen's favoured rubies. Those who are moved by the romance of history can be present at the birth of major pieces in the royal collection: the very first setting for the legendary Koh-i-noor diamond, or the Indian regal tiara now being worn by Queen Elizabeth, the Queen Mother. These became hallmarks of the British monarchy, and the entries, in flowing copperplate or crabbier salesman's script, detail every single stone, its size and weight, in these important pieces.

The private commissions, the bracelets set with children's portraits, the Scottish pebbles and stags' teeth set in silver, the engraved lockets and mourning rings, shade in the complex character of a Queen who could be at the same time majestical and mawkish, thoughtful with family gifts and insensitive in her distribution of commemorative jewels, whether of her beloved Albert or her unpopular retainer John Brown.

The blond, moustachioed Prince Albert of Saxe-Coburg Gotha, a German cousin on her mother's side, unlocked the romantic, passionate side of Queen Victoria's nature that expressed itself so tangibly in her jewels.

'What a charming pendant he would be to his pretty cousin,' said Prince Albert's Coburg great-grandmother when the two children were in their respective cradles. Prince Albert came to stay at Windsor in October 1839 when the two cousins were both 20. Five days later Queen Victoria summoned

Albert's brooch: a large sapphire surrounded by 12 diamonds – his wedding present to his young bride.

Queen Victoria wore the brooch at her bosom and the Garter on her sleeve.

him to the Blue Closet and proposed. 'Oh! To feel I was, and am, loved by such an Angel,' she wrote in her journal. 'He is perfection.'

Prince Albert sealed their marriage with a brooch, 'Albert's brooch' Victoria called the big sapphire clutched by a dozen diamonds that she pinned to the snow white satin and Honiton lace of her wedding dress. It became a favourite royal jewel: Queen Alexandra perched it among the festoons of diamonds she wore at the Coronation of 1902, a year after her mother-in-law's death; today it beams from the tweedy lapels or the shimmering Garter ribbon of the Queen. Prince Albert made copies of the brooch for his own daughters, and the Queen has given one of these to Princess Anne.

Queen Victoria gave Albert a diamond star, a badge and the diamond Garter, watching him wear the blue ribbon for the first time with affectionate pride. After his death, she symbolically took it back and wore it for the rest of her life as her own.

The wedding of Queen Victoria and Prince Albert took place at the Chapel Royal, St James's Palace on 10 February 1840. It was a time for family gifts, when Baroness Lehzen, painfully aware that her position as guide and governess for the past two decades would soon be usurped, presented Victoria on her wedding morning with a little ring of her own. Her mother more piously produced a prayer-book and a nosegay of orange blossom.

Queen Victoria and Prince Albert of Saxe-Coburg Gotha on their wedding day in 1840. Four years earlier he had given his rosy-cheeked cousin a diamond ring as a token of intent.

The royal wedding was a cause for celebration – the first since the wedding of the high-spirited and doomed Princess Charlotte 24 years earlier. Perhaps because of the youth of the bride and groom, it was a light-hearted and colourful event from the pink and white invitation cards to the guests themselves, who had been specifically asked by the Lord Chamberlain's office not to wear black, or to put on court feathers which would wave in the way of eager onlookers. Even the widowed Dowager Queen Adelaide chose a violet velvet frock, lined in white satin and trimmed with ermine.

The brilliant plumage – 'light blue or green with white, amber, crimson, purple, fawn and stone', according to *The Times* – was mottled with the wedding favours, white ribbons looped into bows, trimmed with silver lace and mixed with sprigs of orange blossom like a perambulating forest as the wedding procession wound its way through the especially constructed colonnade, lit by lamps and the glow of the windows behind.

Queen Victoria on her wedding day was dressed simply by the standards of her time. She wore diamonds at neck and ears; 'my Turkish necklace' she called it, and wore it to her first child Vicky's christening. But this particular jewel, which might have had a special place as an heirloom, passed out of the royal collection. On Queen Victoria's death she left it to Arthur, Duke of Connaught, her third son. The absence of a coronet or diadem was a cause for comment. 'Her Majesty wore no diamonds on her head, nothing but a simple wreath of orange blossom,' wrote *The Times* correspondent, who noted patriotically that the wedding dress (and especially the magnificent lace that cost £1,000) was, like the Duchess of Kent's confection of white satin, silver brocade and ermine-trimmed train of sky blue velvet, 'wholly of British manufacture'.

Queen Victoria had no particular feel for fashion, but she had noted in her journal the French chic of Aunt Louise in her deceptively simple brown silk dress and sky blue bonnet. It was, agreed the sophisticated and worldly Lord Melbourne, impossible not to have French clothes, if one wished to be well dressed, but the young Queen bowed to public feeling and bestowed her patronage at home. The conviction that Princess Diana should be an ambassadress for British fashion is nothing new.

The lack of personal display on the Queen's wedding day was not matched by her surroundings. Every last piece of gold plate was polished up for the Buckingham Place banquet and piled on to a sideboard which was hung with crimson drapes, looped up with white rosettes with a glittering crown in the centre.

The crown was again the symbol at this joyous celebration; multi-coloured illuminated crowns, often with the intertwined V and A, decorated the route. The Reform Club had a particularly enormous crown lit up with gas lamps that flickered dramatically in the February wind.

To the young Queen herself, the symbol of the union was the ring, which Prince Albert slipped on her finger as the guns fired a royal salute. Overwhelmed by this impressive ceremony, *The Times* claimed that the traditional band of gold 'appeared more solid than is usual in ordinary weddings'. The bride's trainbearers each received a special gift: a predatory eagle brooch, its ruby eyes and diamond beak glinting from the turquoise body, its gold claws gripping huge pearls. This dramatic choice was an expression of the romantic side of Queen Victoria's nature. She adored grand opera, and the idol of her teenage years was the great Giulia Grisi, who sang at Kensington Palace to celebrate her sixteenth birthday.

This was the same Victoria who later fell so passionately in love with Scotland that she set the pebbles that Prince Albert picked up on the beach in silver. It was the part of her that reacted with such tragic intensity to her husband's death that her Christmas present to her six-year-old daughter Beatrice in 1863 was a bracelet set with a model of her dead father's eye.

This passionate streak was sublimated for the next two decades in child-rearing and domestic pleasures, in discipline and duty. In ten years, Queen

At the christening of Vicky, the Princess Royal, in 1841, Queen Victoria wore Albert's brooch, her Turkish diamond necklace and the diamond diadem.

Victoria had seven new babies. Vicky, the Princess Royal, and Albert Edward ('Bertie'), the Prince of Wales and future Edward VII, arrived like a volley of gunfire exactly a year apart in November 1840 and 1841.

'I hope you will have no chance of two for some time . . . Bertie and I both suffered (and the former will ever suffer) from coming so soon after you,' she wrote to Vicky in 1858, when her daughter was married to the heir to the German Kaiser and expecting her first baby.

The two elder children were followed by Alice, Alfred ('Affie'), Helena ('Lenchen'), Louise and Arthur; her family of nine was completed by Leopold and Beatrice in 1853 and 1857. New Ministers also seemed to follow one another inexorably as political events unfolded: Lord Melbourne, Sir Robert Peel, Lord Russell, her influential Foreign Secretary Lord Palmerston. Her two most famous Prime Ministers, William Gladstone and Benjamin Disraeli, were yet to come.

Public and private lives were separate. The political unrest caused by the projected repeal of the Corn Laws in 1845 and the Irish potato famine (which finally brought down Peel's Tory government), was set against the calm backdrop of 'blue sky and sea' at Osborne House on the Isle of Wight. Victoria and Albert's first real home was acquired with the assistance of Peel for £26,000 in the autumn of 1844. Prince Albert subsequently pulled down the 'cosy' existing house and built instead an Italianate villa, just as he was to re-create Balmoral Castle from the 'pretty little castle in the old Scottish style' which Queen Victoria described in her journal in 1848. The money for that came from a windfall of £250,000 left to Queen Victoria by an eccentric miser John Camden Nield in 1852, in recognition of the Queen's propriety.

In 1848, Queen Victoria was making some major acquisitions of jewellery. Paradoxically, this was the Year of Revolutions; thrones all over Europe were tottering and the Queen wrote to her uncle, King Leopold of the Belgians, about 'an uncertainty in everything existing'. Three months before there had even been trouble in England; the threat of riots from the Chartists had forced Queen Victoria to fly to Osborne. But five days after penning that anguished letter she spent £1,200 on a large emerald and diamond necklace. By the next summer she was investing £1,400 on a suite of diamonds and rubies (27 June 1849); a large emerald and diamond brooch and matching earrings (April 1850) was followed by a very fine suite of opals costing £1,056 17s (August 1850).

This particular period of jewellery purchase culminated in 1853 with the setting of the Koh-i-noor diamond, that duck's egg of a stone that weighed in at 186 carats when the Honourable East India Company took over the Treasury at Lahore and presented the stone to Queen Victoria in 1851. The Koh-i-noor or 'Mountain of Light' has a fascinating history that takes it back in legend for five thousand years. From the sixteenth century, it can be traced from the Rajah of Gwalior in India to the Moghul Emperors, to Persia and finally back to India. Another romantic chapter was added when the old Duke of Wellington, hero of Waterloo, trotted up to the door of Garrard at 25 Haymarket in the summer of 1852 on his white charger. The Iron Duke helped to cut the first facet of the dazzling brilliant-cut stone which Garrard created

Her Majesty The Queen Dr

1853 April	To Amount brought forward		388	1 9
	<u>Setting the Koh-i-noor Cumberland Diamonds</u>			
April 1	Setting a Brilliant Regal Tiara, consisting of 4 Maltese Crosses, and 4 fleur de lis, with a jointed circlet of 2 rows of Diamonds, enclosing large Diamonds and small Crosses. The large Crosses and Fleur de lis arranged to be removed at pleasure from the Circlet by double springs and sockets, and have also moveable jointed stems and hooks to form Brooches when required. Four Greek Honeysuckle Ornaments with sockets to fit with springs to the Circlet in lieu of the Crosses and fleur de lis. The front Ornament having screws fittings to support the great Koh-i-noor Diamond. Setting the Koh-i-noor Diamond in open frame work of small rose Diamonds, and making for do a large honeysuckle Brooch with screws and fittings. Setting the Cumberland Diamond in circle of large Diamonds closely fitted in with roses to size of, and to fit the same frame as the Koh-i-noor.			
	The whole cont$_g$ 2203 Brill^{ts} and <u>662 Roses</u> 2865 Diamonds			
	For making the Regal Tiara with Crosses & Fleur de lis		493	
	Do the four Honeysuckle Ornaments & fitting with moveable springs to the Circlet		87	10
	Setting the Koh-i-noor in open frame work, thickly set with small roses and arranging to Tiara, and large Brooch		56	
	Making large Greek Honeysuckle Brooch of small Brilliants, and arranging fittings to receive Koh-i-noor or Cumberland Diamond as centres		57	
	Carr'd over		1081	11 9

and set in a regal tiara for the Queen. (History had it that the stone brought ill-luck if worn by a male ruler.)

The Koh-i-noor was set like a giant bloom in an open trellis framework garlanded with roses. There were altogether over 2,000 diamonds in this splendid tiara, which became a mine of gems for future generations. It was broken up and its stones used as the basis of Queen Elizabeth's new crown at the Coronation of George VI in 1937.

OPPOSITE *The Garrard ledger sheet for 1 April 1853 showing the original setting of the newly acquired Koh-i-noor and the historic Cumberland diamond.*

THE POOR OLD KOH-I-NOOR AGAIN!

1. THE KOH-I-NOOR.
2 2. THE DUTCH ARTISTS.
3 3 3. THE REQUISITE MACHINERY.

4. THE "DOOK" MANIFESTING GREAT INTEREST IN THE PRECIOUS GEM.
5 5 5. EMINENT SCIENTIFIC MEN WATCHING PROCEEDINGS.

The cutting of the Koh-i-noor was a cartoon joke in Punch.

In April 1853, Queen Victoria also spent £2,880 9s 3d on an impressive ruby necklace and £2,200 19s 3d on a diamond and opal tiara in the oriental style, its curlicues and spires now familiar on the head of Queen Elizabeth, the Queen Mother. The tiara was originally set with 17 enormous opals (which are still in the strongroom store today). Queen Alexandra considered opals 'unlucky' stones and had them taken out after Queen Victoria's death. In their place went the rubies we see glittering now – culled from the Maharajah's gifts that the Prince of Wales brought back from his visit to India in 1875/6 (Chapter 2).

Between April and November 1853, Queen Victoria spent £6,030 2s 3d at Garrard – an enormous sum which suggests an urge for acquisition, a sensuous feeling for the beauty of jewels, and a confidence in the stability of the British throne. This was the period when the royal couple, in their early thirties, were the centre of society in a way that did not happen again for 20 years, after Bertie, the Prince of Wales, and Princess Alexandra of Denmark were married.

The Great Exhibition of 1851 was not just a personal triumph for Prince Albert. ('It was the happiest, proudest day in my life,' said Queen Victoria.) It was also a celebration of art and industry that marked the beginning of what we now describe as the Victorian era. As Queen Victoria, puffed with pride, dressed in pink and silver and wearing the Koh-i-noor and a small crown, drove in an open carriage to Paxton's great temple of glass, Prince Albert seemed to her to embody the Victorian ideal of the marriage of art and commerce.

Prince Albert was interested in design. It was he who supervised the interior of the new Balmoral Castle, completed in 1854 in all its tartan splendour; he redecorated the ballroom at Buckingham Palace for his daughter Vicky's coming-out and designed her dress – all lace flounces, ribbons, embroidery and a wreath of convolvulus and jewels in the hair. The geranium-embroidered dress he created for Queen Victoria for the state visit in Paris in 1855, supposedly as a foil for the Koh-i-noor, was a similar floral fantasy.

His jewellery designs seem more certain in taste: flowers were the main-spring from the enamel and emerald necklace he gave Victoria for Christmas in 1842 to the later necklace of golden oak leaves and semi-precious stones that set a fashion in society. At the time of the Great Exhibition, the Prince Consort presented his wife with a bracelet of gold leaves which he had designed to mark the twelfth anniversary of their engagement. These natural-istic leanings were quite separate from Queen Victoria's more conventional taste. He was temperamentally attuned to the budding Arts and Crafts movement, and to the nineteenth-century Revivalist jewellers who used history and archaeology for inspiration; he looked forward towards the later idealised naturalism of Art Nouveau.

It is interesting to speculate how Prince Albert might have affected the royal jewel collection if he had lived to see the gems coming in as Imperial tributes and demanding to be reset. He might have turned to the great Revivalist jeweller the Roman Castellani, a favourite with the Empress Vicky and her sister Alice (who married another German Prince, Louis of Hesse), who sent a Castellani brooch to Queen Victoria for her birthday in 1873. Both the Queen and Princess Margaret own necklaces by the other famous Revivalist jewellers Carlo and Arthur Giuliano – the Queen's a delicate foliate design with multi-coloured sapphires growing among green enamelled leaves.

Did Queen Victoria herself have any taste and judgement such as Queen Mary was to show? Certainly she was overwhelmed with delight at Albert's creations. 'My beloved one gave me such a lovely unexpected present,' she wrote on 10 February 1846, 'a wreath, going right round the head, made to match the brooch and earrings he gave me at Christmas. It is entirely his own design . . . the leaves are of frosted gold, the orange blossoms of white porcelain and four little green enamel oranges meant to represent our four children . . . such a dear kind thought of Albert's.'

The first 20 years of Queen Victoria's reign were marred by a dispute over jewellery. Immediately she acceded to the throne in 1837, King Ernest of Hanover claimed as his some of the royal jewels which had been given to Queen Charlotte by her husband George III, but which both had understood to be part of a Hanoverian inheritance. Queen Charlotte had kept them in a separate chest and, according to the evidence given to a commission set up by

Queen Victoria, considered them personal property and decided to 'give the said jewels to the House of Hanover in her will'. She died two years before her deranged husband in 1818.

Queen Victoria wore the disputed jewels, which included some exceptionally fine and historic pearls, especially a necklace of 37 lustrous stones which had been given to Mary Queen of Scots, purchased from her by Queen Elizabeth I and given by James I to his daughter Elizabeth of Bohemia and passed by inheritance to the Electress Sophia of Hanover and thence to the British crown. Among a quantity of other jewels, including a mighty diamond stomacher and a small crown, was the Cumberland diamond, presented to the Duke of Cumberland after the battle of Culloden and already set into the brilliant regal tiara which Queen Victoria ordered for herself from Garrard on April Fool's Day 1853.

The commission was eventually set up by the British Government in 1857. It consisted of three independent law lords whose dry-as-dust legal arguments and the mass of evidence contained in the papers now lodged at Windsor give no sense of the emotion that this royal dispute caused, or of Queen Victoria's anguish and rage when the judgement finally went against her in 1858. (She did not hand back the last of the jewels until 1866.)

Her daughter Vicky, by then married to the heir to the German Kaiser, boiled with indignation for her mother: 'I hear the Queen of Hanover wears the jewels. It makes me so furious that anything which you have worn should be worn by anyone else,' she wrote in 1859.

By that time, Victoria had received a torrent of Indian jewels which had been taken along with the Koh-i-noor from the treasury at Lahore in 1851, after the Punjab was conquered. Her disappointment at the commission's finding had nothing to do with greed, pride or pique. It was because the judgement struck at the heart of her right as sovereign to decide which jewels were the property of the state or Crown and which personal gems to dispose of at will.

During the 1850s Queen Victoria bought and acquired important jewels yet her emotional involvement, according to her commissions in the Garrard ledger, remained with private and personal pieces. These suggest that, unlike Prince Albert, she had little interest in design and was a captive, rather than a creator, of 'Victorian' taste.

The first Balmoral holiday in 1848 was marked by a series of 'Scotch' trophies: a pebble set in silver as a brooch (cost £2 10s); another pebble was polished up with the care bestowed on recutting the Koh-i-noor. Deers' teeth from Prince Albert's teutonic massacres of game (much criticised by British sportsmen) were mounted as brooches, a bracelet, half a dozen of them even set in enamel and gold as waistcoat buttons. The stag horns that still poke spikily from the walls of the grand staircases at Balmoral were also turned into ghoulish *objets d'art*. On 23 October 1850, a desk set was made from a buck's horn mounted as a paper knife, a doe's horn banded in gold and set with an eraser and deers' teeth set as a pen rack.

There is something macabre about Victoria and Albert's passion for commemoration, which pre-dated the mawkish relics in the Queen's widowhood. Thirty years before Queen Victoria struck a set of silver and gold medallions on the death of her Scottish retainer John Brown in 1883, Albert laid out marble limbs moulded from their babies on red damask cushions in his study at Osborne.

Queen Victoria not only ordered a gold miniature bracelet with 'Louise' spelt out in gems; she also hung mementoes of 'Affie', Vicky, Alice or 'Lenchen' on herself. 'I had your picture on my arm (a little photograph in the wedding dress) and Affie's in a locket, and your pretty locket . . . round my neck,' she wrote to her daughter Vicky. Prince Albert's moustachioed portrait bracelet competed with a blue and gold enamel bracelet in six compartments containing portraits of the children and given to her by Albert on her birthday in May 1845. He gave her a similar bracelet with portraits of their younger sons in August 1854. Queen Victoria left all these pieces to her son Edward VII as Crown property with the words 'All these were given to me by my beloved husband'.

Birthdays became a rite, each child's arrival scored into metal. Engraving was such an essential part of Queen Victoria's jewel purchases that she summoned an engraver to Windsor as frequently as the pearl stringer. The stately setting of the Koh-i-noor diamond in 1853 was completed at the same time as a gold charm bracelet (cost £11 15s) engraved with the name of the new baby Leopold. He was a delicate, sickly child who was found to be suffering from the 'bleeding disease' haemophilia. Thirty years later, when her 'special' son, as Queen Victoria described him for his incurable condition, died at Cannes, all the stationmasters along whose rails the coffin passed were presented with commemorative gifts.

'To the Medical Gentlemen at Berlin', reads the inscription on the diamond studs that the grateful Queen Victoria sent off in February 1859 at the safe delivery of her first grandchild. Vicky had married Prince Frederick William of Prussia the year before, thus fulfilling her father's dearest wish to unite the crowns of England and his native Germany. At the same time, the departure of his favourite daughter at the age of 17 depressed his spirits. Vicky's son, the future Kaiser William II and perpetrator of the First World War, was born after a traumatic breech birth which left him with a permanently withered arm. His grandmother sent him a small gold locket with 'W' in turquoise blue enamel.

Later grandchildren were more likely to be treated to a miniature of the late Prince Consort with a standard engraving 'To our dear little granddaughter/ son from her/his affectionate Grandmamma VRI'.

The Queen's obsession with birthdays was finally enshrined in the Birthday Book, a massive tome which she carried with her in old age so often that onlookers thought that it was the Bible (as indeed it was to her). Everyone who ever visited her had to enter name and birth date and, by the end of her life, the Birthday Book was coded into such a baffling series of volumes that Fritz Ponsonby, Queen Victoria's Private Secretary, made Sarah Bernhardt sign the wrong volume. When the Queen sent him back to the theatre in Nice with the correct 'artists' book, the great French actress finally signed with all the drama she had brought to her recital at the Hotel Regina for the Queen.

With such overwhelming importance already attached to dates and their ritual observance, it is not surprising that Victoria expressed her anguish at her husband's death in memento mori and in the mourning jewellery that became an integral part of the Victorian age.

But it was not the Prince Consort's lost battle against typhoid fever at Christmas 1861 but her mother's death earlier in the year that first plunged the court into mourning. A veil was instantly thrown over the ruby red and emerald of the Queen's favourite jewels. The young Queen who had so loved colour that she hung the State bed in Windsor in fuchsia pink and emerald green, was now dressed in unremitting black. All her jewels were now in onyx: sombre lockets and bead necklaces, studs and snaps to contain locks of hair, onyx pins with discreet onyx centres. Into an oxidised silver frame went two miniatures of the Duchess of Kent emblazoned in gold with the word 'Grandmamma'. The mother whose relationship with her young daughter had been uneasy and never really affectionate, was mourned with all the fervour of a guilty heart. The first amethysts, that sad half-mourning stone, were bought at this time, with a black enamel ring, and rows of beads.

The most ancient superstitions concerning reflected images of the dead meant that matt finishes – both for jewellery and fabric – were considered the most suitable. Rules for etiquette were already established; the length of the first and secondary mourning periods varied according to the closeness of the dead relative and personal feelings. Strictly speaking, a widow remained in total mourning for a year and a day and came out of her widow's weeds after two and a half years, although after Albert's death Queen Victoria remained in black for the rest of her life.

No jewellery was allowed at court during a short period of deep mourning. Male courtiers even removed decorative shoe buckles, buttons, watch chains and swords, replacing them with matt black substitutes. Second Mourning meant 'white necklaces and earrings', the pearls and diamonds in which Queen Alexandra was smothered after Queen Victoria's death. Today, the royal family interpret 'white jewellery' as suitable for all mourning. At the funeral of Earl Mountbatten at Westminster Abbey in September 1979, both the Queen and the Queen Mother wore black with pearl and diamond jewellery.

Queen Victoria was 42 when Albert died of typhoid fever on 14 December 1861 – a day that became enshrined in the family calendar as Mausoleum Day. Her eldest daughter Vicky and her first grandchild were in Germany; her son and heir, Bertie, just 20, sowing wild oats and in need of a wife; the wedding of her second daughter Alice was imminent; her youngest daughter Beatrice was 4½.

Albert's memory was kept alive in a life-size marble bust that appears like a ghostly presence in family photographs. Queen Victoria slept with a photograph of Albert's death mask hanging above her bed; his dressing room at Windsor was kept exactly as he had left it; every night his valet prepared a ewer of hot water and fresh clothes just as Uncle Leopold had left Princess Charlotte's blue cloak hanging on the back of the door at Claremont.

Queen Victoria and her daughters embroidered mourning handkerchieves – the Queen's a snowy square of lawn stained with black embroidered tears and marked 'VR'. Nine photo miniatures of Prince Albert went into nine gold

DYNASTY OF DIAMONDS

Five generations of the royal family have worn the diamond collet necklace (1). It was made for Queen Victoria from stones taken from a Garter badge and sword. They weigh a staggering 161 carats. The detachable diamond drop was originally part of the Timur ruby necklace. It is also used in the Queen Mother's crown. Queen Victoria (2) wears the small diamond crown she ordered for her personal use. It is very light in weight.

Queen Mary (3) is wearing another historic jewel: the diamond fringe tiara inherited from the Hanoverians and also worn as a necklace. 'Albert's brooch', the sapphire and diamond circle given to Queen Victoria on her marriage, is on Queen Mary's bodice.

The Queen Mother (4), photographed by Cecil Beaton in 1940, also wears the diamond fringe tiara. She removed two of the collets from the necklace in 1937 to make her drop earrings, replacing the stones from the second necklace of 42 diamonds.

HM the Queen (5) wears the diamond diadem, a completely circular head ornament decorated with symbolic roses, shamrock and thistle. It was made for George IV and worn by Queen Victoria for many of her formal portraits. Queen Alexandra was particularly fond of the diadem. The Queen wears the diadem for the Opening of Parliament and it also appears on postage stamps.

Albert's death plunged Queen Victoria into mourning. Her lady-in-waiting Lady Julia Abercrombie copied this picture from the famous Angeli portrait and put in Albert's portrait bracelet.

lockets decorated with black pearl drops. Locks of hair were put into onyx pins and lockets. The first of hundreds of medallions and miniatures of the late Prince Consort appeared as brooches, rings, lockets, a bracelet snap.

The shutters went up on Queen Victoria's social life; she was not seen at all in public for four years, when she finally agreed to attend the 1866 State Opening of Parliament (and that was after rumblings of discontent had reached even the Widow of Windsor). She was dressed in a black dress trimmed with crepe. On her head was the evocative widow's cap that was to become a more telling symbol of her reign than the crown. Yet even at this emotional moment Queen Victoria understood the potent majesty of jewellery. At the front of the cap was an aigrette of diamonds and pinned to the Garter sash was the majestic Koh-i-noor as a brooch.

The sad new year of 1862 was taken up with her children who had barely broken out of the chrysalis of childhood. Rings and brooches and diamond-studded snuff boxes were ordered from Garrard for Princess Alice's wedding, although mourning black engulfed this family event. 'More like a funeral,' wrote her mother gloomily as she dressed in her widow's weeds and her 'sad cap'.

The subject which engrossed Queen Victoria at this time was to find a bride for Bertie. Correspondence between the Queen and her daughter Vicky was spiced with discussion of 'suitable' foreign princesses. The beauty, charm and grace of Princess Alexandra of Denmark won the day and the future Edward VII was married in St George's Chapel, Windsor in March 1863, his widowed Mother peering at the ceremony from a secluded closet high above the altar (Chapter 2). The Queen gave Princess Alexandra pearl and opal jewellery, a suite of Indian ornaments, and left Bertie and 'Alix' to take over a society role she had never herself enjoyed.

'There are other and higher duties than those of mere representation,' she wrote in an impassioned statement to *The Times* on 6 April 1864. 'State ceremonies . . . can be equally well performed by other members of her family.' But although Queen Victoria had never been central to society, as sovereign she was the pivot of court life. The Drawing Rooms and Levees were filled with braided uniforms and spreading peacock trains, while displays of fine jewels gave the *nouveau riche* a chance to parade their wealth.

The Court Journal Register, which gave official descriptions of Court events, paints the Queen at Court in a rainbow of colours just before Prince Albert died, in 1859: 'a train of blue silk, embroidered in palm-patterned gold and silver, trimmed with blue net. The petticoat white satin. The Queen wore as a head-dress a circlet of diamonds.' A month later, at the March Levee, 'Her Majesty wore a train of mauve lilac velvet . . . the petticoat of white satin . . . a diadem of emeralds'. In the late spring, 'The Queen wore a train . . . with blue stripes, covered with a running pattern of blue and white flowers'. On her head, 'a diadem of diamonds and opals', probably the regal Indian tiara made five months before and now in the possession of Queen Elizabeth the Queen Mother.

Prince Albert's death drained the colour from the Queen and her attendants, although the maids-of-honour 'with regard to their youth' were permitted white, grey, mauve and purple, except during the recurring bouts of Court

Mourning instituted at the drop of one of the Queen's most distant German relatives. Marie Mallet, a maid-of-honour to Queen Victoria from 1887, complained that she would have to wear black feathers at a Drawing Room in 1888 'so that I shall present a hearse-like appearance'.

But just because Queen Victoria was perpetually in black, it did not mean that she lost her sense of majesty and grandeur. The big jewels, a major diadem and necklace, and the beribboned and glittering orders, were worn right through her reign, while Princess Alexandra set a fashion for opulence that brought in elaborate swathings of jewels with diamond stars and flowers decorating the dresses (Chapter 2). The court dress, which had a very low bodice and short sleeves, was called, confusingly, a 'petticoat', to distinguish it from the train, which could not be less than ten foot long and hung from the shoulder or the waist. White feathers and gloves (or black in the case of mourning) were *de rigueur*, and these same rules applied right up until 1939 when King George VI and Queen Elizabeth presided over the presentations.

In the last decade of her life, at the Drawing Room in May 1894, Queen Victoria is described in *Lady's Pictorial* as wearing a 'dress and train of brocaded gauze, trimmed with lace and sequinned jet. Her head-dress and veil of Honiton lace was surmounted by a diadem of diamonds. Ornaments — diamonds, the Star and Ribbon of the Order of the Garter, the Victoria and Albert Order, the Crown of India, the Red Cross and the Coburg Family Order'.

The Queen's purchases of jewellery in the 1870s were limited mostly to trinkets: dozens of lockets, in enamel, gold or, increasingly popular, turquoise; lockets clasped with a cherub's head set with a diamond wreath; more lockets suspended from bracelet bands, the persistent commemorative head of her beloved Albert destined for the tiny interiors.

Her other purchases were banal: a new passion for the horseshoe trotted in. There were gold horseshoe collar studs, horseshoe pins set with emeralds, sapphires and rubies or carved out of coral. In May 1884 the list of gifts that Queen Victoria took with her on a journey to Darmstadt is a guide to her personal taste: a gold bead brooch with a serpent border went to Marie Zimmerman, the head of the Queen's household in Darmstadt; the coachman received a gold horse pin with the nails studded in sapphires and diamonds (£7 10s); a gold serpent ring with sapphire head went to the General Manager of Dutch railways; the Grand-Duke Serge of Russia received more of the same – a set of diamond horseshoe studs with black pearl centres (£31 10s).

The gifts presented *to* Queen Victoria increased in number and value, as tributes from Indian Maharajahs filled her jewel cases and underlined the new title she added to her name: Victoria Regina *Et Imperatrix*. On May Day 1876, Queen Victoria was proclaimed Empress of India in Delhi. Indian lask diamonds, blood red rubies and huge flat emeralds were heaped on her, especially during the Prince of Wales's visit to India in 1875/6. In a rare revival of her sensual enthusiasm for jewels and decoration, the Widow of Windsor, with a huge gold crown on her head, decked herself out in these Indian jewels after dinner at Windsor Castle on 1 January 1877. When Disraeli, by then Lord Beaconsfield, asked the Queen whether she had any more Indian jewels, she sent for three large portmanteaux.

From the earliest part of her reign, Queen Victoria received presents from foreign potentates anxious to underline their own wealth and majesty. 'List of Articles sent for Her Most Gracious Majesty, The Mighty Queen, a trifling gift scarcely worth being mentioned,' wrote the Imam of Muscat in 1842 as he presented Queen Victoria with 'two pearl necklaces, two emeralds, an ornament made like a crown, ten cashmere shawls, one box containing four bottles of Otto of Roses'. Four horses were sent separately from Bombay with Lord Aberdeen.

The Empire was also the source of uncut and unset stones that first trickled, then flowed in during her reign and were the raw material of many of Queen Victoria's later jewels. They came not only from India (although that country produced the major tributes). In 1881 a rough Cape diamond was cut as a large brilliant with two more mounted as a bracelet, starting a tradition of gifts from South Africa that was to culminate in the enormous Cullinan diamond in 1907 and the South African necklace of 21 diamonds given to Princess Elizabeth for her 21st birthday in 1947 (Chapters 2 and 6).

Diamonds sprout like mushrooms throughout the pages of the Garrard ledger: 920 appear in 1872, to be mounted as brooch, earrings and necklace, with 336 returned unused for the future. One hundred and three diamonds came off a serpent's buckle and were used with 209 loose diamonds for rose patterned brooches in 1874; two diamonds went into a flower hair pin (10 February 1877). A magnificent pearl and diamond necklace from the Queen's 113 diamonds and 416 pearls was made for her in her old age (11 March 1892).

The opulence and magnificence of the potentate of 100 years ago is overwhelming to modern eyes. Queen Victoria gives a vivid picture of her meeting with the Shah of Persia on his visit to England in 1873 ('Have you seen the Shah?' was the catchword of the moment with the crowds). He wore a jewel-studded tunic with enormous ruby buttons, a large emerald perched in the centre of diamond epaulettes on each shoulder, a jewelled sword and scabbard tucked into a diamond sword-belt, the whole ensemble topped by an aigrette of diamonds on his high black astrakhan cap. The Queen in her 'smart mourning dress' with just a string of large pearls (plus the Star and Ribbon of the Garter and various other orders) sat shyly on a chair in the middle of the White Drawing Room at Windsor with three of her daughters on a sofa behind. The Shah had started his tour in Russia with his three wives, but a public outburst of morality had forced him to send his harem back home. The King of Kings, whose retinue included an official who carried a solid silver stove to heat a solid gold teapot for the royal cup of tea, was so impressed by his meeting with Queen Victoria that when he left Windsor Castle he showed the crowds outside the miniature of the Queen set in diamonds which she had given him, and kissed it with reverence.

The exotic splendours of the mysterious east were immensely appealing to the Queen, whose emotional need for colour and drama was served by her Indian servants in splendid scarlet and gold turbans – a vivid contrast with the tartan furnishings at Balmoral or the bourgeois clutter of Osborne. The contradictions in the Queen's character – her mix of the prosaic and the romantic, the excitable and the dutiful — were expressed in her jewels by the dramatic cluster necklace in opals and diamonds and the domestic pansy as an enamel brooch, the strings of baroque oriental pearls and the whimsical dog and horse portraits.

Was Queen Victoria acquisitive? There is nothing in her Journal or letters to suggest that she was impressed by the monetary value of the objects she and Albert started to amass. Although she was born into debt and grew up relatively impoverished, Queen Victoria had no need to see her jewellery as a hedge against inflation or as security for the future. In spite of the political upheavals in Europe, the Victorian age in Britain was a time of economic expansion and stability. Nothing better symbolises the fruits of industrial and overseas growth than the fact that for 60 years of the Queen's reign, from 1841 to her death in 1901, the annual cup or vase for the Ascot races cost the crown exactly the same amount: an unvarying £200.

The Queen was generous, impulsive and sensitive in her own present giving, from the specially made rosewood luncheon box she gave to Prince Albert (December 1858) for the shooting expeditions she so disliked, to the myriad of gem-studded and engraved lockets she distributed among her family. She chose for her daughter-in-law, Princess Alexandra, a twenty-fifth wedding anniversary present of an orange blossom spray brooch with five rose diamond oranges, white enamel on gold flowers and buds and leaves in silver. Forty years before, Prince Albert had designed the hair ornament of gold leaves, with little green oranges to represent their children.

The courage and fortitude of Florence Nightingale in the Crimean War so moved the Queen that in 1865 she had a Crimean brooch especially made, 'the form and emblems of which commemorate your great and blessed work, and which I hope, you will wear as a mark of the high approbation of your Sovereign!' The jewel was a ruby red enamel St George's Cross on a white field, with VR and a crown in diamonds in the centre, a sunburst of gold around it.

Tiny bracelets spelling out names and initials in gems were ordered for children and grandchildren. One of her last purchases, nine months before her death, was a silver cup proudly engraved 'To William, Crown Prince of the German Empire and Prussia from his affectionate Great-Grandmother and Godmother Victoria RI, May 6th 1900.'

Even servants received thoughtful gifts. 'I hope to meet those who have so faithfully and so devotedly served me, especially good John Brown and good Annie Macdonald,' wrote Queen Victoria in her will made four years before her death. Annie was the Queen's devoted personal maid (and thus in charge of her jewellery, just as Bobo Macdonald, another Scotswoman, is for the Queen today). 'To Annie Macdonald for faithful services to the Queen for XXII years', read the inscription on the oval gold brooch, the figure picked out in roman numerals in turquoise and the Queen's portrait in enamel on the back. It was given in 1879.

The death of John Brown four years later showed the insensitive side of the Queen's commemorative gifts. The hard-drinking Scottish ghillie who became an emotional prop and a physical support in the Queen's widowhood was disliked both by the royal family (who found their mother's attachment to him an embarrassment and a source of public gossip and criticism) and by fellow servants, who were suspicious of this downstairs court favourite. Yet when he died in 1883, the Queen thrust upon friends and relatives the gold and silver medallions, the memorial pins and brooches. Dr Profeit at Balmoral, whose dislike of John Brown was legendary on the Scottish estate, received a miniature of Brown's head set in diamonds as a tie pin. He hid it in his coat pocket so that he could put it in his tie hastily if he saw the Queen; otherwise this unwanted memento mori was kept out of sight away from the mocking eyes of the rest of the court.

At that grand celebration of Queenship in 1887, the Jubilee, Queen Victoria rode to Westminster Abbey in a lace bonnet, but it was decked with diamonds. Twenty-nine years before the contradictory Queen had dressed in an elaborate gown for Vicky's wedding – and scattered her hair with wild flowers.

The Golden Jubilee celebrations of 1887 and the Diamond Jubilee of ten years later brought in a further set of tributes – so many that Garrard charged a fee of three pounds for writing the new entries into the inventory which had been started in 1896. The Crown Jewellers made an heroic attempt to sort, list and categorise the jewels which now filled five large cases lined with white silk velvet and fitted with Chubbs patent locks with steel keys. A royal red levant morocco-bound book with silk facings was purchased and Mr Linton of Garrard spent 10 days at Osborne listing all the jewels and gems.

What was the value of this incalculable store of jewellery that must be measured not only in gems and settings but also in historical interest? From the Garrard ledger we know that Queen Victoria spent £158,000 on jewellery and silver (even though a percentage of this was for gifts to others). On the most conservative estimate, the jewels, gems and orders she received during her reign must have exceeded a quarter of a million pounds (£12.5 million in modern terms) and were probably worth twice that amount. When the single jewel case with which the Russian Empress Marie Feodorovna escaped the Russian revolution was sold off in 1928, the jewels – of great intrinsic worth and romantic associations – were valued at £350,000 before Queen Mary had removed the best pieces (Chapter 3).

By the standards of royalty in her own time, Queen Victoria's jewellery was majestic but not opulent. In 1837, the year that Princess Victoria became Queen, the Czarina Alexandra of Russia showed off her jewels to the wealthy Society figure Lady Londonderry when she visited St Petersburg. The Imperial bedchamber was lined with opals, diamonds, pearls and rubies in glass show-cases. There were more than 500 bracelets, 100 diamond solitaire rings, countless *parures* and diamonds displayed like religious relics.

In one sense Queen Victoria's jewellery was like a Russian icon, a tangible and actual expression of an object of veneration and respect: herself. Throughout the 1880s, the Queen's likeness became the favourite subject for her commissions; 'an oval onyx portrait of Your Majesty (17 March 1883); mounting a small oval enamel portrait of Your Majesty with pearl border and plain gold band as bracelet (28 Jan 1885); a bracelet with opal and brilliant border to contain Your Majesty's enamel miniature portrait (23 November 1889)'.

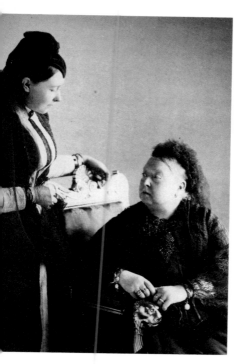

Queen Victoria in her rings, charms and trinkets with her daughter Vicky in 1889. 'I had your picture on my arm . . . and your pretty locket round my neck,' she wrote to her daughter.

This tendency to represent the Queen as an object of adoration and veneration reached its zenith at the Golden Jubilee when portraits of the Queen were stamped on medals, brooches, bracelets, lockets and pendants, even set in a wreath border, with VRI picked out in rubies, diamonds and cabochon sapphires, with gold crown and sceptre thrown in.

A sense of reverence and mystical awe surrounded the Queen in her last years when Queen Victoria's young Assistant Private Secretary Fritz Ponsonby found that diners talked to one another in whispers and spoke in a normal voice only when seated beside Her Majesty. This awe was deliberately fostered by the two leading Prime Ministers of her reign: the worthy Liberal William Gladstone and the intellectual, charming and mercurial Benjamin Disraeli.

Queen Victoria is reputed to have dismissed Gladstone's idea of her as a 'sacrosanct embodiment of venerable traditions' with the complaint that he addressed her like a public meeting. But if Gladstone himself viewed the Queen through a quasi-religious haze of awe, Disraeli, with a more astute understanding of the Queen's character, deliberately encouraged 'the lofty view of her own position which had always been native to Victoria's mind' as Lytton Strachey expressed it. Disraeli supported her idea of assuming the title of Empress of India, and was rewarded by seeing her decked out in the Indian jewels when he dined at Windsor. He couched his own reverence in an allusion to jewels — the traditional tribal totem of majesty — when he spoke of the primroses picked by the Queen in the woods round Osborne as 'the gems and jewels of nature . . . more precious than rubies coming from the sovereign whom he adores'.

That adoration and veneration came increasingly from her subjects, who worshipped her for being sixty years a Queen and forgot their disappointment that she had spent nearly 40 of those years secluded in mourning. The growth of the Empire increased the magic and mysticism attached to the Crown. As Lytton Strachey said, 'Imperialism is a faith as well as a business and, as it grew, the mysticism in English public life grew with it; and simultaneously a new importance began to attach to the Crown. The need for a symbol of England's might, of England's worth, of England's extraordinary and mysterious destiny became felt more urgently than ever before.'

Queen Victoria had taken over a discredited monarchy, and while Europe's other sovereigns tottered or were deposed, she built up the majesty of Great Britain. The final years brought an increasingly mystic sense of grandeur. Her jewellery echoed these lofty feelings by entwining her portrait or initials with images of death and religious glory. There was her Jubilee trumpet brooch with an enamelled VR banner, her gold cupids' earrings, her gold brooch with diamond-tipped wings set with 'Victoria RI' and a crown in rubies, sapphires, emeralds and diamonds.

Even in a God-fearing age, the process of changing the sovereign from leader of state and society into a quasi-divine figurehead had already begun. The jewels were an expression of that awesome Majesty and the heart of the great royal collection.

The monumental Queen Victoria – on her head her personal crown; round her neck the Crown diamonds. Albert's brooch was even carved into marble.

Imperial Alexandra

'It would be dreadful if this pearl went to the horrid Russians.'

Crown Princess Vicky to her Mother Queen Victoria,
about Princess Alexandra of Denmark, 20 April 1861

'May he only be worthy of such a jewel!'

Queen Victoria to her daughter Vicky, 19 June 1861,
about her son Bertie and Princess Alexandra

When Queen Victoria died on 22 January 1901, her image was stamped on the public mind as it was on the coins of her realm: a stern matriarch in a widow's cap and veil, still in mourning for Prince Albert nearly 40 years after his death.

Her daughter-in-law Alexandra, Bertie's wife, had been sent by the royal family to persuade the old Queen that 'the Empire should be ruled by a sceptre and not a bonnet', as Lord Rosebery caustically expressed it. But not even the sweet-natured and gentle Alix could make Queen Victoria exchange her 'bonnet' for a crown at the Jubilee of 1887, or to agree with Lord Halifax that people wanted 'gilding for their money'.

When Bertie was crowned Edward VII at the Coronation of 1902, Queen Alexandra's coinage was the exact reverse. Round her swan-thin neck, beneath her youthful face, the fringe of curls and her new crown, Alexandra had lapped five separate diamond necklaces. Below them was Bertie's necklace, the festoons of pearls and diamonds her husband had given her as a wedding present nearly 40 years before.

Over the bodice of the gilded Indian gauze dress were swags and loops of pearls, a cascade of milky white that poured down to her waist, almost covering her improvised stomacher – the Dagmar necklace with its Danish cross, a proud vestige of her national heritage. From behind the pearls winked the big blue sapphire clasped by diamonds, 'Albert's brooch' as Queen Victoria had always called it because her husband had given it to her on *their* wedding day. She left it to the Crown when she died.

Queen Alexandra looked 'every inch a Queen' in a way that recalled Shakespeare's England: Queen Elizabeth I with her glittering encrustations of gems.

The Edwardian Queen at the Coronation of 1902. Her jewels include the wedding present necklace from Bertie, the Danish Dagmar necklace as a stomacher and Queen Victoria's bows on her skirt. India was the source of her finest gems and the inspiration for her royal image.
LEFT *The Maharajah of Patiala in Coronation year. His family bought Empress Eugénie's jewels.*

This elegant Edwardian Queen was in total contrast with the earlier unsophisticated Danish Princess Alix, 'The Sea King's daughter from over the sea' as the poet Tennyson had described her. Dressed modestly in black, without a single piece of jewellery, the 17-year-old Princess had kissed the hand of the bereaved Queen Victoria on the eve of her engagement in the autumn of 1862.

Princess Alexandra brought little with her as a dowry but her natural beauty and grace and a spontaneous sense of style. 'Not a dazzling beauty but an indescribable charming,' was the vivid, if ungrammatical, description of Alix by Crown Princess Vicky, Queen Victoria's eldest daughter who had married the heir to the German Kaiser.

In the letters mother and daughter exchanged daily for 40 years, the relative merits of various Prussian princesses were discussed as a suitable bride for Bertie. Queen Victoria's son and heir was just 21, had a predilection for pretty girls and, according to his mother's view of his brief affair with actress Nellie Clifden, Bertie was a moral reprobate whose behaviour had caused so much stress to his father that he had precipitated Prince Albert's death from typhoid fever in the winter of 1861. A swift marriage to an available princess could be Bertie's only salvation.

Apart from her beauty and charm, Princess Alexandra was not a particularly 'suitable' candidate – especially as the Germany which had provided Queen Victoria's own family background, and was Prince Albert's native home and Vicky's adopted country, was a traditional enemy of Denmark over the disputed territories of Schleswig-Holstein.

Princess Alexandra had no background of culture or even privilege. 'The mother's family are bad, the father's foolish,' claimed Queen Victoria, referring to the various illicit liaisons which had left the Danish royal family without an heir and had brought Alix's father Prince Christian close to the throne.

Princess Alexandra's immediate family was not poor, but her parents were careful – and the idea that the young bride brought with her on her marriage priceless family emeralds, which were later 'acquired' by Edward VIII and Mrs Simpson, is nonsense (Chapter 4). Alix shared a room in the Yellow Palace (more of a large mansion opening directly on to the street) with her sister Dagmar. This noble Danish name had been given to the symbolic necklace, its cross a replica of the one found on an earlier Princess Dagmar's grave, which the dissolute and sterile King of Denmark, Frederick VII, gave to Princess Alexandra on her marriage.

Princess Alexandra had three brothers and two sisters, but 'Minnie' as the family called Dagmar, was always her favourite. Minnie was to become the mighty Empress Marie Feodorovna of Russia, in another dynastic connection for the Danish royal family. Ten years later she was delighting the London crowds with her fabulous jewels and the girlish delight with which the two sisters rode out together in identical blue and white silk dresses in Hyde Park in 1873.

Part of Minnie's fantastic collection of jewels was to come into the English royal family when they were offered to Queen Mary after the Empress Marie's death in 1928. But in the early spring of 1863, the two unspoiled Danish

Alix's sister Minnie, the Empress Marie Feodorovna of Russia, wearing her fabulous diamonds. The centre stone in the necklace weighed 32 carats.

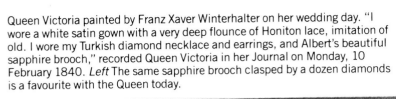

Queen Victoria painted by Franz Xaver Winterhalter on her wedding day. "I wore a white satin gown with a very deep flounce of Honiton lace, imitation of old. I wore my Turkish diamond necklace and earrings, and Albert's beautiful sapphire brooch," recorded Queen Victoria in her Journal on Monday, 10 February 1840. *Left* The same sapphire brooch clasped by a dozen diamonds is a favourite with the Queen today.

Above Queen Victoria had a passion for trinkets and for commemorating her loved ones. Young or old, she would wear a heart or a locket sooner than a Crown.

Above right Prince Albert wearing the diamond Garter and star Queen Victoria gave him the night before their wedding. She took it over when he died and symbolically wore it as her own.

Centre right A mourning ring commemorating Prince Albert after his death from typhoid in December 1861. Queen Victoria's Christmas present to her six-year-old daughter Beatrice was a bracelet with a model of her dead father's eye.

Below right Queen Victoria's children shared her pleasure in personalised gifts. This gold bar brooch by the Roman jeweller Castellani is enamelled with the entwined initials of Queen Victoria's second daughter Alice and her husband Prince Louis of Hesse. It was a present from them to Queen Victoria on her birthday in 1873. A locket on the reverse contains a curl of hair.

Opposite Victoria Regina, every inch a Queen in the diamond diadem — her favourite head ornament, designed for George IV and now worn by the Queen on our postage stamps. Round Queen Victoria's neck are the Crown diamonds; Albert's portrait bracelet is on her wrist. On a red velvet cushion rests the Imperial State Crown, made up for Queen Victoria from family gems at a cost of £1,000. In the centre is the historic Black Prince's Ruby worn by King Henry V on his helmet at the battle of Agincourt. This crown was the model for the new Crown made for the Queen's Coronation in 1953.

Left The duties of Empire . . . Queen Victoria presenting a Bible to the natives, while a stern Prince Albert looks on. On the Queen's wrist is the bracelet containing a portrait of her husband that she wore until the day she died.

Below The spoils of Empire . . . "This is the ruby among the twenty-five thousand jewels of the King of Kings," reads the Persian inscription on the Timur ruby, the 352-carat stone known as the "Tribute to the World". It was taken from India and presented to Queen Victoria in 1851. The Queen has never worn it, although she once planned to have a dress made for it.

Below The legendary Koh-i-noor diamond in a replica of its original setting found at the conquest of the Punjab in 1849. Its history goes back 5,000 years, and a Persian Emperor gave it the name "Mountain of Light". The Duke of Wellington cut the first facet on the stone in 1852. The Koh-i-noor supposedly brings ill-luck to male rulers and is worn by Queen Consorts. It is currently set in the Queen Mother's crown.

princesses sewed Princess Alexandra's trousseau together. The white silk bonnet bobbing with pink roses which Alix wore on her arrival at Gravesend for her March wedding was made at home.

That 'home' was a cheerful mix of warm-hearted family life, practical jokes, physical exercise and local gossip that Bertie was ultimately to find deadly dull. Princess Alix's experience of the wider world encompassed visits to the small principalities of German relatives on her mother's side, and especially the gathering of the royal clans every second summer at Schloss Rumpenheim near Frankfurt, where Princess Alexandra's daughter-in-law, the future Queen Mary, was to spend her formative holidays. At Rumpenheim, Alix enjoyed the family banter and the rumbustious entertainment that echoed the affectionate but completely unintellectual environment in Denmark. Crown Princess Vicky tactfully described Princess Alexandra's non-existent education as 'a natural one – and one of the heart'.

Princess Alexandra certainly managed to capture all hearts as she landed at Gravesend in a dove-grey dress with a violet mantle and the home-made white bonnet to be met by her betrothed Bertie (who, although the most punctilious of men, was unaccountably late). The sweet softness of colour – Alix's own personal interpretation of mourning – not only lifted metaphorically the shroud of black gloom that had descended on England after the death of Prince Albert two years before, it also presaged Queen Alexandra's later style: the mauve and grey, lavender and silver dresses, worn with white jewellery of pearls and diamonds touched with pale amethyst and heliotrope. These were the colours and jewels that exemplify the brief Edwardian decade.

The bejewelled, decorative Queen Alexandra was an imaginative creation that was Alix's contribution to the British monarchy. It was achieved not just with the jewels that flowed to her as Princess of Wales and later Queen Consort, but also with her absolute and unwavering certainty of taste. She showed it when she put on her simplest dress to meet Queen Victoria or when she adapted Victorian mourning dress to her own image. She was 57 when she was finally crowned after a lifetime in Queen Victoria's shadow. By then she was ageing, deaf through an hereditary illness transmitted by her mother Queen Louise; she was surrounded even at her Coronation by a 'loose box' of the King's mistresses. Yet she had absolute confidence in how to dress for the occasion. 'I know better than all the milliners and antiquaries,' she said. 'I shall wear exactly what I like and so shall my ladies – *Basta*.'

Prince Christian described his daughter to Queen Victoria in 1862 as 'a good child not brilliant, but with a will of her own'. It was an accurate summing-up of her character. Gossips were swift to note that Princess Alexandra's dazzling appearance was not matched by a brilliant mind. ('Clever, I don't think she is,' said Queen Victoria a few months after the marriage.) She was also uneducated, obstinate, handicapped by a limp after an attack of rheumatic fever and increasingly cut off from society by her deafness.

She even had a scar on her neck, the result of a childhood illness, and it was a measure of Princess Alexandra's style that she managed to turn this disability to advantage by wearing the 'dog-collar' or choker necklace that she launched as a lasting fashion in jewellery.

Yet the Princess who was in waiting for 40 years and Queen for a brief decade had a luminous quality that outshone her imperfections, enraptured the most doubting and is captured even in the frozen images of Victorian photography.

'She has the accomplishment of being gracious without smiling; she has repose,' said Queen Victoria's Prime Minister Disraeli. 'I never set eyes upon a sweeter creature than Princess Alix,' said Princess Vicky, after she had arranged a 'chance' meeting with the Princess and her mother in Germany. Vicky had engineered an even more tricky 'random' encounter between Bertie and his prospective bride, at Speyer Cathedral, where he complained about Princess Alexandra's long nose and brow. 'Her beauty,' said his sister firmly, 'consists more in the sweetness of expression, grace and manners, and extreme refinement of appearance.'

Significantly, both the Princess Royal and Queen Victoria translated this special radiance into metaphors of jewels. 'It would be dreadful if this pearl went to the horrid Russians,' said Vicky. 'May he only be worthy of such a jewel!' her mother replied.

The first jewel that the Prince of Wales (who was not to be a 'worthy' husband by any means) gave to Princess Alexandra expressed the sentimental Victorian taste that the stylish princess would ultimately eradicate: BERTIE spelled the gems – Beryl, Emerald, Ruby, Turquoise, Jacinth, Emerald – in the colourful ring the 21-year-old Prince gave to his bride, who spent six weeks incarcerated with Queen Victoria at Osborne and won her lasting approval by bursting into tears after an entire evening spent reliving Prince Albert's death. This induction period for potential royal brides is a family tradition. Princess May of Teck, later Queen Mary, was summoned to Balmoral for ten days before she became engaged. Lady Diana Spencer had three months at Clarence House under the gentle wing of the Queen Mother before her wedding.

Marriage brought to Princess Alexandra of Wales her first heady taste of fine jewellery. Bertie's wedding present to her was the delicate looped necklace of pearls and diamonds which is today the Queen Mother's favourite piece of jewellery – a tangible gem-studded link between two well-beloved consorts in the royal dynasty. The jewels were part of a *parure* of diamonds and pearls which included an oblong brooch set with three large pearls and three other pendant drops (much worn later by Queen Mary). The Crown Jewellers Garrard, who made the suite, also produced button earrings and a coronet to match the festoon necklace with its eight fleurettes of brilliants and pearl drops suspended from the front three clusters.

In a dramatic (and slightly mawkish) gesture, Queen Victoria gave Princess Alexandra not just from herself, but also in the name of the dead Prince Albert, a diamond and opal cross threaded on a royal blue ribbon and matching pendant brooches and earrings. She also gave her new daughter-in-law a foretaste of the fabulous Indian gems which she was later to receive: a suite of Indian ornaments with two tasselled necklaces, one of seven swags of seed pearls strung with emerald and ruby flowers, the other an enamel and pearl and gem-set necklet with matching bracelets.

Queen Victoria looked down on the wedding service in St George's Chapel

The pearl and diamond coronet, festoon necklace and suite given to Princess Alexandra of Denmark from the Prince of Wales. The Queen Mother wears the necklace in the fourth colour plate section.

Windsor from Catherine of Aragon's private eyrie perched above the long nave. From the same spot 30 years later, Princess Alexandra ('looking more beautiful than ever in deepest mourning') was to witness the funeral of her eldest son and heir apparent. Eddy, the Duke of Clarence and Avondale, was to die suddenly in 1892; the Crown passed to his younger brother, who became George V.

At Bertie's wedding, Queen Victoria was in 'the plainest of widows' weeds' with only Albert's Garter Star and the Prince Consort's portrait to relieve the black.

Bertie's bride on their wedding day in 1863. She is wearing the necklace, brooch and earrings he gave her.

The bride was in her rustic dress ('Who is this rustic beauty?' Bertie had inquired when he saw her picture), garlanded with orange blossom, in silver tissue trimmed with Honiton lace in a pattern of roses, shamrocks and thistles. A similar pattern inspired the pearl embroidery by Norman Hartnell for Princess Elizabeth's wedding dress in 1947. This patriotic choice created a vision of shimmering lightness in white silk 'that set off her tapering waist and faultless symmetry of form to absolute perfection', as *The Times* grandly expressed it. Lady Geraldine Somerset, a waspish commentator, described the bridal dress as '*très bon gout*, light, young and royal', although among the wedding gifts – the choicest mounted in a baroque display in a temporary structure by the Chapel – was another perfect wedding dress: an exquisite creation in Brussels lace given by King Leopold of the Belgians, Queen Victoria's mentor and father figure. For the first and last time in her life, Princess Alexandra's willingness to do the right thing deflected her unshakeable taste. Later, she would even wear her Garter on the wrong shoulder if it looked better on a dress.

Round her neck, Princess Alexandra was soon to wear the glittering necklace of 32 brilliants presented to her by the Corporation of London and reputedly worth £10,000. This was one of several 'institutional' presents that were added to the generous family gifts. The Ladies of Liverpool all contributed towards a present of a handsome pearl necklace with a suspended diamond cross; the Ladies of Leeds a diamond bracelet. The Ladies of Manchester, like Queen Victoria, chose opals with diamonds for their bracelet, although opals were not at all favoured by the Danish Princess. Immediately after Queen Victoria's death she removed the 'unlucky' opals from the regal Indian tiara and replaced them with rubies – which is how the Queen Mother wears the tiara today.

In the cornucopia of jewels that Princess Alexandra was given as presents, the Dagmar necklace was exceptional – swags of 2,000 diamonds and 118 pearls, the diamond scrollwork in the centre set with pear-drop pearls. From it hung the facsimile of the eleventh-century Dagmar cross in enamel ornamented with pearls and diamonds. (The Queen has now removed the cross and the large pearls to make a less elaborate piece, see colour plates.)

There were personal wedding gifts from all Queen Victoria's children. Vicky, the Crown Princess of Prussia, who had been the principal match-maker, sealed her success with a round gold locket with 'Victoria' in raised letters (designed by herself and just what Dearest Mamma might have chosen). Princess Alice, whose own marriage the previous year to Prince Louis of Hesse had been overshadowed by Prince Albert's death, gave a turquoise buckle bracelet with diamonds spelling out an entwined L and A – for herself and her husband. Bertie's younger brothers and sisters (including Prince Alfred who claimed to be half in love with her himself) gave the Princess a joint present of an oval brilliant pendant set with a sapphire cross.

The Duchess of Cambridge and her family had originally opposed the match, yet she presented a diamond flower spray brooch set with four handsome square emeralds. Princess Mary of Cambridge matched the brooch with an emerald and diamond buckle bracelet. From the Duke of Cambridge came a broad gold and blue enamel bracelet, set with a diamond feather motif strikingly similar to the Prince of Wales' feather pendant which Princess Diana received on her wedding.

The network of German relatives was fuming at the dynastic connection with their Danish enemy. Their long-standing quarrel with the Danes over the Duchies of Schleswig and Holstein was to erupt into open war the year after the royal wedding. But even Prussian princes produced jewels large and small for Princess Alexandra: a gold bracelet and diamond-studded locket pendant from the Grand-Duchess of Mecklenburg-Strelitz, who was later to see her grandniece May marry Alix's son and become Queen of England. From the Hesse Cassels and the Landgrave Wilhelm of Hesse came more baroque German pieces – ornaments made like Nibelung gold in heavy twisted circles, part of the trend towards the historical Revivalist style inspired by the Roman jeweller Castellani. There was more of the Revivalist influence in the suite of Saxon armlet, brooch and hairpins from the inhabitants of the outlying provinces of Laaland and the Felater, and a brooch enamelled with Runic ornaments and set with Scottish pearls from the Highland companies of the Edinburgh Rifle volunteers.

The most exotic of all these foreign gifts was the exquisite holder in which Princess Alexandra carried her bridal bouquet. It was carved out of flesh pink crystal, its stem banded with emeralds and diamonds over a crystal ball set with rubies and diamonds, which sprang open to produce four supports – a fine piece of Indian workmanship presented by Maharajah Dhuleep Singh, 'Queen Victoria's Maharajah' as he was called after he was deposed by the British as ruler of the Punjab, settled in England and became a frequent visitor to Windsor.

If Princess Alexandra could have looked into the ruby-studded crystal ball that supported this lovely gift, she might have seen the other wondrous Indian gems she would one day own. At the moment her jewel box, filled as it was with all the wedding gifts, did not really contain anything in her own taste. Just as Princess Diana is wearing jewels that are not yet moulded to her fashion image, so Princess Alexandra danced through the radiant summer season of 1863 as a true Victorian – ringleted hair, crinoline gowns and heavy jewels that were far removed from her delicate later gems.

Over the next decade, the new Prince and Princess of Wales and their Marlborough House set were the lynchpins of society. Queen Victoria had always been shy of social life, and after a brief flutter in her early married life had retreated to a more domestic routine with Prince Albert. 'I have been now

30 years in harness . . . but I am terribly shy and nervous and always was so,' she said to Vicky in 1865. Bertie and Alix became the twin suns round which society spun. The Princess glittered at the ball given at the Guildhall in the summer of 1863 by the Corporation of the City of London – not just in the diamond necklace that the City had given her as a wedding gift, but also in the vast, illuminated picture of herself in front of the hunting lodge in Denmark which formed a lavish backdrop.

Three thousand people crowded in to be presented to the Princess of Wales as she deputised for the Queen in 1863 at her first Drawing Room, part of the official Season at Court. 'She was a bit of a thing, with a white gown and a white face, two curls and a tiara,' said Lady Knightley, a member of Society and of the Court circle. Alix dressed always in half mourning for Prince Albert – in white lace trimmed with mauve ribbons for Ascot; in silver grey moiré silk trimmed with violet velvet for a visit to the zoological gardens; in pale lace over lavender with a jewelled diadem for the Ball given by the Brigade of Guards in the picture gallery of the international exhibition hall at Kensington on 26 June 1863, when the guards formed a gleaming arch of swords and the Prince and Princess danced underneath.

The tight-knit Court circle, still scarcely penetrated by the *nouveau riche* merchant class, did not entirely approve of this 'whirl of amusement' as Queen Victoria described it, but it continued right through Princess Alexandra's pregnancy, which produced (six weeks prematurely) an heir to the throne on a frosty January day in 1864. The new baby, Prince Albert Victor, later Duke of Clarence and Avondale, was always 'Eddy' to his family.

The society centred on Marlborough House, the London home of the young couple, was 'too little royal' according to their critics. Queen Victoria actually suggested that the Prince and Princess should go out in London only to three or four great houses – Westminster House, Spencer House, Apsley House and not even all of these in one year. It is intriguing to see that a century later two of these 'suitable' houses produced potential brides for Prince Charles: Lady Jane Wellesley, with connections to the Duke of Wellington and Apsley House, and Lady Diana Spencer, who became Princess of Wales.

Bertie was a very different young man from his father, and the Queen only occasionally faced up to these fundamental differences between father and son. ('He is my caricature,' she once admitted.) Mostly she complained only of the outward manifestations of his personality: his refusal to study, his supposed weakness of character, his enthusiasm for Society, his passion for fashion. (Prince Albert wrote despairingly to Vicky in 1858 that even when the Prince of Wales went out shooting, he was more concerned with his trousers than with the game, a complaint echoed later by George V about his son Edward VIII.)

The unbending strait-jacket of education into which Prince Albert and his German mentor Baron Stockmar forced Bertie as a child and adolescent had the oddest consequences. Perhaps because he was cut off by his mother from playing a serious role in state affairs, he applied the same strictness, orthodoxy and rigidity with which he had been brought up as future King to the minutiae of social etiquette and dress. 'The Princess has taken the trouble to wear a tiara, why have you not done so,' he chastised the Duchess of Marlborough at dinner.

By 1905, when Queen Alexandra would wear glittering jewellery throughout the day, both the King and Queen scorned the daughter of the British consul in Algiers because she had the poor taste to appear at luncheon 'in flannels'.

The Prince and Princess of Wales must have together created the delicate Edwardian vision that was Queen Alexandra's image as Queen Consort. Although Bertie was in many ways a careless husband, neglecting Princess Alexandra's illness after the birth of their daughter Louise in 1867, and soon amusing himself with other women, they shared a sense of taste and personal style.

Queen Victoria warned the young Princess Alexandra against excessive display: 'I hope dear Alix will not spend much on dress in Paris. There is besides a *very* strong feeling against the luxuriousness, extravagance and frivolity of Society and everyone points to *my* simplicity,' she wrote to Bertie in May 1869. Bertie was already exceeding his income by £20,000 a year, and sinking money into improvements at the Waleses' new country residence, Sandringham House in Norfolk. This had been acquired for the Prince in 1863 but he spent vast sums of money turning it into a suitable royal residence and putting its extensive estates in order. The rebuilding of the old house alone cost £80,000 and the Prince also built other houses, including Park House, where Lady Diana Spencer was to spend her childhood 100 years later.

Queen Victoria also complained at the amount the Prince of Wales spent on gratifying his wife's taste for jewellery, wondering 'what a woman could want with new pieces who already had more jewels than she could ever wear'. (This was from a queen who left five enormous morocco leather cases of jewels when she died.)

The Prince and Princess of Wales created an image for Princess Alexandra that was achieved completely apart from the collection of Crown Jewellery, for although Queen Victoria designated some of her jewels (especially those connected with Prince Albert) as the property of the Sovereign and Consort, this happened only after her death in 1901. Alexandra had no access to the royal jewellery until she was nearly 60 years old, but a quarter of a century before, when the Princess was in her early thirties, she became the recipient of a glittering collection of Indian jewels and gem-set objects.

In the late autumn of 1875, the Prince of Wales, after extracting reluctant permission from his mother and £112,000 from an even more reluctant Parliament, set off for a six-month tour of the Indian Empire, without the Princess, who never forgave him for leaving her behind. (Princess Alexandra, at Sandringham on the eve of her husband's departure, looked, noted Disraeli wickedly, as 'though she were about to commit suttee'.)

When the future Edward VII sailed from Bombay back to England the following Spring in the HMS *Serapis* (where the library was like a gentlemen's club and the ship's band played 'Home Sweet Home'), the vessel and her sister ship HMS *Osborne* were loaded down with an overwhelming assortment of gifts – swords and daggers, solid silver tea services and gold accoutrements for preparing betel juice, suits of armour inlaid with gold, silver spears and lances, shields, a Noah's Ark of animals (dead and alive) and three weighty trunks of jewellery.

Some idea of these Imperial offerings can be seen in the eclectic collection of just one state – gifts presented to the Prince in Benares at the start of his tour of North India in January 1876; 'some gigantic tusks, weapons consisting of jewelled hilted swords . . . a magnificent silver palanquin picked out in gold and lined with red satin and gold emboidery, a large double bedstead of solid silver with canopy and bed of red satin, and a book from the Behar literary society.'

These 'humble offerings' (as the ruling class in the province of Oudh described the solid gold vessels for Princess Alexandra and a massive gold crown hung with limpid emerald drops) were given by the maharajahs to underline their own grandeur and in homage to the distant imperial figurehead in her black mourning dress at Windsor.

The exotic magnificence of this six-month royal progress through India must have had a profound effect on the imagination of the Prince of Wales, who celebrated his 34th birthday on 20 November in Bombay with a two-hour carriage drive in a balmy 88 degrees through streets lined with sentinels of soft lamps and banners proclaiming 'Tell Mamma we are happy'.

Imperial India presented itself to the Prince of Wales as a mixture of alien Hindu ritual, overlaid with a more-or-less comprehensible show of native grandeur and British Imperial protocol. It was expressed in vivid vignettes: the Rajah of Jodhpur receiving the Star of India from the Prince of Wales, and trying to back out gracefully with the robe of the Order sticking out over his voluminous starched pink petticoats; painted elephants in Jumoo swaying towards the Prince with gold and silver howdahs on their backs, their wrinkled grey skins and spreading ear flaps the backcloth for fantastic pictures of deities and animals; the Prince shielded from the blistering sun by a gold umbrella or changing for dinner under canvas on an elephant shoot into his newly invented short dark dinner jacket.

Sometimes the delicate balance between cultures toppled over into the absurd, as when the Christian prince was greeted in Kandy by Hindu urchins whose skins had been painted over with whitewash so that they could appear with gilt coronets and white wands as Victorian angels. A steaming Christmas Day was spent on HMS *Serapis* with cotton wool stuck on the windows as snow. After sitting on a solid silver chair inside the Durbar tent on New Year's Day at an investiture for jewelled Indian princes, the Prince escaped in the evening to watch a performance of his favourite farce, *My Old Dad*.

In the context of the trip, with its torchlight parade of 30 elephants or its solid silver bathtub (and solid gold bed at Gwalior) the gifts presented to the Prince were not so embarrassingly opulent. The problem was the contrast between what was given and received.

The exotic appearance of the maharajahs and the enormity of their offerings were obvious right from the start of the tour, when leading native princes, ablaze with diamonds, emeralds and rubies, lined up to meet the Prince of Wales at a reception in Bombay. Even the nine-year-old Gaekwar of Baroda

THE FRUITS OF EMPIRE

Queen Alexandra's superb diamond necklace (2) was the ripe fruit of Empire. It was made by Cartier in 1904 by dismantling a magnificent Indian necklace. Their ledger (5) shows that it was set not only with diamonds, but with emeralds and rubies. The diamonds were remounted in the Collier Resille – literally a hairnet – a fine example of Edwardian workmanship. The portrait of Queen Alexandra by the French painter Francois Flameng (1) shows the necklace as she wore it. The nine

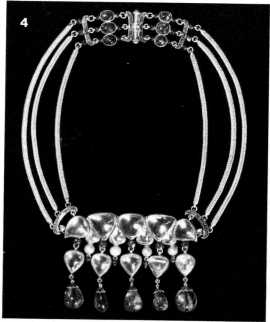

emeralds and rubies were returned to the Queen by Cartier and were the origin of the story of the 'Alexandra emeralds'.

Superb ropes of pearls and diamond aigrette worn by the Maharajah of Mysore in 1903 (3).

The magnificent emerald girdle (6) was from the trappings of a horse belonging to the Maharajah Ranjit Singh. It contains 19 flat emeralds, four intricately carved, 249 lask diamonds and 159 pearls. It was taken from the Treasury at Lahore and presented to Queen Victoria in 1851.

The imposing necklace (4) of lask diamonds set off by emeralds, pearls and rubies was part of the bounty bestowed on Edward VII, then Prince of Wales, in India in 1875/6. It was given to him by the Maharajah Scindiah.

The cat's-eye brooch (7), weighing 313 carats and set in diamonds, was given to Queen Victoria after the conquest of Kandy in 1886.

A pair of Indian enamel amulets (8).

had a gem-studded robe, a diamond-encrusted collar, swags of lustrous pearls and a shimmering brilliant aigrette.

Baroda was one of the first stops on the tour. The elephants wore anklets of solid gold and the Gaekwar was transported in a golden howdah, with cloth of gold canopy and cushions all lit up by the rays of the morning sun. In a formal ceremony, the Prince of Wales received some priceless gifts: a pearl necklace with a huge emerald pendant set in gold (for Queen Victoria), a diamond ring (for himself) and a magnificent diamond brooch for Princess Alexandra; a solid silver tea service in a blackwood cabinet; three swords with gold scabbards, one set with diamonds; two rhinoceros hide shields; a silver tray; two five-foot silver lances; a shawl embroidered with gold thread and an album in mahogany covers.

In return, the Prince of Wales, who received £30,000 from the Indian government for personal expenses, as well as the £112,000 voted by Parliament, gave the Gaekwar a gold watch, a medal, a gold snuff box (the standard overseas gift), portraits of the royal family and a book of engravings of Windsor Castle. In Kandy the Prince presented a pair of leather-bound dictionaries to the priests in a Buddhist temple after they had shown him their holy treasures: a bell-shaped casket studded with gems, standing on an ivory base on a solid gold lotus leaf and containing the largest emerald in the world, four inches long and two inches deep, carved into the likeness of a Buddha.

Because the disparity between the two sets of gifts was so immediately and embarrassingly apparent, the newspaper reporters who accompanied the Prince of Wales on tour stopped listing the native offerings, noting only the Prince's gifts (often described with flourish and hyperbole). They announced merely that 'The Prince received presents of equivalent value.' This suppression of the news most probably stemmed from the editors-in-chief, rather than from the reporters, who made much of the local colour: Indore's 'opium Arch' made entirely out of poppies; the cashmere shawls draped like flags on the streets of Amritsar where the open drains were overlaid with carpets of freshly-picked white roses.

The Times correspondent discussed the disparity of gifts in his despatch to London of 28 December 1875. The presents given by the Prince were, he assured his doubting readers, 'of a very solid and substantial nature'. The native gifts would have been even more costly but for restrictions placed on them by the Viceroy. In his turn, the Prince sought to establish a proximate value, 'but his resources are not boundless'. James Allingham, in his book *Five Months with the Prince in India*, simply repeated the official line that 'the value of the whole of the presents received by the Prince will not much exceed £40,000 and the value of the presents given by the Prince will amount to nearly £40,000'. The *Daily Telegraph* correspondent, in his book of the tour *From Pall Mall to the Punjab*, makes a few discreet jokes about the Prince's choice of gifts, especially the 'sword longer than he is tall' for the tiny Gaekwar of Baroda and the miscellaneous assortment of riding whips, field glasses and flagons given to the 13-year-old Maharajah of Mysore. Diamonds, says James Allingham dryly after inspecting the jewel-studded crown presented to the Prince at Indore, 'seem to be as plentiful in India as blackberries in England'.

The Times of India lists, more or less accurately, the presents given by both sides, although there are still some extraordinary (and presumably deliberate) omissions, such as the impressive diamond necklace given by Maharajah Scindiah of Gwalior and the necklace of magnificent rubies presented by Sir Jung Bahadore in Nepal, along with a menagerie of wild birds and beasts.

The Prince of Wales's entourage had no reason to reveal to reporters presents given in private. The 18-man suite (there were no women in the royal party) was much more concerned with a scandal that broke over Lord Aylsford, a close personal friend of the Prince of Wales and a member of the Marlborough House set. Aylsford received a letter from his wife on 20 February 1876 announcing that she was about to leave him for another of the Prince's friends, Lord Blandford. The departure of 'Sporting Joe' Aylsford on an elephant's back for London and disgrace started a Society scandal that erupted on the Prince's return in England in May, when he appeared in public with Princess Alexandra at Covent Garden at *Un Ballo in Mascera* on the very night of his return in order to defuse the gossip.

Reporters and public alike were therefore not especially concerned with the booty that arrived back with the Prince on the *Serapis* and the *Osborne*. The greatest public stir was caused by the animals, a menagerie that *The Times* correspondent described as including 'two remarkably handsome young tigers', from among the few which managed to escape the gem-studded pistols of the princely big-game hunters. Today the Duke of Edinburgh works for the preservation of wild life. His royal predecessor Bertie (and his son George V) thought prowess in shooting a way of demonstrating royal status.

In HMS *Serapis* were the 'skins, skeletons, heads, horns and hoofs of animals shot or given as presents', including 10-foot-long elephant tusks 'with points as sharp as a needle', reported *The Times*. The live animals included two young elephants, spotted deer, leopards, cheetahs, small bullocks, monkeys, a diminutive pony and a collection of Himalayan singing birds.

This last was the gift of Sir Jung Bahadore, Prime Minister and autocratic ruler of Nepal, whose own bright, bird-like eyes darted above his mauve, green and salmon pink silk outfit and under his magnificent head-dress, encrusted with splendid emeralds, the top of the turban studded 'like the Grand Panjandrum himself', with an awesome ruby. This was a present from the Emperor of China and worth six times the value of the incalculable Koh-i-noor or, as one of the Prince's party put it more practically, worth 'a fine estate in Buckinghamshire'.

The only Maharajah to match him was Patiala, who had bought for £300,000 the magnificent jewels of the Empress Eugénie of France and wore the brilliants that had once sparkled in the Tuileries gardens on his bright blue satin coat and white turban when he met the Prince of Wales in Calcutta.

From many different sources and contemporary accounts, here is a list (certainly incomplete) of the most important pieces of jewellery presented to the Prince of Wales during the Indian tour.

From the Prince and Maharajah Holkar of Indore
A diamond necklace with two large emerald pendants

A pair of diamond bracelets
A pearl necklace with emeralds inserted

From the states of Madure and Trichinopoly
A massive virgin gold belt with figures of Hindu deities
    for the Princess of Wales

From the Gaekwar and Ranee of Baroda
A pearl necklace with emerald pendant
A diamond ring
A magnificent diamond brooch

From Maharajah Scindiah of Gwalior
A necklace of 14 large diamonds set off by emerald, pearl
    and ruby drops (now with the Queen)

From the Maharajah of Mysore
A bracelet set with precious stones

From the Talooqdars of Lucknow and Dewan Mathura Dass
A crown made of diamonds and pearls with emerald drops,
    HRH coat of arms and feathers on front

From Sir Jung Bahadore of Nepal
A ruby necklace with 11 large rubies (used in the Indian
    regal tiara in the Crown Jewellery)

In addition, there were many gold, silver and gem-set objects, including jewel-hilted swords (from Benares), jewelled weapons (from the Maharajah of Kashmir), swords, daggers, guns and a solid gold cup, all set with pearls and diamonds (from Jaipur).

What happened to these jewels and gems, the heritage of the India of the maharajahs, of enormous historical as well as monetary value? The first and last sighting is the vision of Queen Victoria swathed in Indian gems at the dinner to celebrate her proclamation as Empress of India (Chapter 1). In the precise and detailed record of Garrard, the Crown Jeweller, in the ledger for Victoria's reign, there is one specific mention of Indian jewellery during this period. In January 1877 the workshops were repairing an Indian diamond bracelet and 'altering a large Indian diamond and pearl neck ornament by adding joints between the diamonds'.

The major Indian jewels have never been worn in public by any monarch or consort as they were originally presented. They are either in store or have been reset.

In the records of Cartier in Paris, it is possible to trace pieces of Indian jewellery that were reset for Queen Alexandra at the beginning of Edward VII's reign. Six months after Queen Victoria's death in 1901, Pierre Cartier of the French jewellery house was summoned to Buckingham Palace to create an Indian-style necklace to wear with Indian gowns sent to Queen Alexandra by Mary Curzon, the Vicereine of India. The Indian jewellery in the royal collection had been designed for the male maharajahs and was considered too heavy for the Queen. Cartier therefore used 17 pearls, 13 cabochon rubies and 94 emeralds for a new necklace in the spirit of an India which formed an exotic backdrop for European high Society up to and beyond the Great War.

A major piece of Indian jewellery set with nine massive emeralds, nine rubies and diamonds went into the Cartier workrooms three years later (22 August 1904) to emerge as Queen Alexandra's most quintessentially Edwardian piece of jewellery: her *collier résille* (literally 'hairnet'), an airy mesh of diamonds suspended from a choker and laid across the throat like a lace jabot, the whole necklace studded with pear-shaped diamonds and decorated with leafy garlands and diamond bows. The diamonds added up to an impressive 141.4 cts; the nine magnificent emeralds and rubies were returned and may have been the origin of the legend of the 'Alexandra emeralds' which Mrs Simpson is supposed to have received from the royal collection (Chapter 4).

Queen Alexandra wore her *collier résille* in the ethereal portrait by the French painter François Flameng. It hangs in Buckingham Palace, a gentle reminder of the Edwardian Queen as history has identified her — the elegant neck, with its delicate necklace, the pale shoulders in their low-cut gown rising from a mist of white tulle.

The image of Alexandra as Edwardian Queen haunts the imagination long after *The Times* correspondent saw her 'coming through the dark archway of the screen' at her Coronation, 'her crown glittering with diamonds'. She seemed at that point at the apex of social solidity and a symbol of Empire.

Was princely India, in its idea as well as in its torrent of jewels, the source of magnificence which Queen Alexandra saw as majesty? The Edwardian Queen never visited 'that most beautiful and fairylike country', and 30 years after the Prince of Wales had toured India without her, she wrote resentfully to her son Georgie, the future George V, 'I was not allowed to go when I wished it so very, very much.' But as Princess and Queen, Alexandra may have absorbed the exotic splendours of the India she never actually saw. The vision of bejewelled magnificence created by her, with the help and encouragement of her husband Bertie, has an extraordinary resemblance to the Indian maharajahs. Here is the Princess of Wales described by a Society magazine at the theatre in 1900 'dressed in black mousseline de soie, a wide diamond collar supported against the throat . . . a collet necklace and a long chain of diamonds falling over the dress, and in the coiffure an aigrette of diamonds with osprey plume and diamond arrow.' Here is an eye-witness description of the Maharajah of Patiala: 'Around his neck he wore a great collar of diamonds set in platinum along with four or five other massive and beautifully set necklaces of diamonds and emeralds. Another necklace with exquisite diamonds hung from his waist.' In the state regalia of the Maharajah of Mysore was an aigrette of diamonds with an osprey plume that might have been the model for Princess Alexandra's jewelled plume.

Alix showed her enthusiasm for the exotic in the serpent bracelet that slithered round her arm and is still in the royal family today, although the Queen finds it strange and unappealing and shudders when she recalls it.

Princess Alexandra pioneered the passion for display which became increasingly opulent by the 1890s. In the decade after the Prince's tour of India, the Princess of Wales began to establish the style of jewels which we immediately associate with her — especially the dog collars and stomachers pinned to the bodice, both of them in the delicate openwork patterns that echoed the lacy fabrics with which they were worn.

The 'garland' style of the Belle Époque grew from the earlier jewels made for Empress Eugénie in France, who had her jewellery reset in the style of Marie Antoinette recalling the favourite motifs of the eighteenth century: dainty swags of ribbon and garlands of fruit, elaborate ribbons and bows and tassels of diamonds. These were the very jewels that had been sold at the end of the Second Empire and bought and worn in profusion by the Maharajah of Patiala.

The jewel-encrusted fancy-dress costume Princess Alexandra wore to the Devonshire House Ball.

The delicate designs that Princess Alexandra wore were made by setting diamonds and pearls in platinum, rather than the traditional gold and silver of the high Victorian style. The shimmering lightness of the jewellery was achieved by the whiteness of stones and settings and the fact that they were absolutely in tune with the fashions in clothes and fabrics of the time. Another feature of the Belle Époque jewellery was that each piece had a variety of ornamental uses; fleurettes and bows would unpin from tiaras for use as brooches; the tiara itself came off its frame to become a necklace; the stomachers and bodice ornaments were articulated so that they could be used as a centrepiece in a choker, pinned on to a velvet ribbon or used as a simple brooch. Typical of this style was Princess Alexandra's diamond cloak clasp which broke up into five separate parts.

The Prince of Wales himself wore a large diamond star on the shoulder of his elaborate gold emboidered maroon silk cloak in the swashbuckling costume for the lavish Venetian fancy-dress ball which the Waleses gave at Marlborough House in July 1874. This was the seminal moment when Victorian Society seems to be at the cusp with Edwardian. When the young Queen Victoria and Prince Albert held fancy-dress balls, they were deemed to be 'good for trade', bringing work to the dressmakers and tailors. The Venetian ball was unashamedly an aristocratic orgy of opulence, at which the men as much as their wives were smothered in jewels. The Duke of Wellington came as a Spanish grandee wearing the collar and jewel of the Golden Fleece, his Duchess had strewn diamonds across her dress; Bertie's brother Arthur, the Duke of Connaught, dressed as a fairy Prince in a ruby velvet doublet and silver satin hose, with a cloak made out of a complete leopard's head and skin with solid gold claws attached to his shoulders by diamond stars. Re-creating a portrait was a favourite theme, with the Duchess of Marlborough in black satin and lavender after the Blenheim portrait of Rubens's wife. Lady Cornelia Guest's jewellery was baroque in its magnificence. She had re-created a Van Dyck portrait and wore a long stomacher covered in jewels, her hair was plaited with pearls and in her headdress was a gigantic ruby which she claimed was the largest in the world.

At the centre of the throng, leading all London Society into the supper tents hung with scarlet velvet Indian carpets, embroidered with precious stones, was Princess Alexandra, exquisitely elegant in a ruby-red Venetian dress, the blue panel at the front of her skirt sewn with jewels. The ruby red sleeves were puffed with blue satin and the bodice of the dress was swagged with pearls. On her head was a tiny Juliet cap in velvet, encrusted with superb gems.

Queen Victoria, alert to the revolutionary eruptions in Europe, was concerned about an excessive public display of wealth. 'The higher classes, in their frivolous selfish and pleasure-seeking lives do more to increase the spirit of democracy than anything else,' she claimed. The chief contrast between Victorian Court style and the social standards set by the Prince and Princess of Wales, seems to have been the degree of pleasure with which the ritual Courts and Drawing Rooms were enacted.

The jewels worn at Court were a weather vane of changing styles and literally the only mark of individuality allowed within the rigorously enforced rules of dress. The Court circle from which Queen Victoria withdrew as a widow and which Princess Alexandra and the Prince of Wales took over became an elaborate metaphor for Society itself. The old order attempted to barricade itself against the thrusting merchant class with the Court regulations: ritual introductions, rigid standards and the symbolic feathers (two white feathers for a debutante, three for a matron and ultimately four for the Prince of Wales). By the end of the century, as the old social order weakened, the dress rules became immutable.

High Court Dress, according to the Lord Chamberlain's regulations for 'Ladies attending their Majesties' courts' published in January 1908, consisted of 'bodices in front, cut square or heart shape . . . filled in with white only, either transparent or lined . . . sleeves to elbow, either thick or transparent. Trains, gloves and feathers as usual.' The problem of correct dress at court exercised society throughout the Victorian and Edwardian eras. 'What to do with a court train afterwards was, and perhaps will ever be, something of a difficulty' claimed the ladies' pages of the *Illustrated London News* in 1902. One resourceful society lady apparently used her crimson velvet train to cover her grand piano.

It was precisely with jewels that the parvenus were able to outshine the old aristocracy. Lady Violet Greville expresses in 1892 the bewilderment at the breakdown of the old ways. 'Thirty years ago,' she said, 'none thought of going to Court unless they were great personages for whom it was a duty . . . a presentation at Court served as a kind of passport of admittance into good Society . . . It seems strange that there should be no definite rule about going to Court, except that about the regulation costume, so that anyone can be presented if Her Majesty approves.'

Since the Prince of Wales engineered the presentation of his mistress Lillie Langtry (just as Wallis Simpson managed later to be presented at Court) he himself was instrumental in widening the social circle of the aristocracy, or Upper Ten Thousand as he described them to his mother in 1868. During his long apprenticeship to the throne, he set new social standards, just as he set the sartorial fashions for the dinner jacket and the Homburg hat and Princess Alexandra popularised the choker, the dangling rope necklace known as the *Sautoir* and the stomacher.

Princess Alexandra, like all truly fashionable women, believed in simplicity of line. Her rooms at Sandringham and Marlborough House contained an overwhelming clutter of *bibelots* and *bric-à-brac* (including phalanxes of framed photographs and models of all the animals at Sandringham, made by

Fabergé and sent to her from Russia by her sister Minnie). But her dresses throughout the 1880s imprinted on fashion the style that we think of as Edwardian – *a décolleté* dress over a swelling bosom, pulled into a slender waist. (The Princess, unlike her husband, ate sparingly and kept her exquisite figure.) A slim skirt was draped back into a bustle and fell into the requisite court train.

The royal dynasty: Queen Victoria with the future Edward VII and Princess Alexandra in 1883. Alix is elegant in court mourning, with Bertie's coronet, a black velvet choker and a scattering of diamond stars.

These deceptively simple dresses were ornamented with elaborate jewels. By 1894, the transformation of the crinoline and diadem of Victoriana to the bejewelled Edwardian elegance was complete. At the Court Drawing Room in May, the Princess of Wales was in a dress and train of black satin, trimmed simply with bunches of white lilac. On her head was a diamond tiara with feathers and veil. Round her neck and looped across her chest were pearl and diamond ornaments and she wore no less than eight orders – the Victoria and Albert, the Crown of India, St Catherine of Russia, St John of Jerusalem, the Saxe-Coburg Gotha, the Hessian, the Danish family, and Golden Wedding orders.

Even Charlotte Knollys, Woman of the Bedchamber to Queen Alexandra and her faithful companion until the end of her life, absorbed her mistress's style, with the same wide multi-strand choker, a festoon necklace and ropes of pearls falling to her waist. Ladies-in-waiting often mimic their mistresses.

Queen Alexandra's decorative style captured in a painting by a court jeweller. Her scarred neck was swagged in pearls, her lacy bodice festooned with gems, including "Albert's brooch", and the pearl brooch her husband Bertie gave her. On her head is the small diamond crown ordered by Queen Victoria, who is the sombre figure in the painting in the background. The serpent bangle fed an appetite for the exotic but makes the Queen shudder.

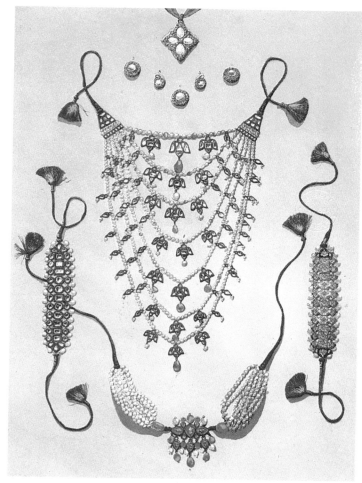

Above Bertie's bride landing at Gravesend from her native Denmark. In her early life, Princess Alexandra wore very few jewels and her white bonnet trimmed with pink roses was made at home with her sister Minnie. By contrast, the future Edward VII was passionate about his dress down to the last stick pin.

Inset Princess Alexandra of Denmark, the elegant new Princess of Wales, painted by Winterhalter in 1864. Victorian ringlets hid the scar on her neck before she set a fashion for chokers. The drop pearl brooch has been inherited by the Queen.

Right A present from her new mother-in-law Queen Victoria, and in the name of the dead Prince Albert: a pearl and diamond cross, brooch and earrings and Indian jewels set with pearls, emeralds and rubies.

Above The Alexandra heirloom: her dowry from the King of Denmark was the Dagmar necklace containing 2,000 diamonds and 118 pearls, hung with a facsimile of the eleventh-century Cross of Dagmar in enamel ornamented with pearls and diamonds.

Inset The Queen wore the Dagmar necklace, without its cross, on a visit to Denmark in 1957.

Far right Fabulous Indian emeralds in a girdle once owned by Maharajah Ranjit Singh. It is in the Queen's possession today.

Right Maharajah Dhuleep Singh's bouquet holder is the centrepiece of family wedding gifts.

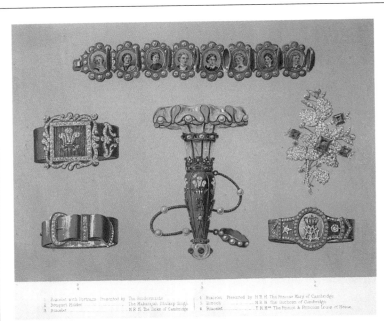

1. Bracelet with Portraits Presented by The Bridesmaids
2. Bouquet Holder   The Maharajah Dhuleep Singh
3. Bracelet   H.R.H. The Duke of Cambridge
4. Bracelet Presented by H.R.H. The Princess Mary of Cambridge
5. Brooch   H.R.H. The Duchess of Cambridge
6. Bracelet   T.R.H. The Prince & Princess Louis of Hesse

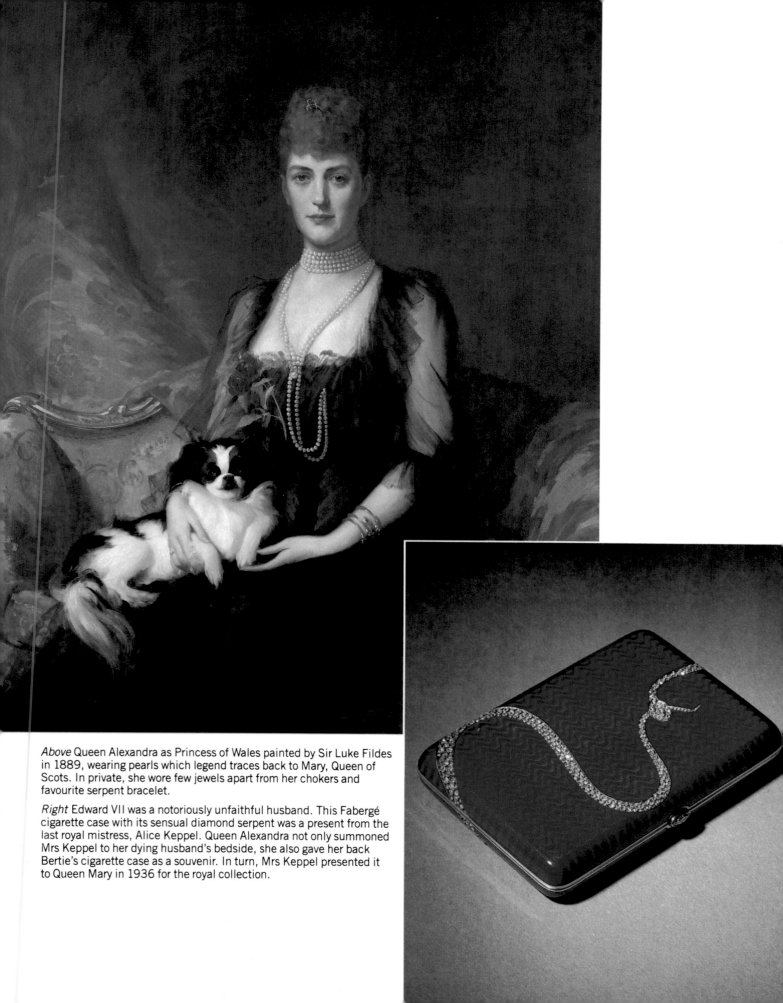

Above Queen Alexandra as Princess of Wales painted by Sir Luke Fildes in 1889, wearing pearls which legend traces back to Mary, Queen of Scots. In private, she wore few jewels apart from her chokers and favourite serpent bracelet.

Right Edward VII was a notoriously unfaithful husband. This Fabergé cigarette case with its sensual diamond serpent was a present from the last royal mistress, Alice Keppel. Queen Alexandra not only summoned Mrs Keppel to her dying husband's bedside, she also gave her back Bertie's cigarette case as a souvenir. In turn, Mrs Keppel presented it to Queen Mary in 1936 for the royal collection.

Lady Susan Hussey pins a fine brooch in her lapel just as the Queen does, and Princess Diana's lady-in-waiting Anne Beckwith-Smith shares a fondness for pearl chokers.

By 1897, Princess Alexandra's transformation of Court style was given its ultimate accolade. For the banquet at Buckingham Palace before Queen Victoria's Diamond Jubilee procession, Alix persuaded Queen Victoria out of her widow's weeds for the first time for 35 years. The old Queen recorded in her Journal how she wore 'a dress of which the whole front was embroidered in gold, which had been specially worked in India, diamonds in my cap, and a diamond necklace'.

The apogee of Court grandeur was reached with the glittering evening Courts instituted by King Edward VII and Queen Alexandra during their brief reign. The idea of changing the time of the Drawing Rooms from afternoon to evening (King George V changed it back to the afternoon and started the garden parties) supposedly came from the debutantes themselves, who dreaded, claimed the *Illustrated London News* of 1901, exposing their 'snowy shoulders' and their complexions to the 'pitiless glare of daylight'. Their plea for evening presentations was neatly expressed by the magazine's columnist I. F. Austin and apparently penetrated Queen Alexandra's increasingly deaf ears:

> When we attend a Drawing-Room,
> We want to wear our evening bloom,
> For evening sheds a gentle ray,
> That makes amends for cruel day.
> O gracious Queen, give kindly light,
> And let us flock to you at night!

To some onlookers, the Queen's jewellery was almost too overwhelming, and her lavish style was later compared unfavourably with that of her daughter-in-law Queen Mary. 'Queen Alexandra could successively wear a great many jewels, but I have sometimes thought her slight figure a little overborne by them,' claimed a contemporary of Queen Mary in 1936, although this was from the viewpoint of a different era. The peeresses at the 1902 Coronation were themselves garlanded in jewels, wearing tiaras rather than coronets. Many of these were in the Russian style, deep fenders of diamonds, following the fashion set by Queen Alexandra's Russian fringe tiara, presented to her on her Silver Wedding in 1888 by the Ladies of Society who all contributed towards the gift.

Publicly, Alexandra may have barricaded herself behind the trappings of grandeur. In private, her style was quite different, and we see here the beginnings of the divide between state appearances and the private wardrobe which is so marked in the royal family a century later.

Princess Alexandra's real defence against her own deafness, lack of intellect and her husband's careless infidelities, was not her jewellery but her family. Her five children – Eddy and Georgie, the girls, Louise, Victoria and Maud, all arrived in the 1860s. The babies ended with the death of the Waleses' premature son Alexander John in 1871 at just one day old; he was buried at Sandringham under piles of white flowers by the Prince of Wales who, in spite of his raffish reputation, shared with his wife a sincere religious belief.

A jewelled cross was one of the ornaments that Princess Alexandra wore in private when she went out with Prince Eddy: he in his jaunty boater and she in a gay polka dotted dress. Prince Eddy was weak and backward, constitutionally languid and increasingly dissolute. Princess Alexandra gave him her unconditional love and support throughout his short life. He died at the age of 28 in 1892, just after he became engaged to Princess May of Teck and 'Motherdear', as her children called her, never quite reconciled herself to May's marriage to her second son Georgie (Chapter 3).

Bertie's gift to Alix for their silver wedding was a ruby and diamond cross. The Christian symbol had a real significance for the Princess, who hung beside her bed a crucifix which had belonged to her close friend Mrs Gladstone, the wife of the Prime Minister. When her dearest friend Oliver Montagu died in 1893, just one year after Eddy, Alix sent a little cross to lie overnight on the coffin so that she might 'take it with me tomorrow as a sad remembrance of my faithful friend'. Montagu, an officer in the Blues and Royals and a younger son of Lord Sandwich, had been a faithful friend indeed, loving Princess Alexandra devotedly and chivalrously throughout his adult life.

It was Princess Alexandra who personally asked for prayers to be said for Bertie during his attack of typhoid and Alix who supported Queen Victoria at the funeral of her son Leopold in 1884.

Princess Alexandra was particularly lonely and isolated during the 1890s, when she was embarrassed by the Prince of Wales's flagrant affairs and by the scandal of the Tranby Croft baccarat case when her husband's *louche* gambling habits were exposed. Earlier she had suffered the indignity of the Mordaunt case, in 1870, when her husband was called into the witness box and acquitted of committing adultery with the young and pretty Lady Mordaunt. He was soon to be involved in yet another sexual scandal with Frances 'Daisy' Brooke, later Countess of Warwick and Bertie's long-time mistress. The Tranby Croft affair in 1890 was less personally wounding to Princess Alexandra but it did untold damage to the future King's reputation

The Russian fringe tiara: solid diamond bars in the shape of peasant headdress. It was a present to Princess Alexandra from the Ladies of Society on her Silver Wedding anniversary in 1888.

and standing in the country. At a game of baccarat at a house party at Tranby Croft in Yorkshire, one of the guests was accused of cheating, and the fact that the Prince of Wales was in the party, and involved in gambling, offended against the code of Victorian morality. Although Princess Alexandra stood by her husband, it was a very public humiliation.

At Sandringham Bertie played squire with a mixture of exuberance and formality that characterised the Edwardian age. A later Prince of Wales, Edward VIII, described Christmas at Sandringham as 'Dickens in a Cartier setting'. It was a well-turned phrase for the blend of Victorian religious morality ('Mamma, with her lady in waiting at the piano, taught us the Christmas carols') and Edwardian bounty – joints of beef laid out in the coach house to distribute to estate workers. Inside the double doors to the Ballroom was the tree, festooned with tinsel and cotton wool snow and ablaze with candles. Laid out on the tables were the heaps of presents – Cartier bejewelled clocks or precious jade masterpieces from Fabergé.

'All this for me,' Princess Alexandra would cry girlishly, as the ropes of pearls, the sapphires and rubies arrived as presents from the Empress and Czar of Russia. Both Alix and Minnie, those two innocent sisters whose romping Danish childhood had been short on material comforts (only one zinc tub as a bath in the Yellow Palace) developed an instinct for acquisition. After Edward VII's final, fatal bronchial attack in 1910, Minnie encouraged her sister to take a Russian view of the role of a Queen Mother. Not only did she think that Queen Alexandra should take precedence over her daughter-in-law, the new Queen Mary, she also stirred up a dispute over which pieces of jewellery belonged to the Queen of England and which to Queen Alexandra herself. This is a question which had bedevilled the British Crown ever since the Hanoverians had won back Queen Charlotte's personal jewels from Queen Victoria (Chapter 1). It is the kernel of the discussion about the presents Edward VIII gave to Mrs Simpson.

Generous presents and fabulous jewellery were part of the royal way of life, particularly before the First World War and the Russian Revolution, when the most public of state visits also meant meeting a royal relative. Queen Alexandra herself was open-handed (and many of her family thought her profligate). In her old age, she would conceal £1,000 in cash in the sofa at Sandringham so that her Private Secretary Sir Dighton Probyn could not prevent her from supporting her favourite charities. By that time, the Empress Marie was back home in Denmark after the revolution in Russia. When asked by her family to economise, she retaliated by letting every light blaze away all night like the Imperial Crown jewels that had once dazzled her court.

As Princess and Queen, Alexandra was thoughtful, rather than lavish with presents. To her mother-in-law Queen Victoria, she gave in 1878 an onyx locket which had originally been intended for Princess Alice of Hesse, Queen Victoria's second daughter who had died of diphtheria in December 1878 on the seventeenth anniversary of her father's death. On another tragic date, the day that Princess May of Teck should have married her darling Eddy, Alix and Bertie gave the bereaved Princess May the diamond necklace that had been intended as her wedding present. Thirty-five years later, Queen Mary reread

Princess Alexandra wore her new tiara, Bertie's necklace and a favourite serpent bangle to the wedding of her son Georgie to the future Queen Mary in 1893.

her diary of that date and remembered how moved she had been by the gesture.

Princess Alexandra was considerate to her staff, pressing a pair of gold cufflinks on a Scottish footman who felt lonely at Christmas even though his 'proper' present was already laid out under the tree. (The Duchess of Windsor was to repeat that gesture by giving a kitchen boy a transistor radio brought back from the United States.) Even at times of great personal stress, Alexandra would still offer her carefully chosen gifts. Two days after her own birthday in 1871 had passed in a nightmare of anxiety when Bertie had typhoid, the Princess gave a birthday present of a crystal watch to Lady Macclesfield, who had helped to deliver Eddy into her flannel petticoat. One of her last gifts was the amethyst heart set in brilliants on a long swag of a necklace that she gave to Lady Elizabeth Bowes Lyon when she married the future George VI in 1923.

The Prince of Wales, whose proudest possession was a diamond pin showing the head of Persimmon, the fine bay which had won the Derby in 1896, was also generous with presents in a careless, aristocratic way. From that first summer of his engagement, when he had rushed to Paris to buy presents for his bride-to-be, Bertie would make large gestures to family and friends. His favourite personal gems for his wife were not just the diamonds made into lacy ribbons and bows. He also chose the leek-green peridot that would hang against a rococo lattice ground; or Queen Alexandra would have a suite of amethysts in her favourite shade of mauve. King Edward VII did not always appreciate the monetary value of the largesse he distributed, scattering gold cigarette cases with the royal cypher of diamonds on state visits. When the King's private secretary Fritz Ponsonby suggested that a silver cigarette case with an enamel cypher – all that was left of a stock of presents after a Mediterranean cruise – was not up to standard for a French racing friend, the King flew into a rage, although he later admitted that his behaviour had been 'shoddy'.

In the spring of 1905, King Edward VII was in Paris, savouring the delights of the Belle Époque, after leaving Queen Alexandra and two of their daughters at the end of a family cruise on the Mediterranean. With him was Alice Keppel, the vivacious russet-haired beauty he had met ten years before, although she, like him, had now grown stout. Queen Alexandra laughed to see 'Tum-tum' and his plump mistress squeezed into an open carriage at Sandringham.

The King's irregular, quintessentially Edwardian arrangements were accepted by Society and (albeit reluctantly) by the Queen herself, who was soon to call Mrs Keppel to her dying husband's bedside, and to return to her a Fabergé cigarette case set with a sensual serpent of diamonds that had been a present from mistress to royal lover.

The dense love life of this 'bon boulevardier' was reflected in the jewels that Edward VII bought from Cartier, the Paris jeweller in the rue de la Paix where the King was received in state as a favoured client. (Twenty years later, his eldest grandson Edward VIII was dubbed by a cartoonist 'le prince charmant de la rue de la Paix'.)

Side by side in the ledger of Cartier, as they were in the King's affections, are the commissions for Her Majesty Queen Alexandra and those for Mrs Keppel

Queen Alexandra at home in 1904 wears a simple cross and chain instead of the elaborate swags of jewels.

(who was still impressing Sir Henry 'Chips' Channon with her diamonds after the Second World War). For the Queen, there was a necklace of pearls and brilliants, trembling with a double pendant of diamonds, a stately piece using impressive stones from the royal store. For Mrs Keppel, there was the piece of jewellery that the Queen herself had made fashionable: a broad choker with a removable diamond centre, made up from dismantling six smaller pieces including a Maltese cross. Alice Keppel became such an important patron of Cartier that she advised them on the Bond Street site of their new London shop in 1909; the year after Queen Alexandra was crowned in a blaze of diamonds, Mrs Keppel had her own private crown – a Cartier tiara shaped like a laurel wreath.

Queen Alexandra's crown of paste. The central stone represents the mighty Koh-i-noor.

Queen Alexandra won the fashion palm. She is the Queen who stamped an image on the monarchy with her jewels and made jewellery synonymous with majesty. Yet very few of those delicate Edwardian jewels are now worn and only the Dagmar necklace is now on show among the Queen's jewellery; the rest of the pieces are either languishing in the vaults or were broken up by Queen Mary; or they were distributed among Queen Alexandra's relatives (she died intestate) or given to her grandson Edward VIII (Chapter 4).

One piece remains – and with it a mystery. The new crown made for Queen Alexandra for the Coronation now nestles inside a domed sapphire blue velvet box from the jewellers Carrington. Every single glittering stone is intact in its intricate frame (made in platinum, rather than the traditional gold for the stylish Queen). But today, in place of the great Koh-i-noor winking from the front cross, gripped by other diamonds, all the jewels are fakes. Why did Queen Alexandra break up the crown, when she already possessed rivers of diamonds? How did the jewellers manage to prise out the stones and make paste replicas without damaging the frame in any way?

Years later, in 1953, the grandson of Queen Alexandra's close friend Gladys, Lady de Grey, told the society photographer Cecil Beaton that his grandmother used to bring back to Queen Alexandra from her visits to Paris 'a great selection of false jewellery which she, the Queen, preferred to the Crown Jewels.' She wore these even to the opening of Parliament, for on one occasion the long row of artificial pearls broke and scattered all over her carriage.

Could it be that Queen Alexandra ('I shall wear exactly what I like . . . *Basta!*') chose to be crowned with a lightweight more comfortable crown rather than to have her head weighed down with real stones? Did the splendid, stately Queen Alexandra, a vision of Majesty in her maharajah's ransom of jewellery, become Queen of England before God and her King in a crown of paste?

Majestic Mary

'Queen Mary glittered with five diamond necklaces about her neck.
She was in blue with literally mountains of jewels. Pamela Berry
whispered to me – "She has bagged all the best." She has.'

Chips: The Diaries of Sir Henry Channon,
16 November 1938

In the cold, raw spring of 1929, three-year-old Princess Lilibet and her grandmother Queen Mary were making sandcastles in the garden of a modest house in Bognor. In the sun room sat King George V, convalescing from the first and dangerous bout of chest infection that was to drain away his strength for the last five years of his life.

Behind them in the world of real ancestral castles and royal palaces, the King and Queen had left a heavy box laboriously bound round with tape. It had arrived from Denmark two weeks before the onset of the King's illness and now it lay in a safe at Buckingham Palace. Inside were some of the most superb jewels of the fabled Romanov royal collection – ropes of lustrous pearls graduated from a central stone the size of a cherry, globular cabochon emeralds, deep blue sapphires and fistfuls of rubies in a bright military red that was the King's favourite colour. (He had chosen it for the walls of his ship's cabin of a study at Sandringham.)

The jewels had belonged to King George's Aunt Minnie, the Empress Marie Feodorovna, who had married into the Russian royal family at the same time as her sister Alix married Queen Victoria of England's eldest son. In a strange historical parallel, Minnie had first been engaged to the Czarevitch, who died, and then married his brother, just as Queen Mary had married George after his older brother's death.

The Dowager Empress Marie had escaped the Russian Revolution in 1917. She had survived her murdered son the Czar and his family and had withdrawn to her native Denmark, to the seaside villa washed by the sea at Hividore near Copenhagen which she and Queen Alexandra had bought together as a holiday hideaway. She died in 1928.

The single casket of jewels was all that remained of the collection which had stunned London Society when Minnie had visited her sister in 1873, seven years after her marriage to the heir to the Czar. Dressed in identical blue and

Queen Mary wears 'Granny's Chips' – the third and fourth parts of the enormous Cullinan diamond, pinned to her Garter ribbon. The Koh-i-noor is in her crown. The diamond necklaces were divided among her children. The broad diamond bracelet is now worn by the Queen.

51

white foulard silk, Princess Alexandra was judged the prettier sister, but Minnie's jewels the more glittering.

Throughout the 1920s, King George V supported his aunt in exile. He had insisted that Captain Andrup of the Danish navy should take charge of both the Empress's finances and the key to her jewel case, for he was acutely aware of the chaos surrounding the disposal of the Russian royal family jewels. Minnie's daughter Xenia had given her matchless pearls to a pair of cheap crooks who had pawned them for £20,000. The swindle had been exposed publicly in Court in 1923, to the hilarity of English Society and the embarrassment of the royal relatives.

It was precisely because the Grand-Duchess Xenia had so naïvely handed away a fortune that she and her sister the Grand-Duchess Olga eagerly waited for the King to recover from his illness. He had offered to supervise personally the sale of their mother's inheritance – valued in Copenhagen at half a million pounds. In the event, it was the stately Queen Mary who walked into the room at Buckingham Palace with the Grand-Duchess Xenia to meet Mr Hardy from Hennell and Sons (the jewellers favoured by the Prince of Wales for trinkets for his mistresses).

Fritz Ponsonby, the King's private secretary, who had arranged to snatch the jewel box from Copenhagen before Empress Marie's funeral from under the noses of her Russian and Danish relatives, withdrew discreetly from the room as the first of the Imperial baubles tumbled from the box. All he knew was that Mr Hardy was willing to advance £100,000 on the jewels and that the King and Queen asked him to set a value on each item and take his time to sell them. The last remnants of the gems that had once lined two walls of the Imperial bedchamber inside their glass cases fetched, claims Ponsonby, £350,000, and the King most properly put the money in trust for the Grand Duchesses.

Nobody at the English Court, even perhaps the King himself, knew until forty years later that Queen Mary had taken a more than cousinly interest in the Grand-Duchesses' gems. *She had picked out the choicest items for herself and had offered half the Hennell's valuation price or had simply never paid up at all.*

The truth came to light when a Mrs Olga Koulikovsky died in a humble flat above Ray's Barbershop in a shabby suburb of East Toronto, Canada, on 24 November 1960. She was the Grand-Duchess Olga Alexandrovna, the youngest daughter of Czar Alexander III and the Empress Marie – the same Olga who at the age of seven had watched crates of Cartier baubles unpacked in the family palace each Christmas.

In 1964 the Grand-Duchess's memoirs were published, and that book gave a rather different account of Ponsonby's story. She had told the author Ian Vorres that she and her sister Xenia had received only a fraction of the money from the jewels. Sir Edward Peacock, the Director of the Bank of England between 1929 and 1946, confirmed the story that only about £100,000 had been paid.

The Grand-Duchess Olga was an intelligent artistic woman who sloughed off her Romanov past and dismissed the story of the missing money. 'There are certain aspects of this affair which I could never understand,' she admitted, adding, 'I know that May was passionately fond of jewellery.'

Other relatives now point out that George V had paid out £10,000 a year for the upkeep in Denmark of the exiled Empress Marie, that King George also helped and supported distant Russian relations and even their servants, and that 'anything that was not paid was compensated for'.

Grand-Duchess Olga's younger son, Guri Koulikovsky, was not satisfied. He began to bombard Buckingham Palace with letters demanding an inquiry. After a lengthy correspondence between Guri (who has since died but is survived by his brother Tikhon) and the Lord Chamberlain's office, the matter was put in the hands of the Queen's solicitors. They examined the papers – which have now been sent to Windsor – and discovered the truth: Queen Mary had held on to the jewels until 1933; she had then claimed that the Depression and the collapse of the pearl market had reduced their value; she paid only £60,000.

In 1968, 40 years after the Empress Marie's jewels had cascaded from their box, Queen Mary's granddaughter, the Queen, settled the debt.

This story tells us a great deal about Queen Mary and her passion – perhaps it should be described in more psychological terms as a 'mania' – for collecting.

To her grandmother, Queen Mary, the Queen owes the bulk of her superb collection of jewels. She first received a glittering diamond tiara, bandeau, stomacher, bow brooch and bracelets as a wedding present from Queen Mary when she married Lieutenant Philip Mountbatten in 1947. On her grandmother's death six years later came a cornucopia of jewels, from the tremulous marquise peardrop to the massive diamond heart brooch and the large diamond ring that were all 'chips' cut from the Cullinan diamond (see later in this chapter).

How did 'Granny', the serious, reflective, determined Princess May of Teck whose family had to flee to Florence in 1883 to escape their debts (£18,000 to the Kensington traders alone) amass such a wealth of personal jewellery? And why, considering how much had flowed in during her reign as presents, from family, officials and as tributes from the Empire's mines and maharajahs, did Queen Mary continue to bargain in the 1920s for jewels salvaged from the shipwrecked European monarchies?

Perhaps it was because Princess May's background was so financially insecure that she was throughout her life so conscious of possessions and so eager to acquire them. Her mother, Princess Mary Adelaide, was a large, impulsive, generous woman, a granddaughter of George III by his son Adolphus, Duke of Cambridge, and therefore a cousin of Queen Victoria.

In spite of this impeccable royal connection, and mostly because of her enormous girth, Princess Mary Adelaide married very late in 1866, at the age of 32, a minor German Prince, Francis of Teck. His mother had been a Countess, but not a Princess, and this cost the Duke of Teck the succession to the German principality of Württemberg. It also meant that he was penniless. The Tecks muddled their way financially through 31 years of marriage, baled out by relatives and friends, and making protracted tours of all the German relatives when the debts had mounted at home.

From her mother, and especially from her mother's sister Augusta, the Grand-Duchess of Mecklenburg-Strelitz, Princess May imbibed a sense of family history. From her father, she inherited a passion for order and an aesthetic pleasure in collecting and arranging *objets d'art*. She sorted and categorised all the jewels first in 1910 on Edward VII's death, when she sent seventeen historic royal rings to Windsor Castle. Among them was a portrait ring belonging to Queen Charlotte, the wife of George III, with whom Queen Mary identified and liked to think she resembled. Another major sort-out of the royal jewels came in January 1926 after the death of Queen Alexandra. On Saturday, 9 January, the King and Queen and two of Queen Alexandra's three daughters, her spinster helpmate Princess 'Toria' and Maud, gathered at Sandringham to divide up the jewels. 'It was interesting but sad,' Queen Mary confided to her diary. (In the same way the death of Queen Elizabeth the Queen Mother will be followed by a major family assessment of the large number of jewels at Clarence House.)

Many of the royal jewels in store today have labels in Queen Mary's precise writing, detailing their family history. Even as Princess May she had a reverence for the concept of monarchy and an insistent interest in everything royal. This sense of family pride was fostered by Aunt Augusta, who had married into a stiff Teutonic court at Neu Strelitz in northern Germany, but who never forgot until the day of her death at the age of 94 that she was a granddaughter of George III.

The young Princess May watched her father arrange jewels on her mother's large — enormously large — person. She saw her effervescent mother put on mourning dress, cut down at the front in the Court style, garnets glittering like black diamonds on her ample white bosom. She squeezed into the carriage beside her mother at Kensington Palace and watched her being greeted affectionately as a member of the royal family. She stood singing hymns with her invalid grandmother, the Duchess of Cambridge, in the shadowy apartments at St James's Palace (which would one day be her first married home). And Princess Victoria Mary Augusta Louise Olga Pauline Claudine Agnes realised that she was of English royal stock. '*Une vraie petite anglaise,*' as she wrote priggishly to Aunt Augusta at the age of 9. She had been born in the very room at Kensington Palace that Princess Victoria had shared with her own mother. Princess May's birthday on 26 May was just two days away from Queen Victoria's. 'I like to feel your birthday is so near mine, that you were born in the same house as I was and that you should bear my name,' Queen Victoria wrote to her granddaughter-in-law May in 1896.

But the Wales cousins — Eddy and Georgie, Toria, Maud and Louise — who played with May and her three brothers, never let their cousin forget that she was not *quite* as royal as them. May was better educated, widely travelled through the continental courts of her German family, more intelligent, cultured and self-reliant than they were, but the morganatic marriage on her father's side put her right on the outer edge of the royal pale. Her Serene Highness, not the absolute HRH, was Princess May's title. She was too royal to marry a 'subject' and not royal enough to marry a royal prince, whispered her relatives as May grew up and the German princelings refused to consider her (aware of the complexities of heredity in the tiny principalities which were soon to be devoured by the advance of Prussia or snuffed out by the Great War).

'Now she has drawn the *first* prize,' crowed Aunt Augusta from Strelitz in December 1891 when Princess May of Teck became engaged to Eddy, the Duke of Clarence and Avondale, heir to the throne of England.

For stout, ebullient, irrepressible, debt-ridden Princess Mary Adelaide and the tetchy protocol-obsessed Duke of Teck, there had been an earlier moment of triumph. The proud parents, who had only just returned to England from their ignominious (but socially enjoyable) financial exile in Florence, watched Princess May at her first Drawing Room in March 1886, standing in the inner royal circle next to the Queen. She wore a snowy white dress studded with Aunt Augusta's diamond brooch (a Confirmation present) and a large diamond star from her grandmother the Duchess of Cambridge (who was ultimately to drop those great green translucent Cambridge emeralds into the royal jewel collection). Round May's neck, below the dull gold waves of hair that had been put up for the occasion, was her mother's small diamond neck-lace. On the bodice of the dress which Aunt Augusta had paid for – the tight-fisted Cambridges were soon expostulating with Princess Mary Adelaide about the profligate price of £40 for one of her daughter's ball gowns – Princess May wore other diamond brooches. They were pinned on, as her father deli-cately put it, '*à la mode*'. The fashion of stomachers and jewels to fill the bodice from neck to waist was to be her hallmark as Queen, when her jewels made an inverted triangle from her shoulders down her bosom to her navel.

Princess May's Confirmation – an essential ceremony before 'coming out' into Society with a Court presentation – had given her a first taste of fine jewels. As well as Uncle George Cambridge's clasp, with its locks of Queen Charlotte's and George III's hair framed in diamonds and set in dark blue enamel, the Duchess of Cambridge (who had stumped up a meagre £2 for her granddaughter's seventeenth birthday) gave Princess May a set of diamond stars. These were the height of fashion in the late Victorian period. Dressed in Court mourning in 1887, Princess Alexandra wore eight diamond stars pinned across her low neckline and pretty shoulders and running vertically like celestial buttons down the front of her jet black gown.

Beaten gold bracelets, another fashion of their day, were offered to May by Uncle Wales and by her Russian-born Aunt Marie Edinburgh, whose home at Clarence House, filled with jewelled icons lit by burning oil lamps, fascinated Princess May and her brothers almost as much as Aunt Marie's harrowing tales of the icy Russian winters. The Prince of Wales's bracelet was studded with jewelled flowers; Queen Victoria, still mourning the death of her haemophiliac son Prince Leopold, gave May a diamond butterfly brooch. It was left to her own parents to give Princess May her first important diamonds. Princess Mary Adelaide passed to her daughter a diamond necklace of her own, diamond and pearl earrings and three yellow diamond wheat ears, just as for May's seventeenth birthday she had presented her own carbuncle and diamond star earrings.

Princess Mary in her coming-out gown and court feathers.

Princess Mary Adelaide was open-handed and warm-hearted, with a well-developed social conscience and no sense of money. She drew into her social orbit wealthy friends like Baroness Burdett Coutts of the banking family who gave her straightforward gifts of money and Mr Peter Wells who funded the purchase of a piano and discreetly settled up with the traders in Florence after the Tecks left. The Duchess of Teck wore herself out with good works (the Needlewoman's Guild started as a charity in the parlour of her home at White Lodge), but she also loved fine jewellery and clothes. One of her earliest presents to her daughter was a tiny blue stone heart that she brought back from a trip to Frankfurt. The boys, Dolly, Frank and Algy, got Hamburg hats. Princess Mary Adelaide was considered so particularly knowledgeable that Princess Alexandra sought her advice on where to get a jet diadem made. Queen Mary had two jet tiaras and a bandeau, all worked as delicate wreaths of flowers and ivy leaves, and a jet brooch 'In Memory of My Dead Brother'. (Her feckless but much loved brother Frank died in 1910 at the age of 39.)

The sensitive Duke of Teck, whose favourite sports were to rehang pictures, move furniture and complain about precedent and protocol, is generally credited with having given to his daughter – by blood and upbringing – her aesthetic sensibilities. These were shared also with two of her three brothers, 'Dolly', Adolphus, 1st Marquess of Cambridge, and Frank, who fell out with his sister when he allowed his mistress to wear the Cambridge emeralds after Princess Mary Adelaide's death. These gems had been won by the Teck family in a lottery in Frankfurt in the early nineteenth century but despite such raffish beginnings have played an important part in the royal collection.

Princess May's feel for jewellery must have come partly from her mother, who continued to hang on to her tiara and diamonds during the worst crisis of the Tecks' muddled financial life, when they were forced to sell up the contents of Kensington Palace and close White Lodge in Richmond Park, which May and her brothers considered as home. The Tecks' wide horizons – the early exposure to the 'Royal Mob' (as Queen Victoria called the relatives who congregated at Schloss Rumpenheim near Frankfurt every second summer), visits to Aunt Augusta at Neu Strelitz and to her father's eccentric sisters at Reinthal – gave the observant princess a chance to see the Court jewels and royal treasures. Majesty to Queen Mary meant diadems and jewels and orders, all the glittering outward trappings of monarchy. As an impressionable young girl she imbibed this message from the clockwork ritual of the Grand-Ducal courts, where the gentlemen in livery and cocked hats and the ladies in low gowns and jewels would stand in formal, frozen postures to receive the visiting English royals. At the German state banquets, where the ritual was still that of the Middle Ages, each princess was allowed two pages who spread her train and covered it with napkins before the feast was served.

Princess May was ultimately to take sweet revenge on the relatives who had looked down on her in her youth. On the very last gathering of the Royal Mob, in 1913, she appeared at the wedding of the Kaiser's only daughter in a glittering dress of Indian cloth of gold, its gold-embroidered bodice studded with diamond bows, pearl drops and diamonds, a diamond collar and the Crown diamonds around her neck and a pearl and diamond crown on her head.

Augusta became Princess May's mentor, intellectual stimulus and soulmate. 'I am much more like her daughter than her niece,' said May of the aunt who fulfilled the same role as 'Uncle Leopold' to the young Queen Victoria or Uncle 'Dickie' Mountbatten to Prince Charles. In 1884, a wide-eyed seventeen-year-old Princess was describing to her aunt the bejewelled Russian nobility who treated Florence as a playground. One royal princess appeared every day wearing twelve ropes of perfectly matched pearls – perhaps the very pearls that Queen Mary was to covet forty years later when she opened the Empress Marie's jewel box or bargained for the fantastic treasures sold by the Grand-Duchess Vladimir. Her conception of royalty was nurtured by her continental travel and those formative experiences were reflected in the rows of milky pearls that lapped the throat and poured over the pale dresses of the majestic Queen.

After her Confirmation and Court debut, Princess May was out in Society, although she was still as shy and tongue-tied as in the days when she had been taken to Signor Taglioni's dancing classes and practised her curtsy with a chenille tablecloth as a train. (Both Princess Diana and the Princesses Elizabeth and Margaret Rose went through the same ritual with the redoubtable dancing teacher Miss Vacani.)

Her Serene Highness Princess May passed her days serenely, as helpmate-cum-secretary to her chaotic mother; Princess Mary Adelaide once accidentally set ablaze the pile of papers on her desk. She sorted parcels from the Needlewoman's Guild until she had 'housemaid's knee'; she read George Eliot under the tutelage of Helene Bricka (who became a friend, confidante and later a rather unsuccessful governess to her boisterous children). The steady progress of the turning year was punctuated by royal events like the marriage of Auntie Alix and Uncle Wales's daughter Louise to the dour 'Macduff', Duke of Fife, a subject rather than the expected royal prince. May was a bridesmaid to her cousin, frilly in rose pink faille, and the recipient of a sturdy gold bangle set with L and F in diamonds, a crown and coronet. These bridesmaids' gifts were designed by Louise herself and dismissed by May as not very pretty. More to her aesthetic taste was the feast of jewellery laid out at Marlborough House for Auntie Alix and Uncle Wales's silver wedding in 1888. May especially admired the spiked diamond fringe tiara presented to Princess Alexandra by the 'Ladies of Society'. It was to become one of her own personal favourites and of the present Queen, who wore it on her visit to the Vatican when the spiky rays gleamed above a dramatic black dress.

Six weeks after Princess May gazed covetously at the Waleses' magnificent presents, her own jewel box began to fill up. For her twenty-first birthday on 26 May 1888 her grandmother, the Duchess of Cambridge, who died the next year, presented her with a fine cameo surrounded by diamonds and pearls. The rest of the Teck family – her mother, Uncle George Cambridge and Aunt Augusta – clubbed together to buy Princess May a serious jewel: a pearl and diamond heart brooch. Gemset brooches and bracelets came from Aunt Marie Edinburgh and the Prince and Princess of Wales.

'May is indeed a pearl of great price,' was Princess Mary Adelaide's verdict on her dutiful daughter. It was an unconscious echo of the words of Queen

Victoria and her daughter Vicky as they selected Alexandra as a bride for the heir to the throne. The Tecks had set their sights on the current royal heir, the dissolute, lethargic Prince Albert Victor, who had inherited a swanlike neck from his graceful mother, Princess Alexandra, a foppish love of clothes from his father and a nickname 'Eddy Collar-and-Cuffs', which may also have referred to his penchant for pretty boys and the persistent rumours that Queen Victoria's grandson was a homosexual.

Eddy's problem was not that he avoided young girls but that he seemed to change them as often as his high starched collars. An apparently passionate attachment to the Roman Catholic Princess Hélène of Orléans ran concurrently with a promise of undying love to Lady Sybil St Clair Erskine. Prince Eddy was twenty-eight, immature, under-educated and lacking in character. What he needed, the family decided, was a wife, which is why Princess May and her brother Prince Dolly were summoned to Balmoral in October 1891. Queen Victoria announced to her daughter Vicky that May was a nice girl, quiet, cheerful and sensible. When Eddy proposed two months later, the 'sensible' Princess May picked up her skirts and danced round her bedroom. Six weeks later she was laying her bridal wreath of orange blossom on Prince Eddy's coffin with nothing left of her 'bright dream of happiness' but the ring that Eddy had given her.

Princess May, looking like a 'crushed flower' as Queen Victoria described her, was still wearing a ruby ring on her engagement finger when she returned with her mother from an extended tour of the South of France and her German relatives. But she had received another token from the Wales family. Half a century and two World Wars away, Queen Mary, banished to Badminton House in Gloucestershire to escape the bombing, relived that bleak year of 1892 and noted in her diary that Uncle Wales and 'Motherdear' (as she now called Princess Alexandra) had marked what was to have been her February wedding day by giving her the diamond necklace originally intended as her wedding present.

At Christmas 1892 there was another token of intent, a brooch from Georgie, Eddy's brother, who was recovering from a debilitating attack of typhoid and the shock of his brother's death. Princess Mary Adelaide, with embarrassing zeal, had thrust May and Georgie together when both families were staying separately in the South of France.

Princess May of Teck and Prince George, Duke of York (as he became in May 1892) were married in the Chapel Royal at St James on 6 July 1893. May, with characteristic efficiency, gave George not one wedding ring but a couple to try for size. (In a similarly unromantic gesture, Prince Charles summoned Garrard to Windsor Castle with a selection of eight engagement rings to offer his prospective bride.)

The Duke of York's bride wore a fairly simple white and silver dress. (Her entire trousseau cost £1,000.) For the wedding a diamond Rose of York fastened her discreet lace veil. It was like an 'elongated lappet!' Lady Geraldine Somerset, the late Duchess of Cambridge's companion, claimed. She was quite put out at the rise in Society of Princess May.

Festoons of midsummer blooms – all in crimson and white for the houses of

Lancaster and York – were sent from the gardens of Osborne and Frogmore on the luminous blue July wedding day. 'Queen's weather', the Victorian crowd called it, sensing some of Queen Victoria's mystique rub off on young Princess May, although Queen Victoria's own wedding day had been dull and grey and out of climatic character. The flowers at the Chapel Royal outpointed the most lavish royal wedding decorations: fragrant blush pink tea roses from Sandringham intertwined with laurel leaves caressed the pillars at St James's Palace. The heavy scent of exotic white plants filled the staircase that led up to the bride's and bridesmaids' rooms. Even the armoury had been turned into a conservatory, its sharp metallic tang overlaid with sweet-smelling flowers.

More snowy white flowers among the massive gold plate smothered the altar cloth, embroidered by the Ladies' Working Guild under its President

Princess May of Teck and the future George V on their wedding day in 1893. In those early days, his decorations outshone her simple jewels.

Princess Beatrice, whose mother Queen Victoria sat in her chair of state to the right of the flower-decked altar.

As the sunlight struggled 'under architectural difficulties', as *The Times* put it, into the gloomy chapel, it lit up the jewels of the Court ladies sitting in full evening dress (but without trains). The Duchess of Buccleuch had the most impressive diamonds – a photo finish with the Duchess of Leeds and a close win over the Duchess of Abercorn's sapphires. Princess Mary Adelaide, who had driven in the glass coach with the Queen of England, re-lived her glory, tiara and all, when she sat later for the Danish painter Tuxen for the official wedding picture, where she appears symbolically as a plump presence set apart from the inner royal group.

Even Queen Victoria herself seemed to capture the lightness of Princess May's wedding day with a glittering diamond crown and a 'profusion of white lace' worn over her perennial mourning black. It was half a century since her head had been crowned with a wreath of orange blossom over a veil of Honiton lace as she stood beside Prince Albert at the altar where Georgie and May were now. The last wedding ceremony in the chapel at St James's had been Vicky, the Princess Royal's, thirty-five years before, when Albert was still alive, and the Queen had shaken so much with nerves and tears that the family photograph was blurred.

Princess May's wedding was a family affair, but there was an important difference between it and the earlier weddings of Queen Victoria in 1840 or of Princess Alexandra thirty years before. The Duke and Duchess of York's wedding presents – 300,000 pounds' worth that had been laid out at White Lodge and were later stampeded by visiting crowds – expressed all the wealth, stability and confidence of Victorian England.

Whereas the major royal presents had previously been from members of the family – Prince Albert's sapphire and diamond brooch for Queen Victoria, Bertie's *parure* of diamonds and pearls for Alix – the most glittering of Princess May's prizes were the tributes from the local boroughs and counties. Her new husband's present of pretty diamond bow brooches, one set with a diamond heart, the other with twin pearls, was eclipsed by the bold diamond bow and its tremulous pendant pearl from the inhabitants of Kensington.

The Russian relatives produced some fine jewellery: sapphire and diamond bracelets from the Emperor, an emerald and diamond brooch from the Czarevitch and a cabochon sapphire and diamond brooch from Princess Alexandra's sister the Empress Marie Feodorovna. (Queen Mary later acquired the more flamboyant cabochon sapphire brooch set in a double rim of diamonds given by Alix and Bertie to Minnie for her own wedding 27 years before.)

The new Duchess of York's favourite present was the delicate, spiky diamond circlet ('Granny's tiara' the Queen always calls it) which she received from the Girls of Great Britain and Ireland. They had collected £5,000 for a wedding gift, and this collection was echoed throughout the country. From the County of Surrey came another diamond tiara, a diamond ring from the Mayor and people of Windsor, a diamond bow from the County of Dorset. This trend towards public gifts to mark royal events had been growing

Queen Mary's wedding presents include the diamond bow and drop pearl brooch that is a favourite now with the Queen.

60

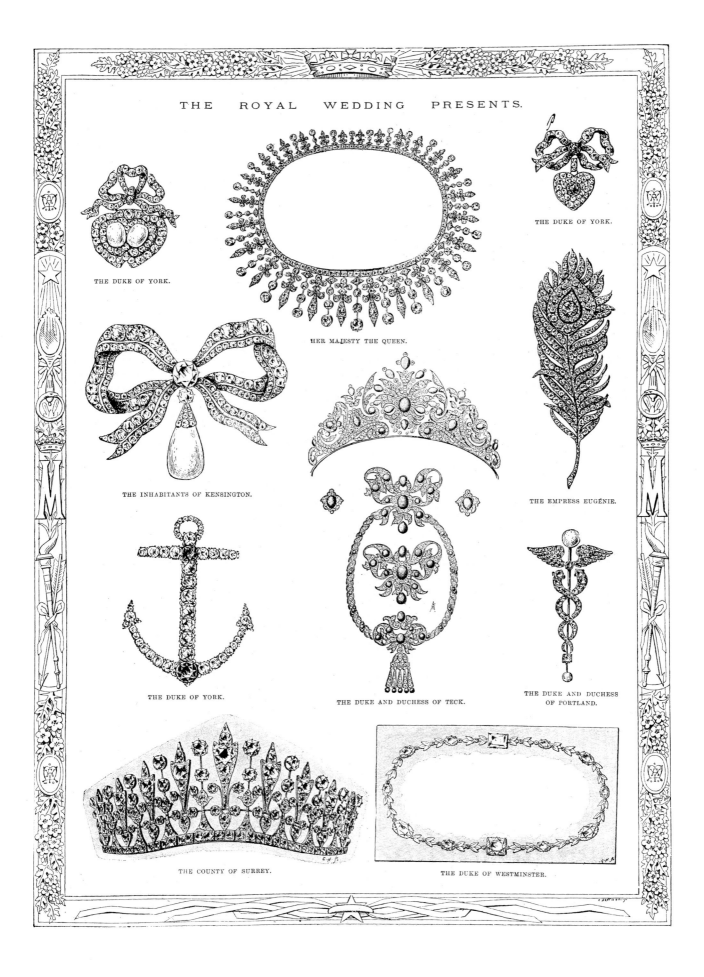

THE ROYAL WEDDING PRESENTS.

THE DUKE OF YORK.

THE DUKE OF YORK.

HER MAJESTY THE QUEEN.

THE INHABITANTS OF KENSINGTON.

THE EMPRESS EUGÉNIE.

THE DUKE OF YORK.

THE DUKE AND DUCHESS OF TECK.

THE DUKE AND DUCHESS OF PORTLAND.

THE COUNTY OF SURREY.

THE DUKE OF WESTMINSTER.

throughout Queen Victoria's long reign. Princess Alexandra's most important Silver Wedding present in 1888 had been her diamond tiara from the Ladies of Society; Queen Victoria's Jubilee brought into the royal collection the diamond and pearl Jubilee necklace presented by the Daughters of Empire at the time of the building of the Albert Memorial in 1887. A prosperous and expanding Britain made other tributes to the young Princess May: the diamond and pearl pendant brooch which Queen Mary wore at the christening of her great-granddaughter Princess Anne in 1950, a necklace and pearl earrings from the Ladies of Devonshire and a diamond and ruby bracelet from the County of Cornwall.

King Edward VII cut the aristocratic bonds that trussed up the old royal court. Already, as Prince of Wales, he had widened his social horizons by making friends with bankers like the Rothschilds and theatrical stars. Although the Duke and Duchess of York were uncomfortable in the racy Edwardian social milieu, Princess May's presents reflected her father-in-law's catholic taste in friends. Alice de Rothschild, who had played hostess to the Tecks in the South of France when May was recovering from Eddy's death, gave Princess May a diamond watch. The ladies of the stage, so many of whom owed so much to Bertie, presented his new daughter-in-law with a diamond spray brooch. Mrs Gladstone restored a Victorian moral tone to the wedding by offering a Bible.

Two final gifts were thrust into the royal blue upholstered train as Princess Alexandra's private carriage took the newly married couple off to Sandringham – May in her white going-away dress trimmed with gold, pink roses bobbing in her bonnet. Two baskets were offered to the bridal pair – one filled with crimson and white roses, the other with succulent strawberries from the fruitful English summer.

How did the young Duchess of York feel about the flood tide of personal presents, as well as the princely gifts of silver, porcelain, furniture (and an inkstand in the shape of a police helmet from the Marlborough House police)? The opulent display went on show at the Imperial Institute to raise money for charity. The favoured pieces of jewellery were locked away in a safe at York Cottage on the Sandringham estate by Princess May's elderly French maid Tatry ('None of the Princesses who married ever had a Lady younger than themselves,' decreed Queen Victoria.)

York Cottage, an awkward, Victorian neo-gothic house standing beside a frog-filled pond at Sandringham, was to be May and Georgie's home for 33 years, until long after they were Queen Mary and King George. It had been built – like Princess Diana's birthplace and childhood home Park House – by Edward VII to take the overflow from the Big House, and before the Prince's change of marital status was ominously named 'Bachelor's Cottage'.

'Nothing and nobody can or shall ever come between me and my darling Georgie boy,' wrote Princess Alexandra after Eddy's death. Constant visits from Motherdear (who had helped the man from Maples furnish York Cottage) showed that the Wales family had no intention of losing another son, even to his bride. Over at the Big House, Eddy's room had a silk Union Jack draped over his bed and the soap in his washstand changed regularly. Its presence threw a long shadow across the pheasant-filled meadows and towering beech trees to York Cottage.

But Princess May showed every sign of revelling in her new position and her new possessions. When she and Georgie left Sandringham to spend Cowes week with Queen Victoria at Osborne, May listed lovingly to her mother every detail of clothes and jewels that she wore for the family festivities. On the first evening there was 'the Combined Counties pearls' on a 'lovely little grey gown' with 'Richmond's pearl and diamond brooch in my hair'. (Princess May's very first speech had been made in reply to an address from the people of Richmond, with its royal connection with White Lodge and Cambridge Cottage, the home of Princess May's late grandmother, the Duchess of Cambridge.)

Even at the age of twenty-six, and in the first flush of married life, provenance played an important part in Princess May's attitude to her possessions. She listed her new jewels precisely to her mother: 'the Iveagh tiara, Grandmama's necklace, the Kensington Bow in front of the bodice and the Warwicks' sun on the side. I wish you had seen me . . .' Twenty years later, Queen Mary's dresser was writing down these jewels with the same precision. 'Nattier blue brocade gown . . . Richmond and Hampshire diamond brooches,' reads the entry for Ascot 1913 in Queen Mary's Dress Book.

'What I liked best was wearing Grandmama's crown,' Queen Mary told Aunt Augusta after her Coronation in 1911. The Grand Duchess fed this appetite for history. She was pleased that the family emeralds were taken to India, she told May after the Delhi durbar when the new Queen Mary was celebrating the return of the Cambridge emeralds into the royal fold after the death of the family's black sheep, Prince Frank of Teck, in 1910.

For the last seven years of the nineteenth century, the Duke and Duchess of York were 'in the shadow of the shadow of the throne'. Another heir to Queen Victoria's mighty empire – May's first son – appeared in June 1894. (The exact same pattern of a June baby following a July marriage was echoed by Princess Diana nearly a century later.) Prince Edward Albert Christian George Andrew Patrick David, known to his family as David and destined for the briefest flutter on the throne as Edward VIII, was followed the next year by his brother Bertie.

'I am delighted that they have got their King guarded,' said Princess May's brother Frank. Prince Albert, who gave up his nightly chess game at the insistence of young Queen Victoria, would have appreciated the metaphor. The new Prince Albert, Bertie to his family and King George VI to his subjects, was born on 14 December 1895, the anniversary of the Prince Consort's death and 'Mausoleum Day' to Queen Victoria's family as they gathered annually at his tomb at Frogmore, on the Windsor estate.

Death and life chased each other across the Yorks' early married years. Princess Mary Adelaide died in the autumn of Jubilee Year in 1897. To the end she was giving generously of her time to charity work and still taking handouts of money from Baroness Burdett Coutts. Her namesake Princess Mary, May's only daughter, had been born that April, just before her mother's thirtieth birthday. After the death of the Duchess of Teck, May helped her father to divide up the family jewellery. Her most emotive keepsake was a pearl brooch, its large central stone surrounded with a plait of diamonds with a large one suspended in a half circle and three pearl drops hanging from that. This imposing, lavish and rather chaotic brooch seemed to represent the spirit of Queen Mary's ebullient mother.

Two more sons for the Yorks appeared as old lives were extinguished. The century opened with the death of the Duke of Teck in January 1900 and the birth of Harry, later Duke of Gloucester, in March. In the new year 1901 the Imperial span of nineteenth-century England came to its symbolic end with the death of Queen Victoria, surrounded by her family and in the arms of her grandson the Kaiser who was to destroy the web of royal connections that his grandmother had spun. In the middle of the dynastic changes that brought Motherdear and Uncle Wales to the throne, May produced a fourth son, Prince George, Duke of Kent in December 1902.

In 1901, in spite of Queen Victoria's death and the burgeoning babies, the Duke and Duchess of York left on a seven-month tour of the Empire. As the stately SS *Ophir* steamed from Gibraltar to Malta, Colombo to Singapore, to Australia for the opening of Parliament, to New Zealand, the Cape and Canada, Princess May and George had their first experience of the enormous Empire they were later destined to rule. Princess May suffered from sea sickness, but she diligently read up the Empire's history. She also received the first of the many gifts that would be a feature of the next visit to India in 1905 and, especially, of the great Delhi durbar which she attended as Queen. The enamel maple leaf spray which was presented to the Duchess of York by the ladies of Montreal was mirrored forty years on by the flame lily brooch presented to Princess Elizabeth (later the Queen) from the children of Southern Rhodesia.

The Yorks returned to England in November 1901 to be met at Portsmouth by the new King and Queen and the news that George was to be proclaimed Prince of Wales. The Coronation of King Edward VII and the reverberating splendour of Court social life initiated a new period in Princess May's life. Her breeding years were not quite over. Prince George was born six months after the Coronation and her final tragic son John in 1905. (He died of epilepsy at the age of thirteen.) But by 1905 Princess May had mentally drawn a completed circle round her family of five and regarded this final pregnancy as 'the penalty of being a woman'. (Her great-granddaughter Princess Anne was to express the same sentiment when she pronounced children 'an occupational hazard of married life'.)

The Duke of York was at odds with the Edwardian era. He was temperamentally, even fanatically, conservative, unable to express his affection to his wife except in his many letters to her. He was strict and terse with his children, who learned to dread a summons to 'The Library', their father's tiny study lined in military red cloth and as trim as the ship's cabin he had sailed in as a boy.

Although David, as the family called their eldest son, draws an idyllic picture of his mother at York Cottage, he and his brother Bertie were sent away very young to train as naval cadets. The new reign was for the Yorks a period of duty, consolidation and waiting; and there was no real focus on family life.

Life at York Cottage and in London was set apart from the Edwardian social setting, but its colourful style must have affected the new Prince and Princess of Wales. Just as David and Bertie used to run up the hill at Sandringham to the glittering red, blue and gold saloon (the royal racing colours), so Princess May must have absorbed the splendour of the Court settings. The passion for display, and in particular the opulence of jewels in contrast to the strict Court etiquette of dress, reached its peak in the reign of King Edward VII. Queen Alexandra, at the apex of this glittering social pyramid, appeared in swathes of jewels for the Coronation, or for the State Opening of Parliament in 1902 when the girdle of diamonds round the Queen's waist reached down to her knees.

In 1900 Princess May's taste in jewellery was still unformed so she followed her mother-in-law's style. With her pearl and diamond tiara she would wear a wide eleven-strand pearl choker linked with diamonds. (She later gave this necklace to Prince Harry's wife, Alice, and it is worn today by the Duchess of Gloucester.)

But although both Queen Alexandra and Queen Mary saw jewels as a tangible expression of majesty and part of their role as the sovereign's consort, there was later a clear distinction between their royal style in jewels. Queen

Queen Mary as a young woman. The diamond and pearl earrings were given to the Queen. The Duchess of Gloucester has inherited the 11-strand pearl choker with diamond flowers.

Alexandra was a creature of fashion. An instinctive sense drew her away from high Victorian taste and towards the neo-Romantic jewellery that expressed itself, especially in France, in delicate re-creations in diamonds of lace motifs, of ribbons and bows. This 'garland' style lent itself to her favourite choker necklace, the corsage ornaments and stomachers that seemed to grow out of the fabric of her pale dresses. May always saw Aunt Alix after Eddy's death in pale sweet colours – white, dove grey, the palest wistaria. Her jewels were also pale – soft white pearls, white diamonds set in pale platinum; the only coloured stones were amethysts or King Edward's favourite watery green peridot.

During the nine-year reign of King Edward VII and Queen Alexandra, Princess May's own taste developed along different lines. Her psychological urge to distance herself from Edwardian style was reinforced by practical circumstances. On to Queen Mary's generous bosom (not for nothing was she known by the French as 'Soutien-Georges' – a pun on her support for her husband and on the French word for brassière) dropped the cleavings of the largest diamond in the world.

The Cullinan diamond, named after the owner of the premier mine in the Pretoria, was found when the blood-red South African sunset refracted in myriad points of light in the wall of the mine on 26 January 1905. The stone weighed a staggering one and a half pounds, it measured an impossible three *thousand* and twenty-five carats and was presented to Edward VII as a token of loyalty by the Transvaal people at the end of the Boer War. In order to fool potential thieves, it was sent to England by parcel post, while a dummy stone was transported by ship in a safe in the captain's cabin. The 'great and unique diamond' would be preserved, said the King (who had originally been advised by Lord Esher not to accept the gift), 'among the historic jewels which form the heirlooms of the Crown'.

From the stone, two major and magical gems – purest diamonds of the first water, weighing in at 516½ carats and 309⅓ carats – became part of the Crown Jewels: the pear-shaped Star of Africa set in the royal sceptre and the other set in the brow of the Imperial State Crown.

When the mighty stone was cleaved Mr J. Asscher of the diamond company Asscher's in Amsterdam fainted as the two great Stars of Africa and another beautiful marquise of 11¾ carats broke away from the mass. Edward VII presented the smallest of the three to Queen Alexandra the year before he died and this personal jewel was inherited by Queen Mary, who attached it as a trembling pendant to the Cambridge emerald necklace.

The rest of the Cullinan stones – six large brilliants and ninety-six smaller diamonds (each of these still major stones by the standards of ordinary jewellery) were bought from Asscher's by the Union of South Africa and presented to Queen Mary by the High Commissioner, Sir Richard Soloman, on 28 June 1910.

King Edward VII had died seven weeks before and May asked Aunt Augusta to approve of her new name – Mary. It was odd, said the new Queen, 'to be rechristened at the age of 43'. Queen Mary was also discussing with the Grand-Duchess the problem of getting Motherdear to hand over the royal jewels ('Alix retaining the lovely little crown I do not approve of,'

The most valuable brooch in the world made from the third and fourth parts of the Cullinan diamond. The pear-drop diamond of 92 carats hangs from a square-cut stone of 62 carats.

said Aunt Augusta). Exactly one week later Queen Mary had her 'chips'.

With exquisite upper-class English irony, the royal family refer to all the pieces set from the cleavings of the Cullinan as 'Granny's chips'. It applies to the heart-shaped brooch (Cullinan V) that Queen Mary planted in an emerald and diamond stomacher or in her crown at her son's Coronation. The most magnificent Cullinan brooch (now Crown property) is the tremulous diamond teardrop suspended from a solid diamond square (Cullinan III and IV) that Queen Mary hung from the centre of her bosom (and wore in her new crown made for her husband's Coronation). There is yet another brooch of an oblong and marquise diamond (Cullinan VII) and a flawless pear-shaped diamond set in a claw ring (Cullinan IX).

The death of Edward VII in May 1910 brought the new Queen Mary all the Crown Jewellery – at least after it had been gently prised away from Queen Alexandra. Two other events then combined to produce a glut of fine jewels that fed Queen Mary's appetite for gems and helped to create her physical aura of majesty. In the summer of 1910 May's feckless, engaging brother Frank unexpectedly died after a nasal operation, at the age of 39, bringing to Queen Mary (after a family upheaval) the heirloom emeralds from the Cambridge family. In December of Coronation year, 1911, the Delhi durbar produced some imperial tributes.

Both these events have an element of mystery, and from this time dates a reticence and embarrassment about the royal jewels which do not apply to the Edwardian era.

Prince Frank of Teck resembled in spirit his ebullient, spendthrift mother Princess Mary Adelaide, Duchess of Teck. His two other brothers, Princes 'Dolly' and Algy were sensible and sober like their sister May, whom Frank described as 'head nurse' in his mother's declining years. But it was 'darling May' who came to the rescue of Frank when he blew £10,000 – a truly enormous sum in 1895 – at Punchestown race course in Ireland. The newly married Duchess of York paid up, hushed up the scandal and sent Frank off to India, where he was cheerfully unrepentant and threatened to send a betting book to his sister as a Christmas present in 1896. Princess May could forgive Frank his profligacy. She loved her brother and for the only time in her reign wept publicly at Prince Frank's funeral at St George's Chapel, Windsor in 1910. But ten years before that there had been a major rift between brother and sister, and the cause of it was jewels.

Princess Mary Adelaide had died intestate in 1897 and around that time Prince Frank acquired the Cambridge emeralds, which had come into the family in a way that he must entirely have approved: the globular green cabochon gems were won in a lottery in Germany in the early 1800s. Augusta of Cambridge, the daughter-in-law of George III, had left them to her daughter Princess Mary Adelaide, Duchess of Teck. Prince Frank gave these jewels to his mistress, Ellen Constance Kilmorey, the none-too-faithful wife of an Irish Earl. Lady Kilmorey was one of Edward VII's 'loose-box' of royal mistresses given favoured seating arrangements for his coronation in 1902. Frank of Teck's liaison with her prevented him from fulfilling his mother's heart's desire – that he should marry the Waleses' daughter Princess Maud.

BELOW *The jewels in the eye of a royal storm. The Cambridge emeralds, originally won in a lottery, were Queen Mary's Teck family heirlooms. She added as a pendant the marquise diamond, the sixth part of the Cullinan, which Edward VII bought for Queen Alexandra.*

RIGHT *Prince Frank of Teck. An incorrigible gambler and womaniser, Queen Mary's feckless brother gave away the family emeralds to Lady Kilmorey.*

RIGHT *Queen Mary wears the Cambridge emerald suite which she clawed back from her late brother's mistress. She allowed Lady Kilmorey to keep one brooch to hush up the scandal.*

No one has ever named this 'elderly paramour', as Queen Mary's official biographer James Pope-Hennessy describes her, but society gossip at the time related that after Prince Frank's untimely death, Queen Mary prevailed upon her to hand back the family jewels. These consisted of eight large cabochon emeralds set as a necklace, to which Queen Mary added an emerald drop and the marquise pendant of the Cullinan diamond given to Queen Alexandra by Edward VII. The rest of the suite was made up of emerald and diamond earrings, a brooch with pendant drop, a stomacher and two bracelets. There were also some loose emeralds which Queen Mary later used as interchangeable drops for the diamond circle tiara she acquired from the Russian Grand-Duchess Vladimir.

But is there more to the story than history has yet revealed? A royal source claims that Lady Kilmorey's silence was bought with an emerald brooch from the same suite which she continued to flaunt and gave to her daughter-in-law on her marriage in 1920. The recipient of the brooch died in April 1985 in Ireland, although her family believe that the brooch was stolen in a robbery at her home ten years ago.

More mystery surrounds Prince Frank's will, the document which might reveal the fate he intended for the Cambridge emeralds, which his friends claimed that his mother had specifically given to him before she died. The basic details of Prince Frank's will were published in *The Times* on 22 February 1911. Prince Francis of Teck 'left estate of the gross value of £23,154, with net personalty amounting to £670.16s'. Probate was granted to his two brothers but by order of the President of the Probate Division of the High Court, dated 17 February, probate was granted *without annexing a copy of the will and codicil*.

Prince Frank's will was therefore 'sealed', a practice followed after all subsequent royal deaths but previously unknown. Four centuries of royal wills are deposited at the Probate Registry in London. They have caused disputes, as in the case of the Queen Charlotte's will and her jewels (Chapter 1). Until this time the wills of the Kings and Queens of England, Princes and Princesses of Wales and every branch of the blood royal have been studied by historians and are open to public scrutiny just like those of ordinary people.

According to the legal historian Michael Nash, the earliest sealed will preserved at the Registry is that of Prince Francis of Teck, and an internal report compiled for the President of the Family Division in 1980 states that the practice of sealing up royal wills did not exist prior to this present century. One can only speculate why Prince Frank, the brother of the Queen but with little royal blood, was accorded this very special treatment. It suggests that there was something to hide.

In the Coronation Year of 1911, Queen Mary started to keep a book listing the clothes and jewels she wore in the orgy of opulence that took place throughout the summer. The maroon Morocco leather book, with its watered silk and tooling of gold fleur-de-lis, was a fitting choice to record the grandeur.

On a showery and overcast 22 June 1911, Queen Mary sat in the Golden Coronation coach wearing her new crown above a white satin gown embroidered in gold with the design of rose, shamrock and thistle which was to be

Lady Kilmorey's daughter-in-law unwittingly wore the emerald brooch from the Cambridge suite at her bosom to a family wedding in 1922. Queen Mary's brother, Dolly, Marquis of Cambridge, cut her dead.

repeated in jewel-encrusted motifs on her granddaughter's dress in 1953. Just as Queen Mary had methodically listed the possessions of her late brother Frank, so her dresser noted all her jewels.

> Collar formed of rows of diamonds with large row under.
> Diamond Cockade arranged with drops to form stomacher
>   with four diamond bow brooches under the pearl drops.
> South African pendant brooches on sleeves of gown.
> Diamond bracelet with blue enamel clasps with V.A. in
>   diamonds on clasp.

The listings continue in loving detail as Queen Mary swept in to dinner at Downing Street in her sapphire blue satin gown with the 'diamond fringe tiara, sapphire and diamond necklaces, under diamond collar, large sapphire brooches and *sautoir* of diamonds'. Old friends appear: the sapphire anchor brooch that Georgie had given her on their marriage was pinned to her navy blue serge coat and skirt for a naval review; the 'City collar' from her wedding came out for the Ghillies' Ball at Balmoral that September; the 'Hampshire pearl and diamond brooch', the 'Surrey diamond tiara' and the 'Richmond brooch', all wedding presents from nearly 20 years before, went off with her on the great Imperial fling in India in December, 1911.

The Delhi durbar was the apogee of jewelled splendour. The King Emperor entered the arena in Delhi with his Consort wearing the new Imperial Crown of India, made up for the occasion (at a cost of £60,000) and glittering with over 6,000 diamonds, four enormous sapphires, four rubies and nine emeralds, including the splendid central stone. After some dispute, the cost of Garrard's creation was borne by the people of India. The original supposition was that the Rajput princes would donate enough stones for a new crown, but the Viceroy advised against such flagrant royal begging. Then the British Government suggested that the stones should be hired from Garrard in the old Hanoverian tradition. 'I really do think,' wrote the Viceroy in 1911, 'it should have been considered where the crown was to come from.'

The oriental magnificence of the tent city set up by the 135 ruling princes was overwhelming. The Maharajah of Kashmir's camp, with its 20-foot-high carved entrance towers covered with gleaming copper and gold in a re-creation of a Hindu temple complete with solid panels of carved walnut, competed with the Maharajah of Sikkim's hand-painted flying canopy that formed the roof of his reception pavilion. The Indian princes were equally colourful in themselves as they advanced in procession to the throne-dais to be presented to the King Emperor and his Queen Empress, who were protected from the glare of the sun by scarlet and gold umbrellas. Each prince had his own distinctive dress and head covering from Gwalior's long coat with gold epaulettes to the Maharajah of Kapurthala's salmon pink turban. They also competed with their jewels, and on that morning of 12 December 1911, the swags of pearls, the glittering diamond aigrettes, the monumental rubies and emeralds were a magnificent sight.

The Persian word *'Darbar'*, or durbar, means literally a grand court, and this particular durbar of 1911 was also a Coronation celebration for King George V in the heartland of the British Empire. A feature of the traditional durbar was the giving of tributes, or *nazar*, and according to an account by the Maharajah of Dewas Junior, this homage was paid to the King Emperor. His daughter Shashi Wallia describes the scene as her father told it to her:

> First was the Nizam, who gave the King a ruby necklace in which each ruby was as big as a pigeon's egg. Then other princes followed – Baroda, Gwalior, Mysore, Kashmir – each presenting the king with other items of jewellery which must have been lying in their coffers for centuries . . . His Highness of Panna presented . . . an umbrella for his throne which was at least twelve inches in diameter, carved out of a single piece of emerald from his emerald mines. Sir Tukoji Tao of Indore, dressed in gold and silver brocade clothes, walked up to the dais twirling a gold stick with jewelled engravings and with a hilt carved out of a single ruby. Unfortunately he slipped on the polished wooden floor, put his weight on the stick . . . and it shattered, so he was very put out.

The Maharajah Dewas Junior himself gave the King an engraved silver box from his family treasure that was 'so old that in places the faces on the figures had been rubbed smooth'.

Even allowing for exaggeration and embroidery, it seems implausible that this vivid and picturesque eyewitness account could have been entirely invented. Yet there is no report of any such presentation ceremony in the extensive newspaper coverage of the time, either in England or in India. This scene apparently took place in private, and the jewels and tributes, if they were accepted by King George V and Queen Mary, absorbed into the royal collection.

There is one other eyewitness account of the Delhi durbar, by the then Crown Jeweller, William Bell of Garrard. This comprehensive and apparently fascinating story, written in the excitement of the moment and completed on the return journey from India in 1912, would presumably give a full description of the scene through the eyes of a jeweller. It is today in the possession of the Crown Jeweller, Mr William Summers, but Buckingham Palace did not feel able to make it available to the author.

Queen Mary did receive a magnificent gift in her own right – emeralds presented by a group of Indian ladies headed by the wife of the Maharajah of Patiala, who was later to take his glittering treasury of gems to Cartier in Paris, where his remodelled Crown Jewels (including a diamond, ruby, emerald and sapphire nose ring) created a sensation at an exhibition in 1928.

Queen Mary, who was cementing ties with a country she had first fallen in love with when she visited India as Princess of Wales in 1905, gave a warm speech of thanks: '. . . the jewel you have given me will ever be precious in my eyes, and, whenever I wear it, though thousands of miles of land and sea separate us, my thoughts will fly to the homes of India . . . Your jewel shall pass to the future generations as an Imperial heirloom and shall always stand as the token of the first meeting of the English Queen with the ladies of India.'

The *Statesman of India* describes the jewels as 'a large square of emeralds of historic interest engraved and set in diamonds, and a necklace and pendant of

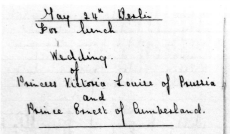

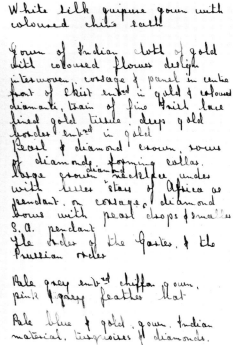

Queen Mary's jewels and gowns were listed in her Dress Book, preserved at Windsor Castle. She decked herself in diamonds for the marriage of the Kaiser's daughter in Berlin in 1913. It was the final gathering of the Royal Mob before the First World War.

emeralds set in rosettes of diamonds'. According to the Crown Jeweller, the carved emerald was made into a brooch and is in the Queen's collection, although he has never seen it worn. Queen Mary's dress book records that she wore both jewels at the Coronation durbar.

'Diamond collar, emerald and diamond necklace under the new Indian necklace of emeralds between large carved emerald brooch' reads the entry for 12 December 1911. The 'emerald and diamond necklace' was in fact the Cambridge emeralds. 'Mamma's emeralds appearing *there* amused and pleases me,' wrote the Grand-Duchess of Mecklenburg Strelitz. 'What would she have said to her Grandchild's Imperial glory?'

In that Coronation year of 1911, Queen Mary established the grandiose, Imperial style, in jewels and in dress, that was to be set for the next 40 years. Diana Vreeland, the doyenne of American fashion as editor of *Vogue*, describes Queen Mary as history remembers her: 'She also wore matching clothes. The toque. You know the Queen Mary toque. Then the fox. Then the tailleur. Then the boots. All the same colour . . . pale blue fox to go with the pale blue kid laced boots.' Chips Channon fills in the jewels on this ice-pale vision. She received him at Buckingham Palace in 1938 glittering 'with five diamond necklaces . . . She was in blue with literally mountains of jewels.' A year earlier he had seen Queen Mary at the royal garden party 'looking like the Jungfrau, white and sparkling in the sun.'

This ossification of style was due partly to the King, who was obsessively conservative about dress. His tyrannical refusal to allow his wife to shorten her hemlines was matched by his eagle eye for correct Court dress and the etiquette of orders. A king, said George V to the Aga Khan, looks on a man with an improperly worn order with the same distaste the public would feel for shirt tails hanging out. The King himself wore a frock coat in the daytime and the Prince of Wales (the future King Edward VIII) was obliged to keep a pair of conventional trousers to wear in front of his father as fashionable turn-ups were greeted with the scornful cry of 'Is it raining in *here?*'

In 1913 Queen Mary set forth in all her regal splendour to visit Germany for the wedding of the Kaiser's daughter Princess Victoria Louise. The indomitable and unapproachable Queen – almost unrecognisable to the relatives who remembered the young Princess May at Schloss Rumpenheim – was in Indian cloth of gold, her massive train borne up by two pantomime pages in white silk knee breeches and with Teutonic hair-cuts.

She listed her jewels in her dress-book: 'Pearl and diamond crown. Rows of diamonds forming collar. Large Crown diamond necklace under, with Stars of Africa as pendant on corsage. Diamond bows with pearl drops and smaller South African pendant. The order of the Garter and the Prussian order.'

Queen Mary's pale spring-like toilettes, her magnificent jewels and her grand style were much admired in Paris when the King and Queen made their last state visit in 1914 before the lights went out on a Europe engulfed in the First World War. 'Abroad is awful,' was King George V's verdict on the continental Europe that had played such an important part in his wife's peripatetic childhood. It was perhaps a reaction to the horrors of the front, which the King visited during the Great War.

The Europe that emerged from the maelstrom was in absolute contrast to the settled world of privilege and protocol that Princess May had known. Principalities, thrones and royal relatives had all been blotted out by war and revolution. Alicky and Nicky, the Czar who looked like Georgie's twin when he came to stay at Balmoral in 1896 (and left a £1,000 tip for Queen Victoria's servants), had been murdered. Soldiers crippled by war returned home shocked and sullen to an uncomfortable world. Thrones, Lord Esher tactfully explained to the Queen, were 'at a discount'.

Against this sombre backcloth and the terrible experience of World War, Court life restarted like the reprise of a half-forgotten tune. To refresh the fading memories of ritual, a dancing master had to be called in to teach the Dukes of Northumberland and Abercorn a stately quadrille.

In spite of King George V's 'private war with the twentieth century', as his eldest son described it, there was a new development at Court in the lean post-war years. The *al fresco* Court – the forerunner of the current Buckingham Palace garden party – replaced King Edward VII and Queen Alexandra's glittering evening Courts. Everyone 'except perhaps the dressmaking fraternity' looked forward to the prospect of the first afternoon Court in the summer of 1919, although those with longer memories remembered that Queen Victoria's Drawing Rooms had always been held by daylight, when the 'dowagers and debutantes had to face the trying ordeal of dressing themselves up in lowcut gowns, trains and feathers before luncheon', as the Social Notes column in *The Queen* expressed it in June 1919.

Punctually at 4 pm on 5 July 1919, with pink geraniums in big stone jars mounting sentry over the steps, the royal family made their way across the lawn from their private apartments at Buckingham Palace. Any notion that the afternoon Court was to be a low-key affair was dispelled by the sight of Queen Mary. She wore sky blue crêpe-de-chine with flower embroidery in blue beads on the cross-over bodice (a fashion taken up by her daughter-in-law Elizabeth, now the Queen Mother). Over the snowy tulle at Queen Mary's neckline fell a heavy string of pearls; on the corsage was pinned Queen Victoria's diamond and sapphire brooch, with earrings to match. A diamond arrow pierced the front of her favourite toque hat in blue and gold iridescent silk. Many of the society ladies at this open-air court were wearing not only elaborate jewels but ermine wraps and broad-brimmed, feather-trimmed hats plucked from the Edwardian era.

For the next sixteen years, through the bitter general strike and the Depression, during the rise of Ramsay MacDonald and his new Labour party, the rules of court etiquette, the length of the trains and the depth of the necklines remained as immutable as Queen Mary's personal style of grandeur. A quarter of a century later at the royal garden party after the Second World War, when wartime fashion meant severe suits, military shoulders and hair in the Victory Roll, Queen Mary advanced slowly through the crowd in a magnificent cloth of gold coat. 'My cousin May,' whispered a relative, 'is rather overdressed.'

But to most of her subjects and courtiers, Queen Mary's grandeur was monumental. If her manner was 'like talking to St Paul's Cathedral', as Sir Henry Channon irreverently claimed, the Queen's façade was 'floodlit with splendour'. 'I have never known any Empress or Queen who could wear a quantity of superb jewels with such ease and simplicity and without appearing in the least overladen', wrote a contemporary in 1936.

At the Courts still held inside Buckingham Palace, King George V and Queen Mary would be flanked on their dais by the 'Scots in their tartans, their laces, their velvets, their daggers, their sporrans', remembers Diana Vreeland. On their other side would be the Indians 'in all their regalia, with their sapphires, their pearls . . . their emeralds, and their rubies'. The setting is eloquently described by Mrs Vreeland as 'luxury *in depth*'.

At the centre was the King, in full dress uniform of an Admiral of the Fleet or Field Marshal, and beside him the Queen 'dazzling with jewels' as she proceeded majestically towards the crimson and gold throne with her train carried by two pages-of-honour dressed in scarlet. Behind the King and Queen on the dais would be grouped the Princes and Princesses of the Royal Blood and the household, ready to receive first the diplomatic corps (including an Ethiopian in a leopard skin), then the ladies who were to be presented by their sponsors.

Lady Cynthia Colville recalls in her memoirs the day her mother took her to

Court for her debut. She wore a white tulle dress, embroidered by Norman Hartnell with silver and pearls, with the traditional ostrich feathers perched on her head, as she swept her best court curtsy (taught by Miss Vacani) to Queen Mary. When she lifted her head towards the figure on the golden throne under the great canopy of state, she saw the Queen, dressed in gold brocade bisected by the royal blue Garter ribbon, emeralds and diamonds at her neck and an emerald and diamond coronet on her silver hair.

The extraordinary thing about this grand Court life that so contrasted with the threadbare years of the Depression, was that for nearly twenty years it was the only social life that the King and Queen had. Throughout the 1920s and until the King's death in 1936, the royal couple ('a Darby and Joan such as we are,' May said to George) dined at home in their private apartments, the King in his tail coat and the Garter, the Queen always in a tiara for dinner.

All the children's lives were changing after the War. One life burnt out: the shadowy Prince John whose epileptic fits had set him physically apart from the rest of the family died in 1919 in a cottage on the Sandringham estate. On 21 January, Queen Mary buried her son at Sandringham church where Prince Eddy's funeral had taken place nearly thirty years before.

Happier family events began to crowd in on the 1920s. The King and Queen's only daughter Princess Mary married Lord Lascelles in 1922 and produced their first grandchild George a year later. In 1923, Bertie married Princess Mary's close friend and bridesmaid, Lady Elizabeth Bowes Lyon, and their first child Elizabeth (or 'Lilibet' as she soon called herself) was introduced to her cousin George and his younger brother Gerald.

The great houses of London that had been turned into hospitals during the war were refurbished and opened up, with formal dinners served on gold plate by footmen in the family livery. But the King and Queen did not go out in Society. The Marchioness of Cambridge remembers that at family dinners the King, worn out by the War and perhaps by the early effects of his debilitating illness, would say 'We won't talk, will we?' Queen Mary's natural gaiety, always masked by a reserve, was apparently extinguished.

The King and Queen made no social background whatever for their growing children nor introduced them to anyone outside the Court circle. The Prince of Wales was sent off on a perpetual peregrination round the Empire and on his brief stops home plunged on his own into the Society that was to dance through the Depression to the beat of jazz. He made his own friends among the cosmopolitan world outside the stuffy court, and there he met Mrs Wallis Simpson, the American woman who was to become his wife.

The flint that sparked Queen Mary's imagination was not her family, but her collecting. 'Just imagine . . .' she would tell her niece by marriage, Dorothy Cambridge, eyes agleam with the story of how she had found a particular little treasure or unearthed at Buckingham Palace the last of a set of chairs or managed to beat down an antique dealer to a bargain price. The redoubtable Queen Mary who met death or duty with an impenetrable carapace of majesty, was girlishly enthusiastic when sifting and sorting and adding to the royal collections. Forays to antique shops were her principal occupation in the post-war years, her own trips in the afternoons (she was always back for tea)

75

being an advance raid or reconnaissance. This would be followed by a summons to a lady-in-waiting or a call to a useful friend or relative, who was told the whereabouts of objects – mostly porcelain or paintings and often something with a tenuous royal connection – and asked to beat down the price. 'He's asking £350 but if you can get it for £250 . . .' would be the royal command that few traders dared to refuse.

It is difficult to decide from this distance how much of Queen Mary's collecting was a genuine passion to possess and how much of the bargaining was just an elaborate game played to amuse her, just as her daughter-in-law Elizabeth (now the Queen Mother) might send out an equerry from Clarence House to a betting shop in Piccadilly.

'She was generous in spirit but extremely mean about money,' says a relative who was used by Queen Mary as an antique spotter and shopper in the 1920s, and later found herself on the receiving end of this bargaining process when Queen Mary offered to buy from her the rococo jewel cabinet that had belonged to Queen Charlotte, wife of George III. Queen Mary offered £1,000; a nearby landowner offered £5,000 and a royal lady-in-waiting announced icily down the telephone that Her Majesty would not be interested at that price. The issue was finally resolved by Queen Elizabeth the Queen Mother, who offered to 'go halves' with her mother-in-law on the £5,000 asking price.

No relative was too distant, no object too small to feed Queen Mary's interest in royal iconography and her acquisitive instinct. Miniatures were especially appealing – tiny gold musical boxes and jewelled watches, Battersea enamels and delicate scent bottles, Queen Alexandra's collection of Fabergé animals and tiny carved ivory tools. For Christmas 1929, the family gave the King and Emperor a regal toy: a miniature Fabergé elephant with cabochon ruby eyes and ivory tusks. An enamelled Indian boy sits on the elephant's back on a yellow gold rug, enamelled translucent green and decorated with half a dozen rose diamonds. One of these diamonds covers the winding hole for a gold clockwork key that sets off the animal at a stately walk, waving his head and tail.

These miniature *objets d'art* found their ultimate expression in Queen Mary's Doll's House, planned for her by Georgie's cousin, Princess Marie Louise. The grand and graceful mansion (so unlike the rambling reality of Buckingham Palace) was designed by Sir Edwin Lutyens, the architect of New Delhi, who wanted to create something that would 'enable future generations to see how a King and Queen of England lived in the twentieth century, and what authors, artists and craftsmen of note there were during their reign'.

From the tiny tablecloths, woven in Belfast to a perfect two-inch square, to the miniature portrait of Queen Mary in the royal diadem, to the water colour sketches in a portfolio in the King's sitting-room, to the miniature books with their engraved bookplates and embossed crown, each especially commissioned – Rudyard Kipling wrote 'If' for the project – the Doll's House was perfection. It was also extremely revealing of the Queen, who played an eager and active role in its creation: the aesthetically beautiful house was empty of family figures, and about as much space was given over to the strongroom for the jewels as to the nursery for the children.

Queen Mary in the interlaced diamond circle tiara with pearl drops, acquired from the exotic Grand-Duchess Vladimir. The Queen wears the same tiara in a large colour plate. On Queen Mary's bosom is the brooch from the pearl and diamond suite Bertie gave to his bride Princess Alexandra on their wedding day.

Above Majestic Queen Mary in her Coronation robes, 1911, painted by Sir Henry Macbeth Raeburn and wearing Queen Victoria's diadem and bow brooches. She listed her jewels in her Dress Book: "collar formed of rows of diamonds with large row under. Diamond cockade arranged with drops to form stomacher with four diamond bow brooches under with pearl drops. S.A. pendant brooches on sleeves of gown. Diamond bracelets with blue enamel."

Right The diamond bow-knot tiara that Princess Diana was given by the Queen as Queen Mary originally wore it — with upstanding pearls above the nineteen hanging drops.

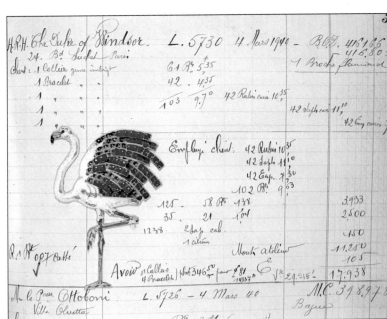

Left In the United States on New Year's Day, 1941, an ebullient Duchess of Windsor wears the flamingo brooch that her husband had given her the previous year.

Above The ledger sheet from Cartier in Paris shows that rubies, emeralds and sapphires for the flamingo brooch were culled from an existing necklace and four bracelets that the Duke of Windsor broke up.

Below The Duchess of Windsor's collection of Cartier cats included this panther's-head brooch. The pugs that followed at her heels were her answer to the royal corgis. Models of the pugs still fill her grand home in the Bois de Boulogne, Paris.

I Broche pince PANTHERE pavée brillants et semi de saphirs
sur I gros saphir cabochon,monture platine,système 2 épingles avec sureté
or gris;

| | | | Platine : | 27gr60 |
| | | | Or gris : | 3gr20 |

28-I-1949	C.A.	Mre	229.866)	
C I400 F	"	27gr60 platine	20.280)	251.000
	"	3gr20 d'or gris	854)	500.000
Lot I5I		I saph. cab.I52.35	pour "	39.200
"		I06 saphirs env.5.00	RSKSK	240.000
"	I5	32I brillants	3.00	72.800
"		62 "	I.I2 TISKS	3.800
"	I5	2 Bts jaune	0.04 pour	59.200
"		68 brillants	0.74 RSKSK	400
"	40	4 roses	0.02 OSKSK	850
		Ecrin		I.I67.250

Top A ledger sheet shows details of the superb panther brooch the Duke of Windsor bought for his wife in 1949. The enormous cabochon sapphire of 152.35 carats cost him £5,000.

Left Wallis wears the glittering panther brooch; its sapphire camouflaged against her blue satin dress.

Above A close-up of the panther, pavé set with diamonds and sapphires, and the Duchess's favourite yellow diamonds as eyes. It was set in platinum.

Were the jewels that Queen Mary acquired for herself in the 1920s substitutes for her departing children and a private pleasure to distract her from her personal anxieties? She had already inherited from the Crown and been given as Empire gifts more jewels than she could ever wear. She did not go out in Society and she did not have in George V (as Queen Alexandra did in Edward VII, Wallis Simpson in Edward VIII and Princess Diana has in Prince Charles) a consort who was interested in beautiful jewels. Georgie did give May presents of jewellery, like the little brooch that had been his first tentative approach to her the Christmas after his brother Eddy died, or the diamond anchor he gave her as a naval Prince to his bride. At Christmas 1928, when the King was just recovering from the removal of an abscess on his lung, he gave May a pink topaz and diamond pendant. But that was when Queen Mary had her heart set on the jewels that lay trussed up in Empress Marie's box in Buckingham Palace. The Romanov Jewels had by then become an indulgence and perhaps an obsession to the sixty-year-old Queen.

Queen Mary had her first taste of the Russian treasures in 1920, when she was grieving over the death of her son Prince John and adjusting to life after the War. Grand-Duchess Vladimir, the wife of one of the sons of the Czar, died in Switzerland in 1920 after a tortuous escape from the Russian Revolution, when she existed for seven weeks on black bread and soup on a refugee train. The Grand-Duchess was a flamboyant character (she liked dressing up in a jewel-encrusted Russian peasant outfit) who had been a pivot in St Petersburg Society and one of Louis Cartier's most loyal customers. She staged an annual Christmas bazaar of Imperial opulence and expressed her colourful personality in the fabulous jewels that were displayed to favoured visitors in the glass cases that lined the walls in the dressing rooms of her palace.

Her favourite jewellery was the Russian tiara, the *kokoshnik* or cock's comb that was the traditional peasant headdress and had been developed by the Romanovs as a majestic jewelled head ornament. Princess Marina of Greece played with her Russian grandmother's tiaras – the trembling aigrettes of diamonds, the weighty ruby tiara, the sapphire *kokoshnik* with a duck egg of a sapphire at its centre and the interlaced circles of diamonds with suspended pearl drops that went to Queen Mary.

'Can I have one too?' said Princess Marina as she playfully tried on the sapphire and diamond tiara.

'Of course you will, when you are grown up', came the prophetic reply from her grandmother. Twenty years later, Princess Marina married into the English royal family as the Duchess of Kent and received from her mother-in-law Queen Mary a magnificent *parure* or suite of sapphires and diamonds.

Queen Mary would have relished that vignette of family history. She must also have appreciated the heroic tale of how the Grand-Duchess Vladimir's jewels made their own escape from Russia, bundled in newspaper in a pair of Gladstone bags. A young English aristocrat named Bertie Stopford befriended the exiled Grand-Duchess and planned a raid into Russia, where he smuggled himself into her old Palace disguised as a workman, located the wall safe and took the jewels out via the British Embassy.

As she was to do later with the inheritance of the Empress Marie Feodorovna,

THE ROMANOV SPOILS

The Queen's most familiar tiara (1) has a romantic history. It was made for the exotic Grand-Duchess Vladimir of Russia (3) who was a fabled collector of jewels; she even created jewel-encrusted peasant outfits for her fancy-dress balls. When she escaped the Russian Revolution of 1917, her jewels were

walled up in a safe in her St Petersburg Palace. A dashing young English aristocrat, Bertie Stopford, smuggled himself into Russia and brought out the tiara and jewels in two battered Gladstone bags.

Queen Mary acquired the tiara after the Grand-Duchess's death in 1921. As an alternative to the pendant pearls, she hung it with the lustrous Cambridge emeralds that she had to claw back from her dead brother's mistress (2). Queen Mary wears the tiara with pearl drops and the brooch that was given to Queen Alexandra by her husband on her wedding day (4).

The Queen inherited the circle tiara on her grandmother's death in 1953 and wears it on many state occasions (5).

Queen Mary 'bagged all the best'. She bought the Grand-Duchess Vladimir's most prized possession, the interlaced ovals of diamonds with suspended pendant pearls. Queen Mary used the spare Cambridge emeralds that she had prised from Frank of Teck's lady love as alternatives to the teardrop pearls and left the emotive tiara to her granddaughter, the Queen.

Other relatives picked over the rest of the Grand-Duchess Vladimir's jewels. Queen Marie of Romania, whose passion for jewels rivalled Queen Mary's, bought the sapphire tiara. The Vladimir emeralds followed new money to the New World, where they were sold first to the Rockefellers and then to the Woolworth heiress Barbara Hutton. Other jewels were divided among the Grand-Duchess Vladimir's children. Princess Marina's mother, the Grand-Duchess Helen of Greece, inherited the diamonds (which had another hair-raising escape into exile from Greece when they were smuggled out by rowing boat in a rickety wooden box along with the family's white Persian cat).

In 1925, the world jewel market was awash with gems sold up by Russian exiles or put on sale by the Bolsheviks, who had discovered a fabulous treasure trove of jewels walled up in the Moscow palace of Prince Youssoupov, husband to the niece of the Czar. Secret passages from behind a gallery of pictures led down to two dungeons filled with 255 brooches, 13 tiaras, 42 bracelets and 210 kilos of jewelled ornaments. In this hoard was a diamond and bow-knot tiara with pendant pearls which may have been the original model for the tiara which Queen Mary had made up by Garrard from pieces of her own jewellery. The Queen inherited this tiara and gave it to Princess Diana on her marriage to Prince Charles (Chapter 7).

In 1925, Queen Alexandra died and Queen Mary finally came into her full royal inheritance. The list of personal jewels she acquired from her mother-in-law is relatively small, but it included some important or historic pieces, including the Dagmar necklace, that Danish symbol that Princess Alexandra had been given on her marriage, and the valuable diamond necklace of thirty-two brilliants presented by the City of London to Princess Alexandra as a wedding gift. The speculation is that Queen Alexandra divided her own jewellery among her children, bestowing the brightest and best on the Prince of Wales who gave this royal inheritance to Wallis Simpson. In fact, Queen Alexandra died intestate and Queen Mary herself supervised the dispersal of Motherdear's jewels. If she allowed any major pieces to be given to her own children at this time, she would have been acting entirely out of character with the rest of her life and her attitude towards the acquisition of jewellery in the 1920s.

The weeding-out of the clutter of Queen Alexandra's objects at Sandringham and Marlborough House was 'a warning to one not to keep too much', Queen Mary said, although her maid regularly removed ninety objects to dust the Queen's rosewood writing table. On 14 October 1926, King George and Queen Mary gave up York Cottage – their home for thirty-three years – and moved to the Big House. But by the end of the decade, clouds of worry were rolling up: the death of the Queen's brother and companion-in-art Prince Dolly; the first bout of lung cancer in the King; the refusal of David, the Prince of Wales, to settle down or move into the traditional Wales residence at

Marlborough House. And while the King's life dimmed and spluttered to its end, the Prince of Wales's affair with Mrs Simpson grew more passionate and more public.

The King died on 19 January 1936, just after celebrating twenty-five years on the throne. In the same fateful week in January, Queen Mary had buried her son John in 1919, her fiancé Eddy in 1891 and now his brother Georgie, her husband. Symbolically (and rather more swiftly than Motherdear) she gave up the Crown Jewels. 'They had been in my care since 1910 – felt very sad at parting,' she wrote in her diary on 13 July 1936.

At the same time, Queen Mary divested herself of all the mourning jewellery that she had collected and inherited. The jet diadems that her own mother Princess Mary Adelaide had recommended to the young Princess Alexandra were handed over to the London Museum, along with jet necklaces and brooches, hair combs and liquorice black butterfly-headed hair pins, the brooch carved 'In Memory of My Dead Brother' and a clutter of memento mori. In one grand gesture, Queen Mary, who had an inborn dislike of wearing black, sloughed off all the paraphernalia of royal mourning that Queen Victoria had amassed as a widow for forty years.

Queen Mary was to live on for nearly twenty years, majestic, indomitable, clearing the woods at Badminton where she was evacuated during the Second World War, facing stoically the deaths of two more of her sons – the Duke of Kent in a plane crash in August 1942, King George VI of cancer ten years later. Once she, and the monarchy that she had nurtured and cherished, had survived the Abdication, both seemed as tough and indestructible as the diamonds she adored.

Some of the Victorian jet mourning jewellery which Queen Mary refused to wear and gave away to a London museum.

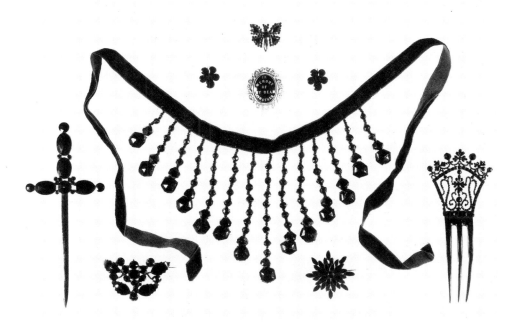

4

The Wallis Collection

Mrs Simpson, she's no fool;
She make her aim the big Crown Jewel.

Bahamas Calypso
from Joanna C. Colcord's Collection
Songs of American Sailormen

On the evening of 16 October 1946, while the servants were eating tea at Ednam Lodge, Sunningdale, the grand and gabled home of Lord Dudley, a thief shinned up a drainpipe and crept through the guest bedroom window. From under the maid's bed he extracted a large black box, which he abandoned on the nearby golf course, scattering the last of the contents. The jewellery belonged to the Duchess of Windsor, paying with the Duke one of their rare visits to an England which had held a frosty welcome since the Abdication. Unwanted at any royal palace and unwelcomed on their arrival, the Windsors had come from their home in Paris for a short stay.

Scotland Yard was immediately called in to hunt for the thief, who was officially estimated to have got away with between £20,000 and £25,000 worth of jewels. Detective-Inspector J. R. Capstick and Detective Sergeant Monk of the Yard, with fingerprint expert Superintendent Cherrill, examined the grounds and the evidence. Two days later, the Assistant Commissioner in charge of the CID, Mr R. M. Howe, and one of the Yard's 'Big Five', Deputy-Commander W. R. Rawlings, took personal charge of the case. A £2,000 reward was offered to anyone coming forward with substantial information.

There then falls over the Case of the Missing Jewels a pall as deep and impenetrable as the mist that shrouded Ednam Lodge that October evening. Nothing was ever recovered and none of the distinctive pieces of jewellery or their individual stones has been seen again. The Duke's Lloyds policy was honoured in spite of the fact that the Duchess had lamentably failed to take the precaution of putting her jewels in the bank or even in the silver store, and that the Duke's dog had failed to bark. The first piece that the Duke of Windsor bought to replace his wife's stolen treasures was, suitably enough, a ferocious panther rampant, outstretched to guard a huge cabochon emerald.

There was only one emerald among the stolen jewels, a solitaire square-cut emerald ring that was relatively small by royal standards (the weight of the

The Duchess of Windsor's fantastic menagerie of diamonds included Cartier's tiger bracelets. She collected canary diamonds like this enormous platinum-set ring. Her other favourite gems were sapphires and rubies.

Golden panther outstretched on a cabochon emerald of 116.74 carats. Bought by the Duke from Cartier in 1948 using the insurance money from the Ednam Lodge robbery.

stone was 7.81 carats). But from this time dates a series of fantastic allegations about the unsolved robbery that are still voiced today. The crime, say the rumours, was master-minded by the royal family itself in an attempt to snatch back Queen Alexandra's emeralds, which had been given to the Danish princess on her marriage. These had previously been the subject of a royal wrangle when lawyer Theodore Goddard, who had represented Wallis in her divorce case, had rushed down to Cannes to see her 48 hours before the Abdication. Lord Davidson, who moved in royal circles, claimed to know that the lawyer had been sent to Mrs Simpson by the royal family specifically to get the emeralds back.

The theft of the Duchess's jewels came almost exactly 10 years after that momentous winter of 1936, when society had heaved and boiled with rumours of the King's infatuation with the American divorcée. Diana Cooper had dined at Fort Belvedere, the King's country home, and Mrs Simpson was dripping in new jewels and clothes. Emerald Cunard was entertaining Wallis at the opera and she arrived in the Royal Box with emeralds ablaze on the green bodice of her black dress. Marie Belloc Lowndes thought that Wallis must be wearing dressmaker's emeralds, because no one could have real jewels so large. Chips Channon had sat next to Wallis at dinner and she was wearing new jewels again.

The diaries of the witty Sir Henry 'Chips' Channon run with the floodtide of speculation: 'Her collection of jewels is the talk of London . . . The King must give her new ones every day . . . he worships her . . . The King is insane about Wallis, insane . . . Cartier's are resetting magnificent, indeed fabulous jewels for Wallis, and for what purpose if she is not to be Queen?'

The ebb and flow and torrent of gossip rolled on until it hit the Abdication on 10 December 1936. The jewels robbery stirred old memories, submerged by the steady new reign, by the War and by the lack of information about the Duke of Windsor and his Duchess who were living abroad, serving out the War as Governor and his lady in the Bahamas and deliberately pushed out of the public's heart and mind by a manipulative British press.

This time there were hard facts to face off the rumours. The list of the Duchess of Windsor's stolen jewellery was published by the assessors, Messrs Summers, Henderson and Company of Leadenhall Street. This is it in full:

> One diamond bird clip
> One diamond and aquamarine brooch
> One platinum and diamond bracelet with six large aquamarines
> One aquamarine ring with solitaire aquamarine (weight of stone 58.2 carats)
> One gold ring set with one golden sapphire (weight of stone 41.4 carats)
> One solitaire square cut emerald ring (weight of stone 7.81 carats)
> One pair of diamond and sapphire earrings
> One pair of diamond ball earrings
> One pair of earrings in the shape of a shell, one set with
>   a blue sapphire, the other with a yellow sapphire
> One double gold chain necklace with one large blue sapphire
>   and one yellow sapphire
> et cetera.

84

This was indeed a 'Wallis collection' as the diamond-bright Mrs Simpson quipped to Cecil Beaton when the besotted King demanded to buy all the pictures that the photographer had taken of her. Beaton described Wallis Simpson's skin as 'smooth as the inside of a shell', her hair so sleek she might have been Chinese, and her *avant garde* flower arrangements – by society's new darling Constance Spry – 'arrangements of expensive flowers mixed with bark and local weeds'.

As in flowers, so in jewels: the Duchess of Windsor was relentlessly up-to-the-moment – '*à la page*' as her friend Diana Mosley described her. There is nothing in the settings of the stolen jewels that remotely suggests the delicate 'garland' style of Queen Alexandra's jewellery or the ornate treasures from Queen Victoria's jewel cases.

The diamond bird clip was typical of the menagerie of jewels created for the Windsors by Jeanne Toussaint of Cartier, whose first birds were caught in diamond cages and made in wartime France as a symbol of occupation. A ruby, diamond and sapphire flamingo brooch bought by the Duke in 1940 became the Duchess's most familiar piece of jewellery and one that she continued to wear after the Duke's death. Although naturalistic brooches were also a feature of Victorian jewellery, this particular diamond bird could not be dated earlier than the 1920s because that was when Louis Cartier invented the clip. The stolen brooch was probably the important jewelled bird, its body a plump cabochon sapphire of 64.80 carats, its tail a long sweep of 322 brilliants, that the Duke of Windsor bought from Cartier on 25 February 1946. This brooch was made by breaking up three diamond rings, three brooches, one with tiny emeralds, the other sapphires including the large cabochon. Five other brooches and two pairs of earrings, all with small stones, went into the complex bird brooch. These particular details from the ledger at Cartier are interesting because they prove that the Duke of Windsor had jewellery to break up in 1946, ten years after the Abdication.

Similarly, the Duchess of Windsor's stolen suite of sapphires, with their bold contrasts of blue and yellow stones, must also have been a modern piece. Mixes of jade and amethyst, sapphire and emerald, rainbows of semi precious stones all came into fashion under the influence of the Fauvist painters and the Ballet Russe. These coloured gemstones remained personal favourites with the Duchess of Windsor. In the 1950s she greeted a guest at the Windsors' home in Neuilly, on the outskirts of Paris (leased from the French Government at a peppercorn rent) in a square-necked purple velvet dress with a striking choker of amethysts and turquoise.

The coloured gemstones painted out the Edwardian vogue for 'white' jewellery so favoured by Queen Alexandra. The double gold chain of the sapphire necklace, the shell-shaped earrings and the diamond balls are all settings of the Art Deco period that is bounded by the 1925 exhibition in Paris and by the Paris Exhibition of 1937. In March 1940 the Duke of Windsor had bought a pair of diamond ball earrings from Cartier that answers the description of the stolen jewels.

The aquamarine brooch, ring and necklace were an impressive set of the pale watery stones that fitted the Duchess's *jeune fille* image of herself. 'The

Duc de Windsor. M 5440 M 5441. CH. M 5471 ᶜᴬ Y/Bod od.
Ambassade d'Angleterre.

démonté d'une bague restant	2 . lts batons —	0.84 .
" de 2 brunettes restant	20 brillants	0.32 —
" d'une bague .	33 "	0 61
" " "	22 " batons	1 27
" " d'une broch	1 Saphir cab.	64.80. X —
" " "	48 Emeraudes cal.	6.28
"	40 saphirs	7.75
" de épingle d'oreille .	44 "	9.80
" " "	34 Emeraudes	5.99 —
" de 2 broches percées .	138 brillants .	5.37
" " "	174 lts batons	10.91 .
" " "	2 lts carrés	1.94 . X
" d'une broch fine lt formes .	64 " formes .	11 91
" broche de cheveux .	79 "	3 65 —
" de 2 broches percées . lt	86 "	4.24 .
les 10 Emeraudes employés Y — 6663 .	12 " batons	1.70 —
démonté d'un motif	1 brillant .	3.30 trisg

Recapitulation

Uer. lts ronds		lts batons.		Saphir		Emeraudes —	
299' 357 . 1753 .		276 . 2837		1 . 64.80		34 . 4	
				84 1755 .		48 .	
				85 . 8235		82 12	
Emploi . 1 . 330		26 . 598 —		1 . 64.80		50 . 78	
322 1319		186 13.42 —		84 1708 .			
au dessin 323 . 16.49 .		212 1940		85 81.88			
Destru —		+ 2 194 .					
23 lts ▭ 761 restu u⁶		214 . 21.34					
pour projet de bague au dessin							

Rendu .   34 lts ronds   1.04 —
    —   24 . — formes   1.70   + 38 lts formes 8.
+ 49 lts formes d'ou/   —   2 Saphirs   047
    —   32 Emeraudes   4 96 —

(a

38 lts 5 33 . pr Coe 5531
reste 8 lts ▭ 030
Rendu u/m Bo . 12100 à Boj 25/2/46 —
Remis à BOJ 2 lts ▭ 194 le 11.3.46 —
Rendu à Boj le 5 4 46 le chaton plus bl 3.30

Reporté au folio 363 — 38 lts formes —

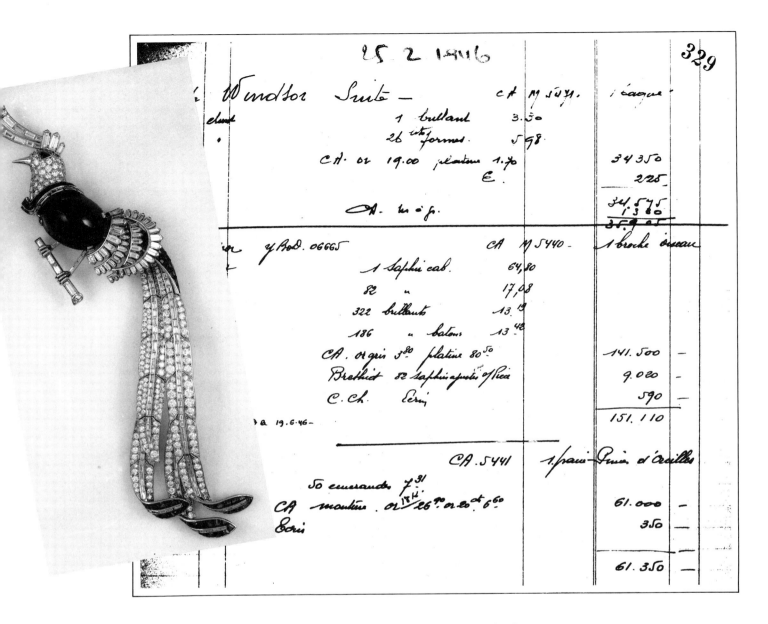

thing I most remember about her clothes is that she dressed very young for her age, in pale pink from head to foot,' says James Viane, who worked as kitchen boy for the Duchess at that time in Paris and who is now the chef at the British Embassy in Paris. The Duke of Windsor bought aquamarine flower clips with large central stones from Cartier on 31 December 1936, just three weeks after the Abdication.

Mrs Simpson first showed her love of aquamarines in a bandeau that gripped her dark shiny cap of hair with its madonna parting and huge aquamarine cross on a thin gold chain that she wore when she and her friend Thelma Lady Furness (both divorcées, but neither officially the 'guilty party') were presented at Court in June 1931. She was wearing Thelma's train, Thelma's fan and Thelma's Prince of Wales feathers – a symbol of the fact that

OPPOSITE AND ABOVE *Gemstones from 16 different pieces of the Duke's jewellery went into the bird brooch in 1946, the year of the Ednam Lodge robbery. The Cartier ledger sheets record the complex unmounting and resetting of rings, brooches and earrings.*

ABOVE LEFT *Diamond bird brooch, its breast a 64·80 cabochon sapphire, its tail a sweep of gems.*

in three years' time she was destined to take Thelma's place as First Lady to the Prince of Wales.

Wallis Warfield/Spencer/Simpson had already come a long way since the teenage dance in her native Baltimore at which she wore a blue-green feather on the back of her head to match her seductive new dress. She was destined to go further still, beyond the wildest imaginings of her Baltimore classmate Mary Kirk Raffray, who eventually married the cast-off Ernest Simpson.

'My Prince of Wales feathers' the Duchess of Windsor called her fan at a Paris ball in 1950. She is wearing her favourite tasselled ruby and diamond necklace.

Mrs Simpson may have climbed a social mountain, but there is nothing in the list of stolen jewels to substantiate the story that, as well as stealing the King, she had also made off with the Crown Jewels. The case for the gossip-mongers rests only on two little words at the end of the list put out by the Duke's insurance brokers, Messrs Hogg, Robinson and Capel-Cure. The list concluded with the words 'et cetera'.

Could 'the rest' have included the fabulous Alexandra emeralds which older members of the court claimed to have seen Mrs Simpson wearing, even though the magnificent stones had been reset? Did the Duke of Windsor deliberately conceal from the British public (and perhaps from his own solicitor Mr Allen, from the police, the assessors and the insurance brokers) just how much was in the stolen jewel case? Was the real value of the jewels which the Duke had

88

heaped on his lady over the previous decade £400,000, as claimed by a member of his staff, and not the mere £20,000 quoted? And did the box contain priceless unset emeralds and rubies which Queen Alexandra had left her grandson and royal heir when she died in 1925?

The first question to ask is this: what are the 'Alexandra emeralds' which are supposed to have been brought by the young Princess from her native Denmark and designated as an heirloom for the British Monarchy? The idea that the impoverished young princess, who shared a room in her modest Danish home with her sister Minnie and whose father's income at £2,000 was one-fifth of his daughter's yearly allowance as Princess of Wales, had a dowry of fabulous jewels is nonsense. Her heirloom gift from the King of Denmark was the Dagmar necklace, made of pearls and diamonds, with a detachable enamelled cross that was a facsimile of the thirteenth-century cross of Dagmar. The necklace was made by Jules Didrichsen, the Crown Jeweller in Copenhagen. It has been worn by the Queen and is in her possession today.

The only emeralds that Princess Alexandra received on her marriage were four square-cut emeralds in a diamond flower spray brooch given by the Duchess of Cambridge (who was later to leave her inheritance of the Cambridge emeralds to the monarchy via Queen Mary). Queen Victoria gave a suite of Indian ornaments containing a few small emeralds but mostly pearls, diamonds and pale pink rubies; there was a sprinkling of emeralds in the diamond and opal band bracelet presented by the Ladies of Manchester; the only predominantly emerald jewellery was a pair of cabochon emerald earrings and a diamond badge set with an emerald leek motif from the Ladies of South Wales. It is difficult to imagine the sophisticated and stylish Duchess of Windsor, whose favourite dish was salmon in a vodka sauce and whose clothes were the essence of *haute couture*, wearing a brooch shaped like a leek.

There are two other possible sources of fine emeralds. Queen Alexandra might have received a suite of the jewels as a present from her sister Minnie, who became Empress of Russia. She sent some generous presents to Alix, like the sapphire and diamond necklace she gave for her sister's silver wedding in 1888. Queen Alexandra, who died intestate, might have passed on such a necklace to her grandson David, the Prince of Wales and later Edward VIII.

If this is the case, the 'emeralds' were a personal bequest which had nothing to do with the British royal heritage. Queen Alexandra had championed her own son Eddy's unsuitable choice of a Roman Catholic bride and helped him to win over Queen Victoria, although Eddy ultimately proposed to Princess May of Teck before his untimely death (Chapter 2). Alix had also condoned her husband's affair with Alice Keppel, and the generous jewels he showered on her, so she would not necessarily have disapproved of her grandson's open hand and heart.

A more likely source of hypothetical 'Alexandra emeralds' is the torrent of real emeralds which poured into Princess Alexandra's jewel box after her husband's trip to India in 1875–6. From Indore, from Gwalior and from Lucknow, the Prince of Wales (later Edward VII) received massive pendant emeralds, including a crown set with emerald drops. Almost none of these princely gifts can be traced today.

Wallis Simpson in June 1931 wearing an aquamarine bandeau and cross and Court feathers borrowed from Thelma, Lady Furness, the current favourite of the Prince of Wales.

Wallis at her wedding: blue crêpe Mainbocher dress, her husband's sapphire and diamond bracelet and her favourite chain of crosses.

When Queen Alexandra's diamond *collier résille* was made by Cartier in 1904, they took apart an Indian necklace containing nine large emeralds and nine rubies, as well as a central diamond star motif and over a thousand brilliants. Some of the diamonds and all the 18 globular rubies and emeralds were returned to the King and Queen. Similarly after another resetting in November 1907, an emerald and diamond choker was remade leaving a residue of 11 emeralds (and over 600 pearls), which were all given back to the King.

If Edward VIII inherited these gems, they could have been made into the ruby and emerald necklaces that so astounded society in 1936, or into the jewels (a different ring not just for every finger but for every day of the year) that the Prince of Wales had given to an earlier mistress, who is still alive today and selling back these jewels, one by one, to the London jeweller who first supplied them.

The Prince of Wales himself was interested, involved and *au courant* with fine jewellery. As early as 1925 (the year that Queen Alexandra died) he was drawn by the French cartoonist Sem as Parisian women clustered round him on his way into Cartier. He was dubbed *'Le Prince Charmant de la rue de la Paix'* by a society that still had vivid memories of an earlier Prince of Wales, later King Edward VII, whose state visits to Cartier had raised the prestige of the house. Hennells, now sited in Bond Street, is another London jeweller which received bountiful commissions from the new Prince of Wales *well before his relationship with Mrs Simpson*. (They were also the clearing house for the Empress Marie's jewels that fed Queen Mary's appetite for gems.)

There is yet another hypothesis about the source of the gems which Mrs Simpson acquired after the warm spring day in Formentor, Majorca when Prince Charming first pressed into her hand a velvet box containing an emerald and diamond charm for her bracelet. (Does Prince Charles, who presents a new birthday charm to Princess Diana each birthday, know that he is following a royal precedent?)

In November 1921, Edward Prince of Wales arrived in Bombay for a four-month tour of India which retraced almost exactly the footsteps of his grandfather Wales nearly half a century before (a fact he frequently mentioned in speeches to his maharajah hosts). The cataclysm of change that had shaken Europe in the Great War had hardly stirred the flap ears of the caparisoned elephants, carefully stencilled with the Prince of Wales's feathers and motto as they paraded towards him at Baroda. When the modern world did intrude on the 'crescendo of gorgeousness' that marked the Prince's tour, it was as a fleet of Rolls-Royces owned by the Maharajah of Bharatpur. ('His Highness owns more than any other person in the world who is not a motor firm.') Or it was the thousands of electric light bulbs that picked out the Prince of Wales's feathers and his motto *'Ich Dien'* against the inky blackness of the Indian sky.

In spite of the political rise of Mahatma Gandhi (who started a gaol sentence on the day that the Prince's ship *Renown* sailed away with the ship's band playing 'Goodbyee'), the reception of the Prince of Wales by the Rajput rulers was almost identical to that of the India seen by the future Edward VII in 1875.

The Prince of Wales made his royal progress through 16 states from the lake Palace of Udaipur with its myriad lights dancing on the water, to Jodhpur, where the royal regent and his court had coats of cloth of gold and gem-encrusted swords. In the desert state of Bikaner, the camel corps rode out to greet him and the evening's entertainment consisted of a native dervish dance on burning cinders and a sensual parade of nautch girls. The Prince tried his skills at pig-sticking, at polo, at tiger-shooting. He sat on a silver chair in a durbar tent: he watched parades of bejewelled elephants and bullocks with their horns covered in solid silver. And everywhere there was 'the usual exchange of visits' with each royal prince.

The one big difference between the tours of the two heirs-apparent, grandfather and grandson, lies in the reporting. Already in 1875–6 the British press found it embarrassing to discuss the magnificent gifts that the Prince of Wales received, and simply suppressed this information, which appeared freely in the Indian press. By 1921, the situation in India had changed. The Prince of Wales was not universally welcomed. ('I feel I am doing no good here at all,' he wrote despairingly home to his father George V.) Gandhi and his nationalistic followers tried to organise a *hartal*, a general strike and boycott of the tour, which was partially successful in the big cities.

Was it considered prudent for this reason to suppress details of the gifts that would normally be given to a royal Prince by the fabulously wealthy maharajahs? On several occasions the reporters in the Indian papers allude to an inspection of jewels in the royal treasuries, such as the reception at Baroda, when the Prince of Wales was garlanded in a heavy gold chain that dropped nearly to his feet and then taken into the jewel room where three million pounds' worth of diamonds and pearls were displayed.

In the context of Rajput India – where an English chronicler of the Prince's trip was rewarded with a 'magnificent ruby' by the Maharani of Bikaner merely because he reported that the Prince was singing happily – it is inconceivable that the royal visitor should have received no gifts. The offering of *nazar*, or princely tributes, was an integral part of the Reception of the Ruling Princes at the Delhi durbar in 1911, and many of these same maharajahs played host to the Prince of Wales ten years later. The custom of giving magnificent gifts was still alive in the year before Indian independence, when the Nizam of Hyderabad presented a diamond bandeau tiara and matching necklace to Princess Elizabeth as a wedding gift in 1947.

In a sapphire blue deep pile velvet book with a silver crest, printed as a double volume in a limited edition to record the trip, there is positive proof of one gift of jewels given to the Prince of Wales. On 11 December, the Taluqdars of Oudh (who in 1875 had given the future Edward VII a pearl and diamond crown with emerald drops) presented publicly to the Prince of Wales 'a beautiful garland, made of gold and set with emeralds, rubies and pearls, a production of fine Indian workmanship'. There is no mention of this gift (only of the reception ceremony) in any British newspaper report of the time, nor in the *Statesman* or the *Times of India*. The garland is not in the list of crown property of the British royal family nor has anything answering to its unique description ever been seen by anyone connected with the royal jewels.

PRESENTS FROM PRINCE CHARMING

In 1925, the Prince of Wales was drawn by the French cartoonist Sem as he went shopping at Cartier in the Rue de la Paix in Paris. (1) 'Prince Charming' had acquired the habit of buying presents for his women friends and the

LE PRINCE CHARMANT
RUE DE LA PAIX.

jewels he bought Wallis Simpson became the talk of the town in Abdication year (3 and 4). The fantastic collection of gems he gave his wife, the Duchess of Windsor, included the serpent necklace (2), the ruby and diamond 'strawberries' on a double gold chain (6), the magnificent opals (8), the dramatic ruby necklace (5), all made by Cartier. In spite of the enduring legend of the 'Alexandra Emeralds', the Duchess of Windsor's favourite jewels were rubies (7) and sapphires, along with the yellow and canary diamonds she collected.

The Duke spent fabulous amounts of money on jewels. On 1 July 1937, the year after the Abdication and in the depths of the Depression, he settled outstanding bills of over £7,000 with two Paris jewellers.

How ironic if the entire edifice of intrigue and suspicion, of feuding and bitterness over the Duchess of Windsor's jewels should have been built on Indian gems that were handed out like sweetmeats by the maharajahs! Could it be that at the very moment these Indian princes were turning over the fantastic jewels in their royal treasuries to Cartier to be remodelled, the new King of England, Edward VIII, was walking through another door to have his presentation gifts reset?

The most straightforward explanation for Mrs Simpson's fine array of new jewels is that her future husband simply bought them for her. Lady Diana Cooper says today that as Prince of Wales and later King he was 'mean' or 'careful', and later accounts of his behaviour as Duke of Windsor suggest that he was more eager to eat a good dinner than to pay for it. Yet in his 'youth' (he was 42 when he abdicated) he was apparently generous, lavishing gifts on his previous mistress of 16 years, Freda Dudley Ward.

He was, in fact, a very wealthy young man, brought up as he puts it himself 'in a special way for a life that disappeared'. He identified not with his autocratic and punctilious father but with the racy, generous Edward VII and the squirearchical surroundings of Sandringham. As Prince of Wales, the future Edward VIII showed his grandfather's careless generosity.

'I got a lovely pin with two large square emeralds for Xmas,' wrote Wallis Simpson to her aunt, Mrs Bessie Merryman, at the start of 1935. Two months later she described on 13 March 1935 'a small diamond that clips into my hair which HRH gave me' and in June 1935 'lovely diamond clips' that were a gift to celebrate the Silver Jubilee of the Prince's father, George V. Wallis's unabashed pleasure at the gifts from her royal admirer reverberates through the early *Wallis and Edward Letters*. Her correspondence bears out society gossip of the time about new jewels.

In the late spring of 1935, Mrs Simpson admitted to Aunt Bessie that she had 'some lovely jewellery to show you . . . Not many things but awfully nice stones.' The next year, the new King Edward VIII was sending Wallis a bracelet from Van Cleef and Arpels and insisting that she wore it 'always in the evening'.

By the spring of 1936, Queen Mary had already expressed her anxiety over jewels her son was lavishing on the woman she described as an 'adventuress'. 'He gives Mrs Simpson the most beautiful jewels,' she said to her lady-in-waiting, Lady Airlie, as they sat reading together at Buckingham Palace. Private accounts for the next year in Paris certainly confirm this generosity. On 29 June 1937, the ex-King settled an account of £6,320 with Van Cleef and Arpels; on 11 July 1937, £1,000 was paid to Cartier.

It was from Cartier that Edward VIII bought the jewels that have become known as the 'Alexandra emeralds' and which have given rise to so much speculation and myth.

In a scrapbook in the billiard room at Polesden Lacey in Surrey (where King George VI and his wife Elizabeth spent their honeymoon in 1923) is a letter which gives a chapter and verse account. The book, like Polesden Lacey itself, belonged to Mrs Ronald Greville, an intimate friend of Queen Mary — so close a friend that the social columns of the day described her as one of only two subjects whom Queen Mary would visit 'without being accompanied by a lady-in-waiting'. Chips Channon describes her, just before her death in 1942, in her suite at the Dorchester 'covered with jewels, sitting on her bath chair'. Those jewels she left to Queen Elizabeth, later the Queen Mother (Chapter 5). Mrs Greville was a very close friend of the new King and Queen at the time of the Abdication, and therefore in a unique position to know what was going on.

Mrs Greville hired a cuttings service, to track down any mention of her own name or especially that of her father the Scottish brewer William McEwen and his family. These cuttings were pasted into scrapbooks, from 1904 to her death in 1942. On 8 March 1937, three months after the Abdication, a letter was published in *Time* magazine from A. E. L. Bennett, an American citizen living in Paris. He obliquely cites Mrs Greville as his source for the information, which he used to counter the impression, prevalent at that time in America, that Edward VIII had been shabbily treated by the British royal family. This is the relevant part of his letter:

> He [King Edward] bought priceless emeralds for Mrs Simpson. These emeralds were the property of Queen Alexandra who left them to Princess Victoria (her daughter), who in turn sold them to Garrard's of Bond Street, where King Edward bought them . . . As to the emeralds, I should have added that Garrard's, the jewellers, who bought them from Princess Victoria, sent them to Cartier's in Paris, and it was actually Cartier's who made the sale, on behalf of Garrard's, to King Edward. As I have said before, these stones are very large and magnificent, but have many flaws. The lady who gave me this information is a personal friend of Queen Mary and members of the royal family, but I cannot tell you her name.

At the end of the letter, pasted into the scrapbook, is Mrs Greville's name.

This then is the truth about the 'Alexandra emeralds'. King Edward VIII did not inherit them from his grandmother, which is why he repeatedly and hotly denied such a bequest. They were not an heirloom that he 'stole' from the royal jewel collection, which is why the closest associate of the Duchess of Windsor continues to deny such rumours. *The emeralds were so little considered as part of a royal heritage that they were offered for sale* to the highest bidder, and that was Edward VIII.

Why then did the Duke of Windsor not announce this fact and refute the rumours with the sheafs of bills from Cartier which he meticulously kept and which are in the possession of the Duchess's lawyer Maître Suzanne Blum today? The answer is money. The Duke of Windsor pleaded poverty and seemed genuinely to believe that he had hardly enough money to get by. Drawing attention to money spent on jewels would have called into question the issue of extravagance and invited discussion about the value of the Duchess's entire collection of jewels. At the time that the emeralds were acquired, the fact that Mrs Simpson had received splendid jewels would have created a major scandal.

'These works brought these people here. Something must be done to find them work,' said the King as he toured the derelict areas of South Wales in November 1936 and saw the dignified desperation of the miners. Three days before, the King had been at Chips Channon's lavish dinner party where 'the

This dramatic lattice necklace studded with rubies and emeralds was made by Cartier in October 1945 by breaking up two gem-set brooches, two pairs of earrings and an emerald ring.

room seemed to sway with jewels'. On 26 November 1936, London society was stunned by the appearance of Mrs Simpson in yet another new suite of jewellery.

If King Edward VIII fed the hopes of the starving miners and Mrs Simpson's jewel box at one and the same time, it may have been morally questionable, but it was no different from upper-class behaviour in general at the time. Alice Keppel, the last of King Edward VII's 'loose-box' of royal mistresses, had received jewels from the King; she had close connections with Cartier and in the 1940s was still glittering magnificently in her sequins and jewels. But Alice Keppel was discreet. 'Things were done better in my day,' she said at the time of the Abdication.

By the winter of 1936 the Mrs Simpson story had become public property and if the revelations about the King's expenditure had been confirmed, it would have stained the reputation of the compassionate monarchy which King George V and Queen Mary had built up during the First World War. The sums that Edward VIII spent were preposterously large in the context of the threadbare 'thirties. Private information in Paris shows that the cruise on the *Nählin* – a scandal in itself in the summer of 1936 because Mrs Simpson was on board – cost the King £4,873. 13s 9d. Symbolically Madame Tussaud's dressed the truly elegant Wallis in the clinging red sheath dress of a scarlet woman when they rushed a wax model of her on to public display just three weeks after the Abdication.

She had a taste for luxury long, long before she found sensual pleasure in choosing between four regal dinner services – the finest embossed with gold oak leaves and the royal arms. Before she had even met the Prince of Wales, Mrs Simpson would shop in Fortnum and Mason, a soignée figure in impeccable white gloves. Ginette Spanier, later directrice of Balmain, served her at Fortnum's and remembers that her favourite indulgence was handbags. When she was too extravagant, the bill would be sent to Ernest Simpson's office in the City, where his wife claimed that 'he is always too busy working to look at things intimately'.

Later she would lavish herself with jewels. The Duke of Windsor's equerry Dudley Forwood describes her as 'blazing with rings, earrings, brooches, bracelets and necklaces and almost stooping under their weight'. But her perception of luxury went deeper than display, right down to the bedrock of the lingerie she bought from the Berkeley Square mews shop run by Diana Vreeland, later the editor of American *Vogue*. The lingerie for Mrs Simpson's first weekend at Fort Belvedere with her Prince was a slither of bias-cut white satin, ice-blue crêpe de chine and a third nightgown with its neck made out of silken petals that rippled as she moved.

If Wallis had been kept by the King in the luxury she craved when she supplemented her first husband's allowance to her with a nightly poker game, no one would have complained. The real problem with Mrs Simpson, in the eyes of Society although not according to her own account, was that she wanted to be Queen. 'I shall be Queen of England,' she announced to Dorothy Cambridge, married to David's cousin, after a phone call from the Prince telling her of the illness of King George V. She was ultimately begrudged not the jewels but the King she took with her when he abdicated for 'the woman I love'. His wedding present to her was a sapphire and diamond bracelet and a lifetime of devotion.

'What a damnable wedding present,' said the Duke when he heard from his brother, the new King, the day before the wedding on 3 June 1937, that although he himself would still be styled 'Royal Highness', Wallis was not to be given the same treatment. But his Duchess – Her Royal Highness as the Duke insisted on calling her, dropping the emotive words, as Harold Nicolson said, 'like three stones into a pool' – created surroundings fit for her King.

The young prince who had chafed at the ceremony surrounding the feudal Indian courts and the stuffy English protocol found that his world had shrunk to a Court circle smaller than the Rajput states, or even than the toy-town German principalities that his mother had visited as Princess May of Teck. First there was the blue and white villa La Cröe, set against the French Riviera landscape; then the Boulevard Suchet in Paris; and their country home with its flauntingly English garden at the Moulin de la Tuilerie. 'I just love your pansies,' said a gushing American guest. 'In the garden or at my table?' quipped Wallis in reply. The Windsors finally moved to the elegant, slate-roofed house in Neuilly, near the Bois de Boulogne, where gilded crowns – one now symbolically fallen – flank the entrance lanterns, and where the Duchess died in April 1986.

The Windsors' home at 4 Route du Champ d'Entrainment, where the butler Georges and his wife Ophélia still kept up the impeccable standards of *Son Altesse*, was a perfect exposition of the Duchess's style that expressed itself so vigorously in her collection of jewels. ('Never quite enough for her and whatever he gave her she would have been slightly disappointed,' says Lady Diana Cooper.) The style became increasingly royal. Whereas the villa at La Cröe had some slightly raffish touches – furniture in the bedroom painted *trompe l'oeil* (a passion with the Duchess) to show stockings apparently hanging out of the drawer or a discarded evening bag, perhaps copied from one of her enormous collection of Cartier pochettes. But the *trompe l'oeil* panels in the Neuilly dining room were quite different in style – *chinoiserie* panels culled from a French château with two miniature musicians' galleries inset, 'like opera boxes' says Diana Vreeland, in the pale blue panelled walls. The Duchess's taste had come a long way since she ordered a pastoral wallpaper and white leather chairs for the tiny drawing room at No 5 Bryanston Court near Baker Street, London, where she, Ernest and the Prince of Wales had so many cosy dinners and later Mrs Simpson and the King more intimate evenings.

The Duchess would greet her guests at Neuilly wearing her *parure* of sapphires in a clear blue that exactly matched her eyes and brought them alive against the frosty blue silk wallpaper with its portrait by Sir William Llewellyn of Queen Mary in her Garter robes and a spiked tiara. ('Well, anyway, a tiara is one of the things I shall never have . . .' said Mrs Simpson to Princess Olga of Yugoslavia three weeks before the Abdication. The nearest she got to one was a circlet of diamonds worn to a Paris ball.)

But there were other jewels, some as graceful as the eighteenth-century furniture that filled the formal drawing room. Especially there was the *parure* of yellow diamonds that picked up the incandescent golden light of the library. The Duchess would sit there in a velvet dress on the yellow silk sofa, its cushions made from a cardinal's cape and as red as the worn leather despatch box, inscribed 'The King'. It had once held state papers which, officials complained, were left around the Fort and stained with the rings of cocktail glasses. Now it lay on a table in the centre of the entrance hall under a pennant with the arms of the Prince of Wales. The box, said the Duke, was the only object he had 'stolen' during the meticulous (some would say pernickety) sifting of royal and private inheritance after the Abdication.

The Duchess saw her jewels as part of her role as a woman who might have been Queen. Twice-married, she may also have collected jewels as a personal insurance policy. She certainly collected canary diamonds. They were the centrepiece of the cluster of gems and jewels she bought in the post-war years in Paris when Lady Diana Cooper remembers that the Duchess and Loel Guinness sallied out together to Van Cleef or Bulgari or Cartier. 'Don't send it back! Don't be a fool! It's money!' the Duchess is supposed to have hissed in 1950 to Lucy Rogers when Lucy planned to return a gold and diamond ring offered by her new husband Hermann, a constant good friend and host to the Duke and Duchess. He and Lucy were both widowed and Wallis's outburst came because Lucy had said that she 'already had' all the jewellery she wanted.

Was the Duchess really 'as hard as nails', an 'adventuress' in the words of her royal mother-in-law, as chic and shiny and glittering as the silver cocktail shaker that the King would use when he played barman at the Fort? A close associate of the Duchess of Windsor insists that her jewels did not contain huge gems – a prerequisite of the gold digger. According to this source, Wallis's preference was for small stones and semi-precious gems; some of her most stunning pieces were actually costume jewellery 'bijoux de théâtre'. 'Wallis wearing costume jewellery! That I don't think,' says Diana Vreeland, who remembers mainly the sapphires and the yellow diamonds, some rubies and no emeralds.

Other friends recall the bird and panther brooches and the crucifixes that the Duke and Duchess both wore. The combination of gold crosses and scantily clad King and Mrs Simpson contributed to the scandal surrounding the cruise on the *Nählin* in the tense summer of 1936.

To the connoisseur, the most important part of the Duchess of Windsor's collection is not gems that might be part of a British royal heritage. It is rather the superb pieces by Jeanne Toussaint of Cartier, the absolute creator of the jewellery tastes of that period. The Windsors, both profoundly attuned to fashion, had discovered Jeanne Toussaint by 1936, when she created a *parure* for Wallis composed of sapphires, pearls and diamonds. Soon she could count the Duke and Duchess of Windsor among her closest friends (her very close friend was, of course, Louis Cartier) whom she asked to dine at her pale and exquisite flat with its few rare objects: the head of a Buddha throwing its shadow on a sculpted screen or a single lily emerging from a piece of Chinese pottery. Coco Chanel (who berated Jeanne for her meek acceptance of her role as Cartier's mistress) and Cecil Beaton were some of the privileged few invited, along with the Windsors, to share the 'intellectual beauty' of this luxurious home.

Flamboyant flamingo brooch in rubies, sapphires, emeralds and diamonds, made in 1940. Details in colour plates.

98

On the floor of Jeanne Toussaint's flat was a panther rug. 'Panther' was Louis Cartier's pet name for her and the jungle cat became a design spring for a prolific period of animal jewellery. The 'Dook', as he started to describe himself in a mocking American inflection, ordered the very first of the great Toussaint panthers for Wallis in 1948 (a collector's item for that reason alone). Its focus was a green cabochon emerald of 116.74 carats over which curved a black and gold flecked panther rampant. The next April (1949), again using the insurance money from the Ednam Lodge robbery, the Duke invested in another fine stone, a cabochon sapphire of 152.35 carats (the gem cost £5,000). On this jewelled prey crouched a diamond and onyx panther with dazzling yellow diamond eyes to make a new brooch. An articulated bracelet in the shape of a panther followed in 1952 – all of these great cats inspired by Jeanne Toussaint's visit a quarter of a century before to the decadent Marchioness Casati, who appeared at a ball in Venice with a panther on a leash and kept another, mechanically operated, in the hall of her Venetian palazzo. The Duchess of Windsor's most lavish Cartier trinket was formed from another animal: a tiger lorgnette she had made in 1954, its rampant body and alert head forming the handle.

The menagerie that animated Wallis Windsor's collection of jewels was reflected in life by the five pugs (looking suspiciously like the royal corgis) which followed her – replacements for the lost 'Slipper', the pug that David had given her as a wedding present which was killed by a snake bite just after their marriage. Oval portraits of pugs hung beneath a fine Stubbs horse painting in her home. Models of pugs, each one standing on a piece of brown felt to protect the polished surfaces, were an eerie echo of Queen Alexandra's collection of Fabergé animals which the Duke had grown up with at Sandringham. 'Dickens in a Cartier setting' was how the young Prince had viewed Christmas at Sandringham in his grandparents' day. It was a prophetic metaphor. 'What does Christmas mean to you now?' the Windsors were asked. 'Getting presents,' said the Duchess. 'Paying for them,' said the Duke.

The Duchess liked naturalistic decoration: a swarm of butterfly brooches fluttered across the lapels of her severe tweed jacket during the honeymoon at the Château de Candé, a grey stone castle near Tours in the château country on the Loire. (The abdicated King tactfully waited to marry until after his brother Bertie's coronation in May 1937, and sent his Garter Star back for Queen Mary to wear.) Cartier created for Wallis Windsor a sensual serpent necklace and two stylised strawberries hanging from a heavy gold chain, both ideas of Jeanne Toussaint, who had also made the Duchess's flamingo brooch. Cartier also created a quintessentially 1940s bracelet shaped like a snail studded with rubies, emeralds and diamonds and made some more conventional and much grander jewels: the sapphires and diamonds; a long necklace of more than a dozen enormous opals (Queen Alexandra would not have approved); a twist necklace of rubies with an asymmetric tassel. The only other piece that the soignée Duchess ever wore off centre was her string of milky pearls with its lustrous drop that slipped askew during the funeral of the Duke at St George's Chapel, Windsor in 1972. It was a signal to her close friends of the turmoil under the composed exterior of the grieving Duchess.

Ruby and diamond and sapphire snail bracelet made by Cartier from the Duke's gems on 8 April 1946. In the centre, an engraved sapphire of 28.77 carats.

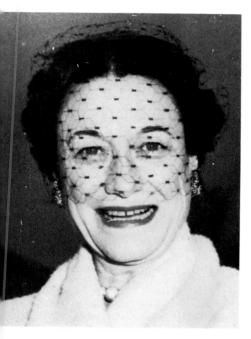

The Duchess of Windsor wears the panther earrings the Duke had made by Cartier on 29 September 1948. He broke up an emerald brooch to get the two cabochon emeralds of 54.04 carats and 50.42 carats. They were mounted in an open-work sunburst frame so that the gems could be detached.

Cartier was the Windsors' court jeweller ('Son Altesse Royale knows more about diamonds than I do!' said Jacques Cartier) but the Duchess also looked elsewhere, to Van Cleef and frequently to Madame Bellpérin at Hertz, also in Paris, who created some of her most striking and colourful pieces, although not with large gems.

It was the Duke of Windsor's wish that his gifts of love should never be worn by another woman. But after his death in 1972, various approaches were made to his *distraite* widow.

In the summer of 1976, a quiet appeal for the jewels was made on behalf of Princess Alexandra and the Duke and Duchess of Kent by Lady Monckton of Brenchley — the widow of the barrister Walter Monckton who first served Edward VIII as Attorney-General of the Duchy of Cornwall and remained a friend after the Abdication. Lady Monckton promised the Duchess that she would escort her body to the royal mausoleum at Frogmore, on the Windsor estate. In return, she suggested a fair distribution of the jewels among the younger members of the royal family.

Hardy Amies and the late Lady Pamela Berry tackled the Duchess at a small dinner in New York, after the Duke's death in May 1972. Their petition was on behalf of the Victoria and Albert Museum. Hardy Amies describes how, after a long pause, the Duchess replied in her quizzical Baltimore drawl, 'I guess I could spare a leopard.' This offer, dismissed with fond and incredulous smiles, was more generous than the suitors realised. If the Duchess of Windsor was offering Jeanne Toussaint's first panther brooch, it would have been a princely gift to the museum.

The only member of the British royal family to have touched the heart and the jewels of the Duchess of Windsor while she was still alive, was Princess Michael of Kent. Her husband, a cousin of the Queen, had built up a relationship with his uncle-in-exile. In the summer of 1978, he introduced his new bride to the 82-year-old Duchess of Windsor, shortly before arterial sclerosis overwhelmed her.

Prince Michael's marriage to the divorced Marie-Christine Troubridge in a civil ceremony in Vienna had some historical parallels with the union between Edward VIII and Wallis Simpson. Marie-Christine's desire for a Catholic wedding, and an attempt at religious annulment of her previous marriage, meant that Prince Michael was to be removed from the line of succession. Princess Michael stressed this bond between her and 'Aunt Wallis'.

Flattered and charmed by the attentions of the vibrant new Princess, the Duchess of Windsor gave to Marie-Christine some prized pieces of her jewellery as a wedding gift. This was, understandably, never made public, but caused a frisson within her circle.

The fate of the fabulous collection of jewels was decided well before the Duchess's death. During her long period of half-life, the jewels were in the safe of her Paris notaire Maître Lecuyer. The Duchess's lawyer friend, the elderly Maître Blum, was charged with executing the Windsors' wishes.

None of the jewellery was to be returned to Britain, for Maître Blum, along with the Duke and Duchess, always vehemently denied that any of the jewels were part of the British royal heritage.

The Duke and Duchess of Windsor had no children. The Duchess had few living relatives and did not choose to leave her possessions to her husband's family, who never forgave her, who ostracised her in the Duke's lifetime and received her grudgingly after his death. She handed over to the Queen the Duke's uniforms, including his Garter robes and all his emotive orders and decorations – all returned to the Crown on the advice of Lord Mountbatten, who had remained loyal to the man he had known as Prince of Wales and served as aide on the far-wheeling foreign tours. Uncle 'Dickie', who had a very close relationship with Prince Charles, may have suggested that the jewels should be left to the new royal generation to heal the running sore of bitterness. That is the persistent rumour.

Yet the Windsors decided that the jewels were to be used for the benefit of medical research at the Institut Pasteur in Paris, apart from some individual bequests. Princess Alexandra and the Duchess of Kent were singled out in the Duchess of Windsor's will, as Lady Monckton requested. Those who like to believe that Wallis went off with the Crown Jewels, and that 'everything' should have gone to Prince Charles and his wife Diana, have been disappointed. The royal family claims to have expected nothing and to have no interest in the jewels.

If the jewels were not replaced in the royal fold, what then? The Marchioness of Cambridge questioned the Queen on this point. 'Jolly good thing,' replied the Queen briskly. 'We've got too much already.'

Precisely. The existing collection of royal jewels is enormous beyond any dream of opulence. Apart from the so-called 'Crown' pieces, there is Queen Mary's personal inheritance, all the gifts the Queen has received during her reign and the unset and mostly unsorted gems in store. There are jewels a-plenty for every living member of the royal family, so much that only the Queen knows the true extent of the collection.

Even if the Duke of Windsor inherited or acquired emeralds the size of an egg or fistfuls of rubies, and gave them to his wife, why should it matter whether they are given back to the overflowing royal vaults? And why should ordinary English people care so passionately about the Duchess of Windsor's jewels that we are speculating 50 years on what she 'got away with'?

The heart of the matter, the conundrum of this entire book on royal jewels, is as follows: which are the jewels that belong to the sovereign in trust for the British monarchy, to be handed over at the beginning of each new reign? And which should be considered personal and private jewellery? It is a question that has puzzled and preoccupied royal families through the ages and throughout the world. The Koh-i-noor, the 'Mountain of Light' that has finally rolled to rest in the British Crown jewels, was treated as a personal trophy and taken by conquest.

Domestic squabbles break out in royal families as in more humble ones. As we saw in Chapter 1, Queen Victoria was incensed when Queen Charlotte's jewels, given to her by her husband King George III, were claimed by the House of Hanover. Queen Alexandra was loath to part with her favourite jewels after the death of Edward VII, who had left his wife all 'his jewels, ornaments, articles of Art or *vertu*, curiosities and other chattels', in order that

Princess Michael of Kent wears her distinctive panther sunburst earrings in October 1985

she could select favourite pieces. To Queen Mary's annoyance (and George V's embarrassment) Queen Alexandra tried to keep a small crown (handed over to Queen Mary just in time for the Coronation), the diamond circlet worn by the Queen at the Opening of Parliament and King Edward's Garter Star.

Queen Mary, with her particular penchant for cataloguing collections, made a thorough survey of the royal jewels. She started this in 1926 after the death of Queen Alexandra (who died intestate) and must have continued until her own death in 1953. The last published information on Crown Jewellery was based on research done by Lord Twining in 1957. From the information which he published in 1960 in *Crown Jewels of Europe*, and amassed in his private papers, it seems that there are relatively few pieces officially designated 'Crown', considering the size of the entire royal collection (Appendix A). Throughout history successive sovereigns seem to have taken a completely personal and eclectic view as to what is their own and what is held in trust for monarch and subjects.

The nearest she got to a crown; the Duchess of Windsor wears a diamond bandeau, with her ruby necklace and flower brooch, to a Paris ball in 1950. The ex-King wears full decorations.

Although no major piece designated as Crown by Queen Victoria or at the time of Queen Alexandra's death in 1925 has 'disappeared' from the royal collection, the public sensed after the Abdication that their new Queen Elizabeth, the consort of George VI, had far less jewellery than the preceding Queens Alexandra and Mary. But this was because Queen Mary's enormous personal inheritance 'skipped' a generation and was left to her granddaughter, the present Queen (Chapters 5 and 6).

It was those subjects, 'the people', who felt most let down and distressed by Edward VIII's decision to abdicate in order to marry Wallis Simpson. It was not precisely her unsuitability as Queen, her slightly *risqué* past and her two divorces which shocked, but the feeling that she had cheated them out of some intangible right. The persistent children's refrain of that December in 1936 expresses the mood:

> Hark the Herald Angels sing
> Mrs Simpson stole our king.

The entire basis for the story of the 'Alexandra emeralds', and newspaper reports that the British royal family was negotiating with the Duchess to ensure that after her death the jewels came to Prince Charles, stems from this public attitude, the instinctive sense that the Windsor story needed an ending. For the public, the jewels had become a metaphor.

The people who had fought the Great War for their country could not grasp that their golden-haired new King, the very personification of hope and belief in the future, could give up the throne of that country and its people for a greater love. The people who continued to struggle through the Second World War and who have seen two monarchs crowned and two new royal male heirs born, demanded a conclusion to the drama that the Duke of Windsor refused to turn into a tragedy by leading an apparently happy life.

The death of the Duchess has rung down the curtain on the Abdication. But the woman who lived for 35 years with her royal husband, and whose name was never mentioned by his family, even at her funeral, did not choose to give the drama a symbolic 'happy ending'. She will be judged harshly and unfairly by her husband's subjects for refusing to make that grand final gesture. If her collection of jewels had been handed back to Britain *virgo intacta*, Wallis Simpson might have made atonement for the King she stole and the bright beam of hope that she extinguished.

The Pearly Queen

'I asked if – perhaps – as much jewellery as possible could – be worn?
The Queen smiled apologetically – "The choice isn't very great you
know!"'

Cecil Beaton, photographing Queen Elizabeth,
later the Queen Mother, July 1939.

By the lake on the Île Enchanté, Queen Elizabeth opened her parasol of
champagne lace, its arc spreading above the pale puffball of her skirt. The
delicate parasols with their diamond handles (more princely gifts from the
Indian Maharajahs) and the ballooning crinolines, recalled another royal
visitor to Paris 80 years before: Queen Victoria, her tiny frame swamped by
the vast skirt embroidered with geraniums that Prince Albert had designed, or
the white satin dress under her enormous diadem for the reception at
Versailles.

The state visit of George VI and his Queen consort to Paris in the summer of
1938 deliberately recreated that vision of Victoriana. King George – 'Bertie' as
he was always known, after his great-grandfather Albert – had not actually
designed Elizabeth's dresses. But as he stood with the couturier Norman
Hartnell in front of the romantic portraits by Franz Xaver Winterhalter of
Queen Victoria in Buckingham Palace, there had come to both of them – the
thin nervous cigarette-puffing King and the eager young designer – an image of
queenly magnificence.

Half a century later, we can point to that visit as a seminal moment when the
style of the Queen Mother, as she has been since her daughter's accession in
1952, was set for a lifetime. Even now, when the fitter and vendeuse from
Hartnell are ushered into the pale green dressing room at Clarence House,
with its marble fireplace and its *chaise longue*, they will be delivering dresses of
much the same kind. There will not be, perhaps, an equal amount of
embroidery and decoration – not the hand-stitched open-work lace design on
white organdie that was reflected as a white radiance in the Galeries des Glaces
in Versailles in 1938. But the silver spangled dress in her favourite sugar pink
(a taste exactly shared with the new Princess of Wales) is very similar in style to
those earlier confections. All the great dresses – the thick oyster satin with its
trailing silver fern worn for the Queen's Coronation, or the Scarlett O'Hara

*Queen Elizabeth, the Queen Mother
in 1963 wearing the tiara she had
made from South African diamonds;
diamond collet necklace and Queen
Victoria's tassel brooch.*

sweep of tiered black velvet seen in silhouette in the famous Beaton photographs – are kept at Clarence House. They hang in ghostly shrouds of white cambric in the tall cupboards and occasionally, when they are brought out, the Queen Mother will greet them with affection. Her most sentimental attachment is to her wedding dress, preserved since 1923 in a snowdrift of tissue paper inside a striped dress box.

The Queen Mother is wearing the same kind of jewels too – an imposing necklace, perhaps, and a grand diadem, probably Queen Victoria's regal Indian tiara, later reset with rubies by Queen Alexandra. It was specifically left to the Crown along with the other state diadems, but the Queen does not mind her mother hanging on to her favourite pieces of Crown jewellery because, as a courtier puts it, 'She knows that Mummie will give it back.'

Queen Elizabeth seems to feel an affinity with Queen Victoria that is reflected not just in the crinoline skirts, but in her jewellery as well. Her favourite brooch, the bold pearl and diamond flower with its distinctive loop of diamonds and tear-drop pearl that beams from the bottle-green velvet lapel of her suit or nestles among the misty blue flowers of a georgette dress, is the brooch that Queen Victoria's household presented to her in the great jubilee celebrations of 1897. Other brooches that you might expect to be more emotive – like the gem-set flowers with dangling drops that Bertie gave his young bride Elizabeth Bowes Lyon on their wedding – are still worn. Others have been put away or passed on to her daughters. But Queen Victoria's brooch appears on every possible occasion from visiting riot-scarred Brixton to Ascot races, or on that mournful day in 1972 when the unquiet soul of her brother-in-law David was laid to rest – the Prince of Wales, later Edward VIII, who in abdicating his throne had precipitated his brother Bertie and his wife Elizabeth into the front line. The brooch seems almost to have become a talisman.

The Jubilee brooch with loops of diamonds and tear-drop pearl.

The Queen Mother wears too the lovely Victorian pearl and diamond necklace, running in great loops and swags across her chest. It was made in 1863 for another Bertie, the future Edward VII, to give to his bride Alexandra on her wedding day, part of a suite that included bouton earrings and an oval pearl brooch with attached drops that Queen Mary seemed to count as *her* talisman, so often did she wear it planted on the centre of her bodice. Her daughter-in-law Elizabeth would pin at that point her 'tassel' brooch, as she calls the circle design with its waterfall of diamonds – another Victorian heirloom. It was chosen for the grand portrait by Sir Gerald Kelly that hangs in the National Portrait Gallery and in which she wears one of her 'Winterhalter' crinolines.

The jewel most closely identified with Queen Elizabeth is the pearl – and not just from the time that she was in mourning for her beloved mother who died just before the Paris visit in 1938. From the first moment that Lady Elizabeth Bowes Lyon emerged from the dark oak and granite towers of her family's ancestral home at Glamis Castle to public view as a potential royal bride (she turned down Bertie twice before the final acceptance) she wore a long double strand of pearls in the fashion of the 1920s with a teardrop pearl at her breastbone. (The Duchess of Windsor had her own superb double string of matchless pearls and drop – supposedly a final forgiving bequest from Queen Mary to her eldest son.)

The portrait painters of the day, Savely Sorine and Philip de Laszlo, pictured the long pearls when the pretty new Duchess of York, as Lady Elizabeth became, sat for them in 1923 and 1925 respectively. In the 1930s, Princess Margaret Rose, the Yorks' second daughter, caught them in her chubby fingers. Lady Cynthia Asquith saw the little Princess Elizabeth using pearls for the reins of the stuffed toy horses on wheels that were lined up under the glass dome at the top of the nursery stairwell at 145 Piccadilly, the Yorks' London home.

Pearls were worn shorter in the 1930s and, according to the fashion of the day, there were three strands of globular pearls instead of the two longer ones. They became shorter still in the Blitz, when pearls were the only jewellery that the Queen felt appropriate when she was viewing the devastation in London's East End or picking over the rubble after the bomb in the royal back yard that scored a direct hit on the Chapel and the swimming pool.

Today pearls – and especially the lustrous string with the ruby snap – are the hallmark of the Queen Mother in both public and family life: having lunch with friends under the trees in the garden at Clarence House, for her 70th birthday portrait by Beaton; for her 80th birthday celebration service; for the racecourse; even for fishing in the river near her Scottish home at Birkhall, when the pearls are worn with a rain jacket with capacious pockets, trousers and sturdy waders.

Her public would judge that the Queen Mother wears little jewellery – and they would be right, for the same pieces recur constantly as though there were not vaults of other gems. It is not that Queen Elizabeth does not care for jewellery. Quite the contrary, for she has a close relationship with several London jewellers and has introduced her own grandson Prince Charles to Wartski, where he buys presents for his young wife. Kenneth Snowman of Wartski in Grafton Street is the third generation to serve the royal family and holds royal warrants for the Queen and for Prince Charles as well as for the Queen Mother.

She enjoys her jewels, not with Queen Mary's sensuous pleasure but 'just to sparkle' any time there is a 'big dressing', as the royal family call the grand evening occasions. Although less voracious than Queen Mary, the Queen Mother is a great collector, and her rooms are filled with beautiful objects – including surprisingly modern paintings, fine china painted with russet pheasants, grander French porcelain and her claret jug shaped like an eagle with glittering ruby eyes.

Lady Elizabeth Bowes Lyon had an unspoiled country upbringing in Scotland and St Paul's Walden Bury in Hertfordshire – the other country home of her parents, the Earl and Countess of Strathmore. She romped with her seven brothers and sisters and especially with her brother David, just two years younger than herself and an inseparable companion for her at the end of the family. But life for the Strathmores was grand enough. Their London home in Bruton Street was a mansion, just a stone's throw away from the Georgian house at No. 26 that Norman Hartnell later converted into his couture salon.

The Queen Mother wears the Jubilee brooch originally given to Queen Victoria by her Household in 1897.

Lady Elizabeth Bowes Lyon. A framed miniature given by her mother Lady Strathmore to Bertie.

The Duchess of York visited there with the two Princesses in the autumn of 1935, she in silver grey georgette, pale arctic fox, dew-drop diamonds and aquamarines. Bunches of forget-me-knots bobbed on the grey pudding-basin hats of the princesses, who were to be bridesmaids at the wedding of their uncle, Harry, the Duke of Gloucester, and Lady Alice Montagu-Douglas-Scott, the daughter of the Duke of Buccleuch and from Scottish aristocratic stock like her new sister-in-law Elizabeth.

The wedding was the moment that the rivers of jewellery poured on to the bosoms of these daughters of earls and dukes. When you married the King's son, the presents were compounded. As a child, Lady Elizabeth Bowes Lyon, in the upper-class tradition, had little chains of corals and pearls to wear on her white broderie anglais party dresses. For her coming of age Lady Elizabeth had pearls. On her marriage at the age of 23, Lord Strathmore presented his daughter with a diamond bandeau of large flower and leaf motifs that came apart – like most of the royal tiaras – to be worn as separate pieces of jewellery.

From King George V – the King and Queen started a new royal tradition of giving presents separately, which was not Queen Victoria's way or Edward VII's style – Lady Elizabeth received a suite of diamond and turquoise jewellery which included a high domed tiara, a bracelet of double drop stones, a brooch and matching drop earrings. Queen Mary (who was to classify the royal collection three years later, after Queen Alexandra's death) gave her new daughter-in-law sapphires and diamonds, apparently a favourite choice of a wedding present since she gave the same stones (but a much grander suite) to Princess Marina ten years later when she married Queen Mary's fourth son, the Duke of Kent.

Queen Alexandra chose her favourite soft mauve stone as a wedding present – very much in the Duchess of York's own taste for sweet colours. It was a large heart-shaped amethyst pendant set in brilliants dangling on a long chain of amethysts and pearls.

Considering the enormous amount of jewellery that Queen Mary had amassed by 1923, including all the Cullinan diamond 'chips', the Delhi durbar emeralds and the Russian collection from the dispersed Romanovs that she started to buy during the 1920s, the spiky sapphire and diamond necklace, with its matching bracelet, ring and pendant, seems adequate rather than generous. (By contrast the eight pieces of jewellery, including two tiaras, that Queen Mary gave to her granddaughter on her marriage to Prince Philip of Greece in 1947, were truly magnificent.) The diamond and sapphire necklace came from her own collection, which she had worn before the Great War. Bertie gave to his bride a pearl and diamond lattice-work necklace very similar in style and also the graceful diamond and pearl bouquet of jewelled flowers.

It was, of course, not long after the War, the Great War, in which Lady Elizabeth had lost a brother and when the grim horror of the trenches had penetrated even the stout stone walls of Glamis Castle, which had been turned into a hospital for 1,500 wounded soldiers convalescing from Dundee Royal Infirmary. 'For Lady Elizabeth,' wrote one of those soldiers in her autograph album. 'May the owner of this book be hung, drawn and quartered. Yes, hung in diamonds, drawn in a coach and four and quartered in the best house in the

108

The Queen Mother in her favourite necklace of festooned diamonds and pearls — originally Bertie's gift to Princess Alexandra on their marriage in 1863. With it, the Queen Mother wears the modern tiara she had made up from diamonds originally given to Edward VII by de Beers from South Africa in 1901. On her Garter ribbon are pinned the family orders of her late husband George VI and her daughter the Queen.

Opposite above The royal rubies: the Queen Mother in the regal Indian tiara made for Queen Victoria in 1853 and set with fire opals. Queen Alexandra removed the "unlucky" opals in 1902 and replaced them with rubies given to her by Sir Jung Bahadore of Nepal in 1876. The Queen wears the new tiara she had made from Burmese rubies and diamonds, and the impressive ruby and diamond necklace her father gave her as a wedding present in 1947.

Opposite below right The three strand pearl necklace is the Queen Mother's hallmark. These pearls have a snap set with diamonds. Pearls with a ruby snap were taken from the Indian Maharajah Ranjit Singh and presented to Queen Victoria in 1851.

Opposite below left The Jubilee brooch, in pearl and diamonds with a pearl centre and drop pendant, is the Queen Mother's favourite. It was presented to Queen Victoria by her Household in 1897.

Above Lady Elizabeth Bowes Lyon painted by Savely Sorine. She married the Duke of York, the second son of George V and Queen Mary, in 1923. Her long strings of pearls set a royal style for the 1920s.

Right Queen Elizabeth painted by Sir Gerald Kelly in 1938, two years after the Abdication had brought George VI to the throne. She altered the diamond collet necklace in 1937 to make her drop diamond earrings. Below are the Crown diamonds and her favourite "tassel" brooch, inherited from Queen Alexandra. The Norman Hartnell crinoline of cream satin, looped up with white velvet camellias, was made for the state visit to Paris in 1938 and is still in store at Clarence House.

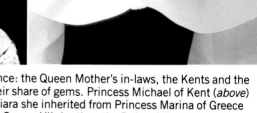

The Family Inheritance: the Queen Mother's in-laws, the Kents and the Gloucesters, had their share of gems. Princess Michael of Kent (*above*) wears the diamond tiara she inherited from Princess Marina of Greece (*inset*), who married George VI's brother, the Duke of Kent, in 1934.

Left The Duchess of Gloucester in the diamond and turquoise suite, given to her by her mother-in-law Princess Alice, Duchess of Gloucester. The clusters and scroll tiara, 28 turquoise necklace and earrings are part of a set of ten pieces of jewellery given as a wedding present by Queen Mary when her son Prince Henry, Duke of Gloucester, married Lady Alice Montagu-Douglas-Scott in 1935. The set was originally a wedding gift to Princess May from her parents.

Top right Princess Margaret's tiara was bought by the royal family from Lord Poltimore for £5,500 as a wedding present. It looks even more impressive with its additional tier of diamonds.

Top left Princess Anne, with her husband Captain Mark Phillips, wears a jewel from the royal pool which belonged to Prince Philip's mother. The choker was made for her by a London jeweller.

land.' Exactly 20 years later, at the Coronation of 1937, his wish was successfully crowned.

After the war had come the parties, the coming-out into Society, the fun that had been snatched away from Lady Elizabeth between the ages of 14 and 18 (she was born, with the century, in 1900). In Bertie's home, King George V, as shell-shocked as a Tommy by the war and by revolution that had wiped out the European royal families and thrones, withdrew from social life. But the great houses were thrown open again and the Prince of Wales and Duke of Kent plunged into this social whirlpool. Both were ultimately drawn out of their depth, Georgie to drugs from which his brother David saved him; David himself to a rootless cocktail set, to Wallis Simpson and the Abdication. Bertie found in Lady Elizabeth Bowes Lyon his safe haven, even if she was at first reluctant to leave her new-found world of parties and balls for domesticity and the rigours of royal life.

The wedding was itself a feast of splendour in a society that had been starved of romance, just as Princess Elizabeth's wedding in 1947 lifted the pall of gloom after the Second World War. This wedding of a truly British bride, and a commoner, to the son of a King was given prominence in *The Times* and greeted with huge enthusiasm by the waiting crowds, who disregarded the uncertain April weather and perched on costermongers' barrows or climbed on to the plinths of statues and peered through the stone legs for a view of the royal family.

The warmest cheers were reserved for Queen Alexandra, resplendent in purple velvet, her cloak trimmed with gold lace, riding in the carriage with her sister Minnie in pale mauve under her Russian sables, dressing to match her sister as she had done when they paraded round Hyde Park together 50 years earlier. It was Queen Alexandra's last great occasion before her death two years later in 1925.

To the music of Elgar's Imperial March, King George V and Queen Mary led the family party in procession through Westminster Abbey, past the bowing guests. The King was in naval uniform like his youngest son Georgie, Duke of Kent, who was grinning merrily. The Queen was in icy blue, the aquamarine and silver tissue of her dress showered with crystal drops over the silver embroidered rose of York; more gems edged the sleeves. Five rows of diamonds were looped round her neck, another was planted in her exotic brocade turban, for all the world as though the Delhi durbar were being re-enacted in Westminster Abbey. On the bright blue Garter sash the Queen pinned the pendulous pear-shaped star of Africa and its cushion square from the Cullinan set.

Lady Elizabeth's mediaeval-looking dress was, claimed the *Illustrated London News*, 'the simplest gown ever made for a royal wedding'. As 'gleam and gloom' chased each other through the Abbey from the scudding spring clouds, the bride seemed to *The Times* correspondent to be touched by sunshine and showers of her own. She walked on her father's arm through the doors in her gentle gown of ivory silk crêpe, with Queen Mary's veil of Flanders lace falling like a cloak over her shoulders. There was a brief hesitation at the Tomb of the Unknown Warrior, then she laid down her

Lady Elizabeth Bowes Lyon, the 1920s bride.

109

5

BERTIE'S BRIDE

When Lady Elizabeth Bowes Lyon married the King's second son in 1923, she was showered with presents. The young Duchess of York received a suite of diamonds and sapphires (1) from Queen Mary, diamonds from her

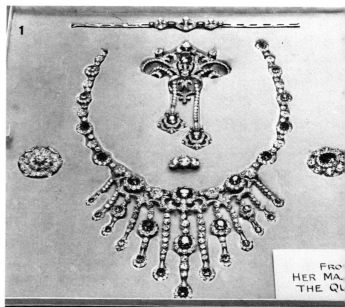

1

FRO
HER MA
THE QU

6

2

husband Bertie (2), a tiara from her father, the Earl of Strathmore (3), and a pearl sautoir from the Citizens of London (4).

The Queen Mother as a young woman wears the long pearl chain (5) with a 1920s style bandeau that she gave to her younger daughter. Princess Margaret wears it on the crown of her head (6).

Bertie's flower brooch with its dangling diamonds that she wore on her shoulder, with the Strathmore tiara (7), is worn today by the Queen Mother, 60 years on, in memory of her late husband (8).

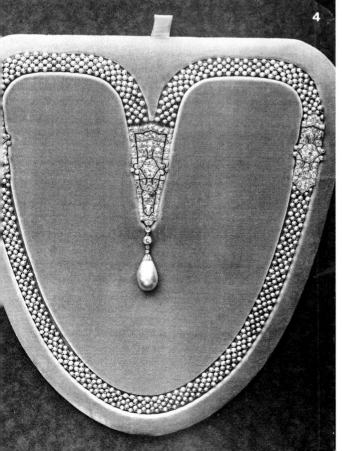

bouquet of white roses in memory of her brother and all the War dead. She walked on towards Bertie, the little white reticule she had abandoned in her carriage (a soldier had brought it back for her) dangling from her wrist. Today, the white silk bag, its wax flowers miraculously preserved, is packed away with the wedding dress at Clarence House. Round her neck was a double row of pearls; on her head, nothing but the veil and a simple wreath of orange blossom with a white rose of York on either side. Feathers were more popular than flowers with the guests, whose birds of paradise and trailing shaded ostrich trembled on hats large and small.

Elizabeth Bowes Lyon, now Duchess of York, drove off in her simple grey crêpe going-away outfit to spend her honeymoon in a house that still expressed an earlier Edwardian grandeur. Polesden Lacey, at Great Bookham in Surrey, was the country estate of the Hon. Mrs Ronald Greville, the daughter of a wealthy Scottish brewer William McEwan and the widow of Captain Greville, who had died in 1908. Through her husband's friendship with George Keppel, husband of Edward VII's last and most celebrated mistress Alice, Margaret Greville was introduced to royalty. She became a close friend of Queen Mary and one of the very few people, outside the royal family itself, who knew the true story about Edward VIII, Mrs Simpson and the 'Alexandra emeralds' (Chapter 4).

Mrs Greville was also a famous hostess who presided over 'intimate' dinners for 40 guests in her house in Charles Street, Mayfair, with 'ropes of milky pearls on her black lace gown' or in 'black paillette and wonderful diamonds', as *The Sunday Times* described her in 1937. (She subsequently left all these jewels to Queen Elizabeth the Queen Mother, 'with my loving thoughts'.)

Elizabeth and Bertie spent more time playing golf in the grounds of Polesden Lacey than entertaining in the ridiculously grand drawing room with its lavish gilding culled from an Italian palazzo. The dark oak-panelled hall (this taken from a demolished Church) made a romantic setting, reminiscent of the oaken interiors at Glamis Castle.

What did the Duchess of York, brought up in comparative simplicity, think of her grand new life and possessions? She had received some splendid gifts, notably the family ones discussed above, but also many other generous presents that rolled back the harsh war years to the more expansive Edwardian age. Antique silver, gold boxes, a Cartier clock in Russian enamel, as well as elegant period furniture and more up-to-the-moment silver cigarette boxes (Bertie was a heavy smoker), competed with personal presents: a diamond brooch, a ruby and diamond pin, a pair of onyx and diamond sleeve links, mounted in gold, from Lady Cunard, another great society hostess, who was to become a close friend of the Prince of Wales and Wallis, but deftly transferred her allegiance back to the Yorks when they came to the throne.

The public presents of jewels were in modern settings, like the diamond and pearl necklace mounted in platinum, with a large pearl pendant drop, from the Lord Mayor and City of London – which recalled the diamond necklace the city had presented to young Princess Alexandra 60 years before. The City of Belfast gave the Duchess of York a platinum bracelet set with diamonds and a matching wrist watch. One thousand gold-eyed needles, offered by the

Needlemakers' Company, might have been destined for the Duke, who spent evenings working at the *petit point* his Mother had taught him.

The royal trousseau that Elizabeth Bowes Lyon ordered suggests the new world that had emerged from the Great War. It also hints at her future style as Queen Elizabeth and Queen Mother and explains why so few of the ornate pieces she was given as wedding presents seemed ever to be favourites. By our standards the trousseau was lavish but at the time it must have struck a tactful note of simplicity in a society heading towards post-war depression. As well as the ermine that King George V had given her, there was a 'full length sable squirrel' and an 'evening wrap of white lapin', its skirt set with a band of velvet brocaded crêpe-de-chine worked with rounds of fur. Even in 1923, there was surprise that the five main dresses did not include anything in her favourite blue, although there was a periwinkle silk edging to her apple-green crepon tennis frock.

The grander gowns included a shrimp pink and silver brocade evening dress 'with pink net sleeves embroidered in silver and pink ribbon'. That certainly presaged her later style as Queen Mother and can be likened to the pink and silver embroidered net evening dress that Queen Elizabeth wears now with her fine ruby and diamond necklace and earrings.

But the 1920s were not a time for decorative jewels, and especially not on the elaborately worked dresses. Edwardian jewellery, with its lacy motifs and corsage ornaments, had been so closely linked to fashion that the jewels seemed to grow from the dresses. Now that mood for elaborate opulence had been overtaken by the new geometry of line which was echoed in Art Deco jewellery.

In 1923, the elegant accessory was a string of long pearls. The lavish decoration came on the dresses themselves, and the pearl and crystal embroideries that were (and are) part of Queen Elizabeth's style, were set by that wedding dress in 1923. The bodice of the dress was crossed with silver lamé embroidered with real pearls, pearly beads and silver thread. More pearl embroidery edged the sleeves and swagged the back under the train of antique lace. The fourteen-year span between wedding and Coronation, her seminal fashion years as Duchess of York, was spent in pearls by day and grand dresses with their own decoration sewn into them at night. Both her wedding dress in 1923 and her Coronation dress of 1937 were made by the same court dressmaker Mrs Handley-Seymour, who also dressed the Duchess of York's mother and sister. (A parallel can be drawn today with Bellville Sassoon, who dress Princess Diana's mother Mrs Shand-Kydd and who make many of the Princess of Wales's evening dresses, even though she deserted them for her wedding dress.)

Temperamentally the Duchess of York seems to have been opposed to Queen Mary's majestic style, which her close relatives began to find excessive, and nothing better illustrates this divergence than the home life of the Queen and her new daughter-in-law. In the 1920s, Queen Mary and King George dressed for dinner, Georgie in his orders, May in her tiara. Elizabeth and Bertie would romp with their little girls: splashing in the bath, playing pillow fights and getting the children over-excited in a way that their nanny Mrs Clara

Knight did not approve of at all. Then, 'heated and dishevelled and frequently rather damp', the young couple would go down from the nursery suite for dinner to chat or read by the fire.

Lady Elizabeth's upbringing in a warm and loving Scottish family was in contrast to her husband's rigid and repressive childhood. 'We were so terribly shy and self-conscious as children,' he admitted. Raised in a bracing country climate with a Fair Isle scarf round her neck more often than jewellery, she was blessed with a sunny, outgoing temperament. 'It is so hard to know when *not* to smile,' she said to Cecil Beaton when he was photographing her in 1939. She had no need to seek stability in the permanence of things or use objects to demonstrate affection that was otherwise hard to express.

But there may also have been more positive reasons that persuaded the young Duchess of York to send a gust of fresh air through the stuffy jewel-laden court, just as today she will escape from the grand life at Clarence House to the rugged Scottish coast and her rock solid Castle of Mey. Even the most insensitive members of the royal family must have realised in the 1920s that the House of Windsor had been fortunate to be spared the storm that had felled so many of its branches. Queen Victoria herself had warned her family against excessive displays of wealth and extravagance. She complained to her son Bertie – Edward VII – about his indulgence of his wife Alexandra's taste for jewellery.

Queen Mary was a part of the old world and could be forgiven the old ways. The younger generation, and especially the Prince of Wales himself, was impatient with Court ritual and formalities. Elizabeth Bowes Lyon, brought up as a subject outside the royal circle, was well-placed to judge the new world in which the first-ever Labour Government under Ramsay MacDonald had been voted into power in 1924, and where royal thrones were, as Lord Esher had explained to Queen Mary, 'at a discount'. Besides, Elizabeth's husband Bertie was the King's second son, not heir to the monarchy and its traditions. Even on his own wedding day, 'our industrial and very industrious Prince,' as *The Times* priggishly labelled him, was in the shadow of his brother and chief supporter, the golden-haired Prince of Wales, whose boyish smile was already 'familiar to half the world'. Dashing David had just returned from his grand tour of India in 1921/22; he was already a veteran traveller. 'What tribute can be paid that would not seem stale news to the whole Empire?' thundered *The Times*. Although the formal Court life of Levees and Drawing Rooms had restarted after the war and the new garden-party presentations were instigated in July 1919, Bertie and Elizabeth were not expected to play any major royal role.

Then, of course, there was Mrs Simpson and the sophisticated world she represented: new money nudging the old aristocracy; cocktails at six to shake up the old social order as well as the smart new drinks. Mrs Simpson herself did not come into the Yorks' life until 1936, when David drove her down to Royal Lodge Windsor, the Yorks' country home, in his new-fangled American station wagon. She describes caustically in her memoirs the domestic scene: Elizabeth presided over tea with the two blonde and 'brightly scrubbed Princesses', and turned her frank 'startlingly blue eyes' on her brother-in-law's sleek American woman friend. The equally snappy American car became the perfect symbol for the clash of old and new.

The fast-paced lives of the Prince of Wales and the young Duke of Kent were already established in the 1920s, when the Yorks were making their first home at White Lodge in Richmond Park and then at 145 Piccadilly, where there were chintzy chairs and warm peach curtains, photographs of golden labradors and a corner reserved for the children's toys (including their scarlet brushes and dustpans for playing housemaid). This was country living in town in the upper-crust English tradition, and no greater contrast could possibly be imagined with the Simpsons' Bryanston Court flat, where the white leather dining chairs and the ocean-liner green walls had a brittle sophistication.

Did the Duchess of York deliberately choose at this moment a personal style as far removed as possible from the woman who stole 'Uncle David' away from his nursery teas with the little Princesses (to whom he had given the newly published Winnie-the-Pooh books)? As Mrs Simpson's blazing emeralds and rubies fuelled society gossip, the Duchess of York stuck discreetly to her strings of pearls and her domestic life, already set into a familiar annual progress between her parents' home at St Paul's Walden Bury in the New Year, their ancestral castle at Glamis in August, Balmoral with the King and Queen in September, Christmas at Sandringham.

The contrasting clothes of the two ladies exemplified the gulf between them. It is hard to believe that the Winterhalter crinolines created for the new Queen Elizabeth in 1937/1938 were exactly contemporary with the reed-slim quintessentially 1930s crêpe dress made by Mainbocher for the Duchess of Windsor's wedding (and a wonderful foil for the magnificent jewellery her husband bought for her).

Even at the age of eight Princess Margaret Rose realised that there was something quaint about her mother's neo-Victorian style of dress. 'When I am grown up,' said the Princess, 'I shall dress like Aunt Marina does.' She had watched the elegant Princess Marina, who married the Duke of Kent in 1934, arrive at Court in an utterly simple white brocade dress embossed with pink and silver flowers, the backcloth for her magnificent jewels – a diamond and ruby tiara with matching necklace given to her by her husband.

But it would be wrong to suggest that the Yorks did not approve of jewellery as an ornament or that they led an ascetic existence and that Elizabeth only put on a tiara when she had to (or when a portrait painter booked a sitting and her staff would find her in full evening dress and regalia in the middle of the morning). Throughout the 30-year period from her wedding to her daughter's Coronation in 1953, the Duchess of York, and later Queen, would choose relatively small, decorative pieces of jewellery in the fashion of the time – the latest clip brooches in sapphires, rubies or aquamarines, always set in platinum; decorative hair clips in the shape of flowers and stars. (She was the first Queen in living memory to perch a tiara directly on the crown on her short hair, rather than fixing head ornaments to a mass of coiffured or false hair.) Her favourite head ornaments were, therefore, the bandeaux of the time, especially the circlet of diamond flowers worn low on her forehead, flapper-

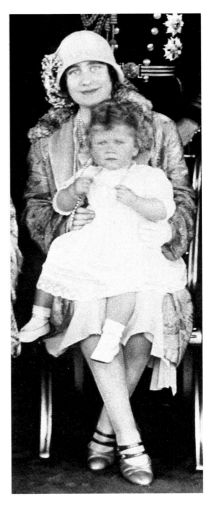

The Duchess of York with Princess Elizabeth playing with her coral and pearl necklet in 1927.

style, throughout the 1920s. This was given to Princess Margaret, who wore it conventionally on the crown of her head.

Ironically, there was a certain similarity between the taste in jewellery of the new Queen Elizabeth and her sister-in-law Wallis, whose name was never mentioned in the York household after the Abdication. They both chose aquamarines at the end of the 1920s; they both chose platinum settings (although the Duchess of Windsor was later to pioneer a return to yellow gold); they both liked rubies and sapphires rather than Queen Mary's favourite emeralds. They also hated each other, but there is no evidence for the story that jealousy over jewels fuelled this hatred or that the return of 'royal heirlooms' is a running sore which still festers with the Queen Mother.

As the maelstrom of the Abdication receded, it left Bertie and his wife becalmed on the throne. George VI's Coronation was in May 1937, and for the new Queen Elizabeth that meant a new crown. 'To Garrard's to see the jewellers working on the resetting of Bertie's and Elizabeth's crowns – Most interesting,' Queen Mary noted in her diary on 9 April 1937.

The Queen Consort's crown had four arches of diamonds. The 16 large stones were taken from the circlet which Queen Victoria had ordered in 1853 to take the great 'mountain of light', the Koh-i-noor, presented to her by the Honourable East India Company in 1851. The Koh-i-noor was also put into the new crown, for tradition has it that the stone is unlucky for male rulers and it is therefore used only by Queens and Queen Consorts. On the cross at the top, above the crimson velvet cap with its ermine trimmings, was another great diamond, taken from a necklace at Lahore and trimmed down in 1937 to a 'mere' 22.48 carats.

Coronation jewels: Queen Elizabeth wears the Koh-i-noor in her crown and the diamond collet necklace; Queen Mary has the Cullinan brooch; Princess Elizabeth wears a gilded circlet made by a theatrical costumier.

The diamond cross blazed on Queen Elizabeth's head in Westminster Abbey on that May day in 1937 as a symbol of the solidity of the monarchy after the earthquake of the Abdication. 'That was an operetta, this is an Institution,' said Lady Diana Cooper, when she contrasted the Prince of Wales's set at Fort Belvedere and the life of the new King and Queen at Windsor. 'The mere thought of the King and Queen having a "set" made us all laugh,' Lady Cunard said.

As the Archbishop of Canterbury lowered the crown on to her head at the most sacred part of the solemn service in Westminster Abbey, the new Queen must have recalled that sad funeral service for her father-in-law George V just over a year before, when a diamond cross had played another symbolic role. In an awful portent of the uncertain transfer of power to a new King, the Maltese Cross on top of the Imperial Crown on the King's coffin had fallen off, the diamonds creating 'a flash of light dancing along the pavement'. Edward VIII describes in *A King's Story* how he watched in horror until the cross was deftly picked up by the Sergeant-Major.

'Felt very sad at parting,' Queen Mary wrote in 1936 of the jewels that had been in her care since 1910. From pictures of Queen Elizabeth as Consort, we can begin to assess what the royal family (and specifically Queen Mary, who catalogued the royal collection) consider to be Crown Jewellery to be passed to a new Queen. This is also the moment to decide whether any major piece of royal jewellery 'disappeared' with Edward VIII at the time of the Abdication.

The first jewel to change royal heads was the diamond fringe tiara with its upstanding blades of diamonds. It was one of the few pieces of jewellery that had been handed down to Queen Victoria. It was originally set in 1830 with brilliants that had been the property of George III, and was worn both as a tiara or unmounted as a necklace. Queen Elizabeth wore it immediately after her accession with the diamond collet necklace Queen Victoria had made from diamonds taken out of a Garter Badge and a sword. It was time, thought the new Queen, for a slight change. In 1937 she removed two stones from the massive necklace (replacing them with three smaller stones) and had a new pair of fine drop earrings made for herself.

Her other absolute favourite throughout her time as Queen Mother has been the regal tiara in an Indian design of flowers and curlicues made by Garrard for Queen Victoria in 1853. Queen Alexandra had the original opals that were set as centres to the flowers replaced with rubies in 1902, using 11 rubies from an Indian necklace presented to the Prince of Wales on his Indian tour in 1876.

The diamond diadem, the nearest circlet to a royal crown with its distinctive square crosses interspersed with a cluster of symbolic rose, shamrock and thistle in diamonds was also slightly altered by Queen Elizabeth, who added an extra row of pearls to the mount in 1937.

Queen Victoria's sapphire brooch surrounded by 12 diamonds, her wedding gift from Prince Albert, sprouted proudly on the new Queen's lapel and is now much worn by her daughter. The diamond bows made for Queen Victoria and also now worn by the Queen were worn by Queen Elizabeth as the Consort of George VI.

Of the rest of the royal jewellery, there is no sign in the photographs of the period. The general public, familiar with the overwhelmingly bejewelled figure of Queen Mary, and before her Queen Alexandra, sensed that familiar pieces seemed to have disappeared. Thus the story that part of the royal heritage was hived off by Edward VIII and given to the Duchess of Windsor stems from this period.

But was the truth quite different? Was it Queen Mary herself who was guarding jealously the royal inheritance and hanging on to most of the fine pieces, *because she personally had divided up the jewels and designated most of them as private property?*

The new King and Queen in 1937, George VI in his decorations, Elizabeth in her pearls and the diamond fringe tiara.

'The choice isn't very great you know,' said the new Queen Elizabeth with an apologetic smile to Cecil Beaton in 1939 when he asked 'If – perhaps – as much jewellery as possible could – be worn?' Queen Elizabeth's remark may not have been upper-class self-deprecation but the literal truth.

Queen Victoria's list of the Crown Jewellery is quite precise and very limited. It consisted, on her death in 1901, of the diamond diadem, the regal Indian circlet and the other diadem broken up and some of its stones used in 1937 to make the Queen Consort's crown. Apart from various splendid orders and swords, there was a cockade and two major pieces of Indian jewellery – a carved emerald girdle and the Timur ruby. The brooches included Albert's sapphire and diamond circle, the Jubilee pearl and diamond brooch given by Queen Victoria's household (and constantly worn by the Queen Mother). The necklaces were the diamond fringe, the collet, another important diamond necklace, two rows of pearls, which belonged to Queen Anne and Queen Caroline, two other pearl necklaces and the magnificent chain of 222 pearls fastened with a ruby snap, taken from the treasure at Lahore in 1851 and reset in 1910, 1937 and 1941.

In addition, there were 21 rings, all but four of which were sent to Windsor Castle on 24 November 1910 by Queen Mary, including a portrait ring engraved 'George III' and mourning rings, named and dated. Like the silver cross with Albert's photograph and a lock of his hair or the blue enamel bracelet set with portraits of Queen Victoria's children, they were primarily pieces of sentimental or historical interest.

The most obvious fact to emerge from the lists of Crown Jewellery is that Queen Mary apparently passed on *nothing* from Queen Alexandra's vast collection of jewels (which Queen Mary sorted out with two of Alix's daughters) to the Crown, and that she herself designated virtually nothing from her own overwhelming collection of Indian jewellery, to be considered, as Queen Victoria had expressed it, 'as belonging to the Crown and to be worn by all future Queens in right of it'.

It is hard *not* to believe that Queen Mary gave to the Crown only those pieces she did not fancy for herself, or that, as Lady Pamela Berry so neatly expressed it, she 'bagged all the best'.

Then there was the war. Two years after George VI's Coronation, all pageantry was eclipsed; the jewels were put away; in fact wrapped in newspapers and stuffed into leather hatboxes in the vaults at Windsor Castle. The Princesses would trot down to the cellars at Windsor with twin jewel cases borrowed from a pair of dolls presented by the French government. The cases were packed with favourite brooches – like the much loved ladybirds given to them by Lilibet's nurserymaid Bobo (still the Queen's dresser). At Buckingham Palace, Mummie was going through the same ritual, the King carrying a corgi, the Queen with her own jewel case as she went down to the shelter when the warning siren sounded. Much of the silver and gold plate, and even Queen Alexandra's collection of Fabergé animals, are now kept in the underground bunker at Buckingham Palace.

After the war that sapped the King's strength much as his father had been overwhelmed by the Great War, there was a brief reprise of splendour. The last

Court ball had taken place in 1937, but Queen Elizabeth glittered with diamonds when she became Treasurer of the Middle Temple in December 1944. The Queen had become more matronly, acquiring her new and identifiable stance – 'a curious sideways, lilting walk', as the witty socialite Sir Henry 'Chips' Channon described it. The year of victory, 1945, had something of the old swagger and the Queen's magnificent rubies with her white dress at dinner at Windsor Castle after the races excited comment. Three years before Dame Margaret Greville, the owner of the house where Elizabeth and Bertie spent their honeymoon, had died. Mrs Greville had a fine collection of jewels which she had long destined for Queen Elizabeth – especially her magnificent pearls and an extraordinary diamond ring, its stone described by *The Tatler* as a 'diamond shaped as a playing card'. From her impressive estate, Mrs Greville left over £1m in all, including £20,000 to Princess Margaret and her house, Polesden Lacey, to the National Trust. Mrs Greville had received some generous presents from Queen Mary, including a superb porcelain 'cricket' cage – an elaborately sculpted china objet d'art designed for collecting butterflies and grasshoppers.

By the next Ascot there was more royal glitter, with the Duchess of Kent emulating her sister-in-law with a parasol, its handle studded with sapphires. The Queen was a vision in white with pearls and rubies and Chips Channon noted her round face bathed in its 'world-famous smile'.

This particular radiance was the reflected glow of the happiness spread through the royal family by the imminent engagement of 20-year-old Lilibet, who was breaking out of the protective chrysalis that her father had woven round his daughters' adolescence. There were cosy family evenings round the fire, when Princess Elizabeth struggled with her war-effort knitting and the high-spirited Princess Margaret would exercise her talent for mimicry; shooting expeditions for father and daughter at Sandringham; wartime pantomimes in which the King took pride and interest. All were coming to their natural end as Lilibet waited for her naval Prince Philip and played on her gramophone the music from *Oklahoma*, which the young couple had seen together.

There was one last works outing together for the 'Family Firm', as King George VI called the royal clan. On 1 February 1947, mother and father and the two Princesses assembled in the Bow Room, with its curving window in front of the garden steps at Buckingham Palace, before their three-month trip to Africa. In April, in South Africa, Lilibet celebrated her twenty-first birthday and proudly received a splendid necklace of 21 diamonds. To this day she calls it 'my best diamonds'. Her mother was given an impressive unset marquise diamond (as well as an 18-carat gold tea set). Princess Margaret had a diamond bracelet with an emerald-cut ring, and all these gifts went on display alongside Princess Elizabeth's wedding presents at St James's Palace in November.

The engagement and the wedding were the high-rise mark of froth and fun in the brief 15-year reign of King George VI and his Queen Consort, who had been dragged unwillingly to the throne by Edward VIII's abdication, thrust immediately afterwards into a sombre and gruelling war and were soon to have their happiness in their daughter's wedding and their first grandson

OPPOSITE *Queen Elizabeth photographed by Beaton in black velvet, the Crown diamonds and the regal Indian tiara. The distinctive diamond tassel brooch is a royal heirloom.* ABOVE *Queen Victoria wears the tassel brooch in 1887.* BELOW *Queen Alexandra also pinned the tassel brooch to her bosom.*

veiled by anxiety over the King's health. For one brief moment, as the war receded and the shadow on the lung had not been diagnosed, all was radiant sunshine.

At the Royal Wedding on 20 November 1947, Queen Elizabeth was like a ripe fruit in her apricot lamé dress that is still carefully preserved at Clarence House. Queen Mary, whose next and last great state occasion was to be the King's funeral, was resplendent in an ankle-length dress and coat of golden tissue embossed with sea-blue chenille. On her Garter sash she wore the Cullinan drop diamond brooch; her neck was encircled with diamonds.

Queen Mary's magnificent presents to her granddaughter – the diamond festoon and scroll tiara, the massive and elaborate diamond stomacher, the diamond bandeau, the bow brooch, the diamond Indian bangles, the ruby and diamond rose bracelet and the bouton pearl and diamond earrings had mainly been presents to herself on her own marriage in 1893. They almost eclipsed in the display the fine pearls and the heavy Indian ruby and diamond necklace and diamond drop earrings from her parents. The King gave his favourite shooting companion a pair of Purdey guns and a pair of sapphire and diamond drop earrings with matching necklace for good measure. Queen Elizabeth and Princess Margaret, almost in defiance of Queen Mary's opulent gifts, gave practical presents: Princess Margaret a picnic basket, a silver ink stand and a set of champagne glasses for her abstemious sister; Mummie, whose favourite escape from royal protocol was to go to the still room and make the Scottish scones and cakes of her childhood, gave an engraved tray, four salt cellars, four mustard pots, four pepper pots and a large toast rack.

The excitement of the wedding was followed by the thrill of the first grandchild, Prince Charles, born in November 1948, followed neatly by Princess Anne in August 1950. The grandparents saw a great deal of the new generation, for following the tradition of iron duty, Princess Elizabeth and her husband undertook a series of royal tours without their children – just as Bertie and Elizabeth had been forced to leave the baby Princess Elizabeth behind when they went on their six-month tour of Australia and New Zealand in 1927. 'The baby was so sweet playing with buttons on Bertie's uniform that it quite broke me up,' she had said, and that searing memory made the Queen Mother give her support to Princess Diana when she decided to break with royal tradition and take Prince William with her in 1983.

On Thursday, 7 February 1952, Queen Elizabeth II walked down the steps of the plane that had brought her back from a royal visit to Kenya to mourn the untimely death of her father and to take over from him as England's sovereign. On the lapel of her black coat was the flame lily brooch presented to her by the children of Rhodesia on the happy African tour the royal family had made together four years before.

Queen Elizabeth the Queen Mother, she who had helped Bertie conquer his stammer and write his Christmas broadcasts, handed over to her 25-year-old daughter the Crown Jewellery. The diadem that had hardly touched her head was now passed on, along with Queen Victoria's sapphire brooches and all the Crown diamonds. She held on to the Indian ruby tiara, for Lilibet already had so much and by the following March was to have immeasurably more. Queen

Mary, who had just buried her fourth reigning monarch and her third son, gave up this life and all its earthly treasures and her glittering collection of jewels was inherited by her granddaughter.

The Queen Mother picked up the strands of her life, withdrawing to the Scotland of her childhood, where she bought and restored the Castle of Mey, its sturdy grey towers standing four-square to the Icelandic winds on the wild Caithness coast. Here was a retreat from the compassionate public gaze, from the all-too-public romance between her late husband's equerry, Group Captain Peter Townsend, and Princess Margaret Rose, whose irrepressible gaiety ('*espiègle*' her grandmother Queen Mary had called her) had been punctured at the age of 21 by the death of a doting father. There was retreat too from the 'grand dressings' and the royal splendours. There were simple pearls in this time of tears and the young grandchildren Charles and Anne to play with them.

But there was also a new tiara, the last grand tiara made for the English royal family, using the South African diamonds presented as a gift to Edward VII by de Beers in 1901. The design for the Queen Mother was quite a contrast to the Jeanne Toussaint panthers – and the jewel-studded tiger lorgnette – that were being made between 1948 and 1954 in the Cartier workrooms for the Duchess of Windsor.

The royal tiara, made by Boucheron, is starkly modern, its triple deck of diamond lozenges linked with geometric precision and surmounted by a more traditional fleur-de-lis. It is a favourite tiara, worn mostly with Princess Alexandra's looped pearl and diamond necklace. This juxtaposition of the romantic old with the new does not surprise anyone who has visited the Queen Mother at Clarence House and seen the paintings by Sickert and Paul Nash and her favourite Augustus John (who painted her in the ruby tiara and a Cinderella gown in 1940) set among the eighteenth-century furniture and the collection of china and *objets d'art*.

The resolute, granite-firm character that lies beneath the sugar-sweet smile is well expressed in the contrast between the paintings, done 20 years apart, of Queen Elizabeth by Augustus John and the same woman as Queen Mother by Graham Sutherland. The first, unfinished picture (the sittings were interrupted by the Blitz) is romantic, even ethereal, with its clouds of white and gold spangled tulle, its fairy-tale tiara and necklace and three splashes of regal crimson where rubies, red roses and plush velvet chair leap out from the deep blue background. In 1960, the year that Princess Margaret found respite in her stormy life in her marriage to Lord Snowdon, Sutherland painted the Queen Mother, again in white against dark blue, again sitting in a gilded chair, with a tiny hint of red on the clasp of her three-strand pearl necklace and more than a hint of uncompromising toughness in her thin line of red lips.

These modern paintings, the new tiara and another geometric bandeau with a fluttering aigrette, exhibited at the International Exhibition of Modern Jewellery at the Goldsmith's Hall in 1961, suggest an intriguing might-have-been. If Queen Elizabeth's time as Queen Consort had not been cut short by her husband's death, might she have taken a keen interest in the old jewellery and had some pieces reset?

Over the last 30 years, during the reign of Queen Elizabeth II, the royal jewel collection has remained almost static. The only major modern piece (a conventional flower design) that the Queen has had made has been the ruby and diamond tiara that Garrard made up in 1978. In fact, we have the Queen Mother to thank for this commission: because Mummie is still wearing the diamond and ruby Indian tiara, the Queen's enormous collection of head ornaments (emeralds, pearls, sapphires, diamonds, aquamarines) was short on rubies.

Garrard have made up two modern diamond necklaces for the Queen from spare collets; Prince Charles is beginning to have some small pieces made for his wife by young designers; Princess Margaret, who received two of her mother's tiaras on her marriage, has taken a serious interest in modern jewellery and has had old-fashioned pieces reset.

The new tiara made from diamonds presented by de Beers to Edward VII in 1901. With it, the Queen Mother wears the necklace the future Edward VII gave to Princess Alexandra as a wedding present in 1863, and the diamond tassel brooch.

The Queen Mother's collection of jewellery swells with every gift presented on the royal progress – visits to shipyards and schools, galas and openings, royal tours and visits to Britain by foreign heads of state. There was the tiny watch given to her by the French on that early visit in 1938, which she passed on to her daughter Elizabeth on her 12th birthday; the antique casket covered in a mermaid's tail of scales of mother of pearl presented by John Brown's shipbuilding yard (who gave Princess Elizabeth an antique flower brooch). None of these gifts (in the case of the Queen now an uncontrollable torrent of treasures) is listed as Crown property. They come under that more confusing category of 'royal heritage' which suggests that they are state rather than personal possessions. In practice, this means that the more appealing pieces are taken over as prized items while the more doubtful are banished to limbo land in a corner of one of the palaces.

The Queen Mother herself has four separate homes. In London there is Clarence House, part of St James's Palace and hers by Grace and Favour of the monarch; she exchanged it in a straight swap with the Edinburghs when they moved out and into Buckingham Palace when Elizabeth II became Queen. In Scotland there is the Castle of Mey filled with the local Caithness glass and Scottish water colours, its tartan hearthrug conveying just a discreet echo of Queen Victoria's tartanitis at Balmoral. And just over the glen from her daughter's Scottish castle there is Birkhall, the Jacobean mansion with its dark oak and Landseer paintings where Prince Charles and Lady Diana Spencer did their courting. There she will wear the full Balmoral tartan rig (the kilt designed by Hartnell) to join her family for a picnic. Royal Lodge at Windsor, with its English country garden which Bertie created (one taste he and his brother the Duke of Windsor shared), is still her weekend retreat and the bowls of fresh flowers – the blue delphiniums and larkspurs, the lilac that Bertie planted – are sent up from Windsor and kept until they drop (and sometimes a day too long) in the sunny garden room at Clarence House.

State gifts of jewels cannot be reset (except after a very decent interval). These jewels, along with commemorative badges and orders, are all meticulously logged by the ladies-in-waiting, who must be able to produce the unworn gift years later when the royal cartwheel again spins towards the donor. Although these records (and presumably an inventory of the Queen Mother's entire collection of jewellery) are kept at Clarence House, her household (themselves 'growing old with Queen Elizabeth') speak only of 'a great clear out' to come 'one day'.

One courtier specifically claims that apart from a few small personal bequests to loyal ladies-in-waiting, such as to Ruth, Lady Fermoy, the Queen Mother's lady-in-waiting and grandmother to the Princess of Wales, all the personal jewellery will go to the newly fledged teens and twenties generation of the royal family. These are the products of 1964, that year of the babies, when the family firm was more productive than it had been since the year of the Royal Marriage Race in 1819, when the dissolute sons of George III were all trying to produce an heir to the throne.

Prince Edward, the youngest son of the Queen, and Princess Margaret's daughter Lady Sarah Armstrong-Jones, both arrived in 1964; they were greeted by cartoons showing the bearskinned guards knitting booties on sentry duty. In the same year the Queen Mother welcomed into the family Lady Helen Windsor, daughter of Edward, Duke of Kent, who had married the Yorkshire-born Katharine Worsley in 1961; and James Ogilvy, son of Princess Marina's daughter Alexandra, who married Angus Ogilvy, the grandson of Mabell, Countess of Airlie who had been Queen Mary's lady-in-waiting and confidante for 50 years, and who had held her hand in silent consolation as the two old ladies watched King George VI's coffin carried past the window of Marlborough House.

The most obvious candidates for the royal bounty are the Queen Mother's grandchildren, especially Princess Diana's close friend Lady Sarah Armstrong-Jones, whose mother Princess Margaret feels keenly that her daughter might be given a few things to wear, suitable for her age, from the royal 'jewel pool'. Princess Anne, on her marriage in 1973 to Captain Mark Phillips, received from the Queen Mother an aquamarine and diamond tiara; she has kept a diamond bandeau from the royal collection. Her own daughter Zara and son Peter are now seedlings of the House of Windsor, which will be spreading further on the marriages of the other grandchildren, Prince Edward and Prince Andrew. The Queen Mother's wedding present to Princess Diana has never been made public. It is believed to be the cabochon emerald choker the Princess first wore on the tour of Wales in the autumn of her wedding year, although this Queen Mary heirloom in fact came from the Queen.

All together the Queen Mother has five young royal relatives – two girls and three boys – of the 1960s generation, none of them with great expectations of an inheritance. The Duke of Kent's children, George, Earl of St Andrews, Lady Helen Windsor and Lord Nicholas Windsor, have more jewels in the family than their Ogilvy cousins Marina and James. This is because their grandmother Princess Marina, in the Greek family tradition, left most of her jewellery to her sons rather than to her daughter Alexandra, on the principle that sons of the family have wives to support. After the death of George, Duke of Kent in 1942, the Kents became the 'poor relations' of the royal family.

'Princess Alexandra and the Duchess of Kent are loyal, hard-working girls, both of them, and they haven't many jewels, you might remember them,' was the request made to the Duchess of Windsor by Lady Monckton of Brenchley, whose husband Walter had done so much to help Edward VIII resolve the marriage question. The Queen Mother may be more receptive to their needs.

There is another younger generation growing up within the royal family, the three children of the Duke and Duchess of Gloucester and also Lord Frederick and Lady Gabriella Windsor, children of Prince and Princess Michael of Kent. They must seem to the Queen Mother, when the family congregates for the Christmas at Windsor or for rites of passage like the christenings of Prince William and Prince Harry, as part of the new generation of great-grandchildren. Because of the sad death of Prince William of Gloucester in a plane crash in 1974, the present Duchess of Gloucester is heir to her mother-in-law's jewellery, much of which, including the delicate turquoise suite of tiara, necklace, earrings and bracelets, she is already wearing. This was a wedding present from Queen Mary to Lady Alice Montague-Douglas-Scott, a daughter of the Duke of Buccleuch whose family possess in the Buccleuch Belt composed entirely of diamonds a monumental treasure which Queen Mary must certainly have coveted.

The 1960s was a time of family partings as well as of new arrivals: first the Queen Mother's beloved brother, Sir David Bowes Lyon, her 'Benjamin' when they were the two youngest in the Strathmore family. Then in 1965 Mary, her childhood friend the Princess Royal, whose marriage to the commoner Lord Harewood had caused a stir in the 1920s and at whose wedding Elizabeth had been placed strategically next to her future husband, Mary's brother Bertie. As the Queen Mother went to Yorkshire to pay her last respects to Mary, she must have remembered the February day in 1922 when she was in Westminster Abbey in her silver bridesmaid's gown with its big silver rose; and how the Lascelles boys, George and Gerald, had played with Princess Elizabeth; and how Queen Mary had taken them to Trooping the Colour and taught them to salute.

Some idea of the scale of the royal jewel collection can be gleaned from the sale of the Princess Royal's jewels at Christie's on 29 June 1966. The family had presumably taken, by selection or inheritance, the pick, but that still left 138 separate pieces of gem-set jewellery. The Princess's sunburst tiara (similar to the Crown fringe and also convertible to a necklace) and a superb diamond collet necklace of classic simplicity were the star items in a sale that realised a total of £52,852. (The necklace fetched £12,500 and the tiara £7,000.) The pieces most obviously linked to the Edwardian era were the stomachers, a vast emerald and diamond triangular piece and an equally unwieldy antique turquoise and rose diamond stomacher in clusters, festoons and with collet drops. There was also a seed pearl, diamond, ruby and emerald collar, which suggests an Indian provenance, and a collection of multi-coloured hinged egg charms, certainly from Russia.

The more personal pieces included the Princess Royal's fantastic collection of owls, in jade, ivory, ebony or rock crystal and a Cartier owl brooch, his round stomach a large cabochon emerald.

If one of Queen Mary's children had such a large collection of jewels (there was even a parcel of unset stones which included 119 baroque pearls and assorted diamonds and cabochon rubies) we can imagine the size of the royal collection of Bertie's wife Elizabeth, increased by a constant flow of gifts over a span of 80 years.

The Queen Mother has a rather charming way of receiving presents, from family and friends or the public, clapping her hands girlishly at the age of 85, saying 'I can't wait to open it', and doing just that. 'It is hard to think of any other person with such a gift for giving pleasure, of making you go away from her dancing,' says a friend and frequent visitor to Clarence House. But it is difficult, say others, to penetrate the famous charm, to work out how much the pleas to stay while her equerry insists she must go, is an actress playing at being gracious. 'Of course there is something of the great actress about her,' said Cecil Beaton in 1953. 'In public she has to put on a show which never fails, but it is her heart and imagination which guide her.'

Her household say that she is a very private person, who puts on her royal

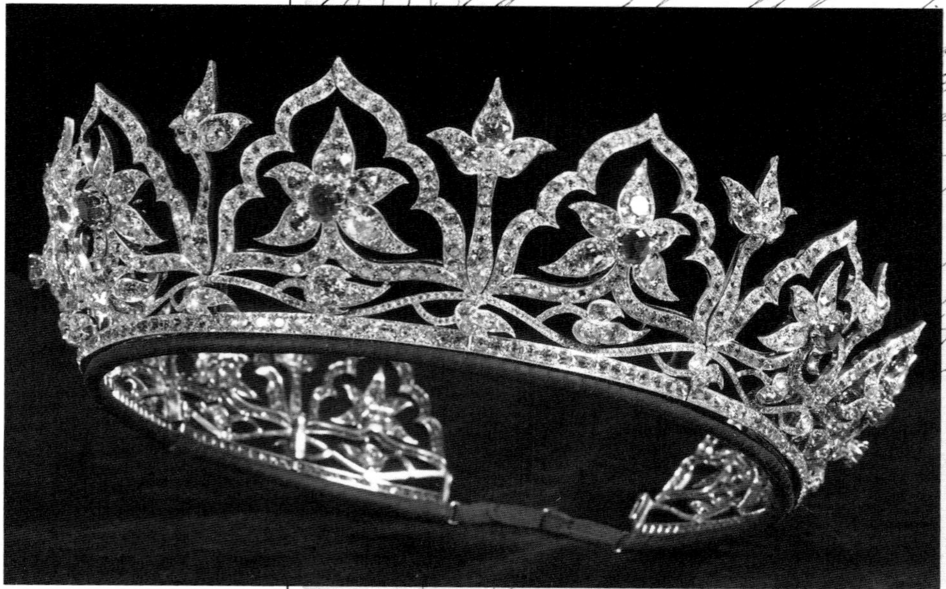

29 *Her Majesty The Queen* Dr

1853		1081 11 9
	…imond…	
	…frames	26 . .
	…or	
	…½ ⅛ 1/16	65 6 6
		28 14 6
	…¼ . 1/16 1/32	54 5 6
	…¼ . 1/16 . 1/64	53 5 6
	…¼ ⅛.	23 . .
	…to Her Majesty	
	503 ½ , ⅛ . 1/32	
	A blue Velvet Case with trays, and lined fitted to &c.	7 5 .
	Diamond and Opal Tiara	
	Making a Diamond Tiara of Oriental design with Opal centres the outer frame ornament and the spire and bush Ornaments made to remove with screws Springs and the spires to be replaced by large single Diamonds to complete the Ornament when a lighter and more simple Tiara is required	
	The whole containing 1348 Brilliants	
	1330 Roses	
	17 Opals	
	Total 2695	
	For setting the above	406
	Furnishing 328 Brilliants ct 41 ½ ¼ . 1/16 1/32 1/64	334 17 6
	Do 1102 Roses	82 13 .
	Do 17 Opals	38 . .
	Used in the above belonging to Her Majesty	
	7 Brilliants ct 18 . ¼ ⅛ .	
	8 Do . 18 . ¼ ⅛ 1/16 1/32	
	7 Do . 14 . . 1/16 .	
	6 Do . 8 ½ . ⅛ 1/16 1/32	
	Carried over	2200 19 3

role, along with her duster coats and her hats and her jewels, and that the Queen Elizabeth who sits alone in her little boudoir with its sombre Sickert painting of King George V is quite different from the idolized image of the public. She hates, they say, the fuss made over her birthdays: 75 and still here; thanking God in St Paul's Cathedral for 80 years; 85 down and more to go. Others say that she is demanding, imperious, expecting everything to be done at a flick of the finger and clicking her fingers anxiously when the staff are late with lunch.

Perhaps one could encapsulate the difference between Queen Elizabeth the Queen Mother and her mother-in-law Queen Mary by saying that the latter had more pleasure from her jewels and her possessions than from her children, and that the Queen Mother values her family far above rubies.

OPPOSITE AND BELOW *The regal Indian tiara made for Queen Victoria on 1 April 1853. It contained 2,678 diamonds and 17 opals. Queen Alexandra removed the 'unlucky' opals in 1902 and the tiara was reset with rubies from a necklace presented by Sir Jung Bahadore of Nepal to the Prince of Wales on his tour of India in 1875/6. The tiara and necklace are Crown property which the Queen knows that 'Mummie will give back one day.'*

6

Queen of Diamonds

'It is yours *and* mine.'

Princess Margaret to J. M. Barrie at Glamis Castle.
Used by Barrie in *The Boy David*

How many crowns has the Queen? Nine in the Tower; ten if you count the diamond diadem, worn for the Opening of Parliament and pictured on stamps. Eleven with Queen Alexandra's paste crown; the skeletal frames of George IV's and Queen Victoria's crowns, which the Queen has gems enough to fill: twelve, thirteen. Then there is the gilded circlet of fleur-de-lis and Maltese crosses, copied from Mummie's crown and worn for the 1937 Coronation with the first grown-up dress – silver bows down the front and an ermine cloak swagging its back: fourteen.

How many tiaras? First, 'Granny's tiara', the diamond festoon and scroll presented by Queen Mary for the marriage of Princess Elizabeth and Lieutenant Philip Mountbatten of the Royal Navy. For the wedding day there was a different royal heirloom: the sunray fringe necklace, inherited from George IV and mounted as a tiara – although it fell apart on the wedding morning and the Crown Jeweller had to be summoned for running repairs. Queen Alexandra's Russian fringe tiara makes three; the Indian regal tiara still with the Queen Mother four; five, the favourite diamond circles with the interchangeable drop pearls and emeralds. Sapphires to go with the King's sapphire and diamond wedding present suite; aquamarines, made for the Brazilian necklace; new ruby tiara made up from the Burmese rubies: eight. Diamonds from King Faisal; English rose bandeau from the Nizam of Hyderabad. Bow knots and drop pearls given to the Princess of Wales. That makes a total of 11 worn, a dozen more in store.

How many necklaces? Jubilee, diamond collet, diamond fringe, triple diamonds, best South African diamonds, two Crown pearls, triple pearls, Dagmar necklace, ruby suite, Indian rubies, Timur ruby, sapphires, Cambridge emeralds, Crown amethysts, turquoises, Brazilian aquamarines . . .

How many brooches? Queen Victoria's sapphire, two bow brooches, Kensington bow, Granny's bow, Granny's double bar, Williamson pink diamond, diamond flower, sapphire flower, emerald brooch, cabochon emerald, cabochon sapphire, cat's eye, Duchess of Teck's pearls, flame lily,

Public and private: the Queen wears the diamond diadem and the fringe diamond necklace presented by the City of London, with the spectacular chandelier diamond earrings given to her by her parents on her marriage. They contain every known cut of diamonds. Another wedding present – part of Queen Mary's eight-inch-long diamond and pearl stomacher – is pinned to her Garter ribbon. On her wrist, the smallest watch in the world, made by Cartier in platinum and diamonds, given to her by the President of the French Republic.

131

diamond fern, Queen Mary's stomacher makes three more brooches . . .

Who is counting? How can anyone add up all the earrings and bracelets, watches and pins and especially those brooches, the mainstream flood from a dozen royal tributaries. And so many presents since the launch of that first ship, *The British Princess*, in 1946, and the first royal tour of South Africa in 1947 – four decades of diamonds among her souvenirs.

They are not all exactly *hers*, of course. Or, as the then Lord Chamberlain Lord Cobbold put it at the time of the Select Committee on the Civil List in 1971, 'In no practical sense does the Queen regard any of the items as being at her free personal disposal.' The Crown Jewellery, like the royal collection of paintings and other treasures, including the stamp collection so lovingly built up by George V, are part of an inalienable national heritage. By contrast those items acquired by the Queen and Prince Philip 'by inheritance, gift or purchase' are private property. 'And only Heaven and Bobo MacDonald know which is which,' as a member of the Lord Chamberlain's office puts it today.

The Queen, her household tell one repeatedly, wears very little jewellery – just her pearls, a brooch on the lapel and her engagement ring, the solitaire diamond that had managed to escape the revolution-riddled childhood of Prince Philip's family. The young naval officer who 'looked like a Viking' inherited the stone from his mother, Princess Andrew, had it made up secretly at the London jeweller Philip Antrobus, and then had to send it back to be made to fit his fiancée's slim finger.

The 'simple' pearls are probably the lustrous globules that once belonged to George II's wife Queen Caroline, 46 fine pearls given to the Queen by her parents on her marriage. The brooch pinned to a tweedy collar on a gusty day at Newmarket will be Queen Victoria's sapphire, 'Albert's brooch', as she always called it, one of the most emotive, historic and personal pieces of the Crown Jewellery. Or it might be the fiery heart of the Cullinan diamond, its 'chip' set in the centre of a brooch that is in its turn part of an enormous emerald and diamond stomacher.

The Queen does not wear her jewels for personal show. Queen Alexandra dressed with elaborate opulence for State occasions, if not in private. Queen Mary brought the royal jewels from the Edwardian evening Courts and into the light of garish day. Queen Elizabeth II has pushed back the tide of jewels and wears them as accoutrements of majesty when the occasion requires: for official dinners, royal tours, the State opening of Parliament.

The rest of royal life is enacted with one 'modest' brooch in front of a one-bar electric fire, as befits the public image of the Family Firm in a democratic age.

This little game is played out right in the bosom of her family, where Queen Mary would, literally and metaphorically, wear her most glittering gems. An elderly relative, staying at Windsor, was complimented by HM on her smart new outfit – which she pointed out was bought from a Cambridgeshire jumble sale. 'Oh Dorothy,' came the reply from the Queen, 'if only I had the time!'

The Queen appreciates her collection of jewels for its history. Her favourite necklace for evening functions is the Jubilee, with its trefoils of diamonds and pearls, made for Queen Victoria for the Jubilee of 1887 using the residue of money donated for the Albert Memorial in Hyde Park. Like that imposing edifice, the necklace is monumental, rather than beautiful. It is usually worn with one of the grand tiaras – perhaps the intertwined circles with trembling drop pearls.

'I gave them my best bits,' she will say after a 'big dressing', when Bobo MacDonald has brought out one of the domed velvet boxes with its silken interior swaddling a majestic tiara. The diamonds sparkle fiercely for visiting potentates on the royal tours – especially in the desert kingdoms – where jewels are equated with status.

The jewel boxes are magical in themselves – shrouds of dark leather worn smooth by human touch. A sapphire tiara nestles on mushroom velvet inside scarlet leather which is as bright as the red despatch box with its gold tooled crown and EIIR. The blood red Timur ruby with its carved stone and its turbulent history has come to rest in a plain, square black leather box, deep at the sides and with a thick hinged lid.

The Queen caresses the Indian jewel and discusses it with Bobo MacDonald in the *Royal Family* film seen on BBC television in 1969.

'It is a fascinating necklace, the Timur ruby one. I think one should get a dress designed so that one could wear it,' she says. 'The history of course is very fascinating. That it belonged to so many of the Kings of Persia and Moghul Emperors. And it has come all the way down until Queen Victoria was sent it from India. It's rather fascinating. It would be nice if one could go on wearing it.'

The 12-year-old Princess Elizabeth, whose grandmother insisted that her school curriculum should be replanned because history was more valuable than arithmetic – has learned her lessons well. But did the Queen – who has never worn that historic ruby – imbibe Queen Mary's taste for jewels, her aesthetic pleasure in their beauty?

In fact she has not once in 30 years asked her dress designers when they call with sketches or for fittings on Tuesday afternoons, to make a dress to suit a piece of jewellery. 'She did once mutter something to Bobo about "that will go with the Cambridge emeralds". Otherwise one just assumes that she will find something from her vast collection,' says one of the royal dressmakers.

The Queen relies absolutely on Bobo MacDonald, 80 now, visibly shrinking and no longer capable of undertaking royal tours, but still with her sharp Scots accent and still in charge of the jewels – just as she was half a century ago when 'My Little Lady' was not even heir apparent and her greatest treasures were the ladybird brooch Bobo had given her, Mummie and Daddy's silver bracelet, Mummie's coral and pearl necklet and the real pearls from 'Grandpapa England'.

Bobo ('PeepBo' the nursemaid would play with the Princess in the nursery until the name stuck) now guards the blue velvet brooch chest. Inside, laid out on separate trays, are all the diamonds, all the sapphires, all the emeralds – rather as, two floors down in the underground vaults at Buckingham Palace, the silver and gold plate is designated special shelves according to its status as suitable for a Number One or Number Two banquet.

JEWELS OF THE QUEEN

A few of the jewels in the Queen's overwhelming collection:

The historic Hanoverian diamond fringe tiara (1), set in 1830 using brilliants inherited from George III. It was worn by the Queen on her wedding day.

'Granny's tiara' of diamond festoons, scrolls and collet spikes (2). Originally given to the future Queen Mary in 1893 on her marriage by the Girls of Great Britain and Ireland.

The Jubilee Necklace of diamond trefoils with a pearl in the centre of each and a crown

and pearl pendant (3). One of the Queen's favourite necklaces, presented to Queen Victoria at the Jubilee of 1887 using the residue of money subscribed for the building of the Albert Memorial.

Sapphire and diamond necklace and earrings (4). A wedding present to Princess Elizabeth from her father King George VI on her marriage to Lt. Philip Mountbatten in 1947. She has since acquired a modern sapphire and diamond tiara.

Triple strand diamond collet necklace with triangular motifs (5). Made up in 1950 by George VI from spare royal gems.

Necklace and earrings of large square-cut aquamarines set in diamonds. A Coronation gift from the President and People of Brazil in 1953 (6). They later presented a matching bracelet and the Queen had an aquamarine tiara made to complete the suite.

Diamond bow brooches (7) made by Garrard for Queen Victoria in 1858 from her own diamonds. Part of a set of three.

Queen Mary knew her jewels intimately, giving them names like favourite children: the 'City' collar, the 'Kensington' bow brooch, the 'Surrey' tiara. When the Queen first inherited this vast 'Family' of jewels, the collection seemed daunting. But there is a new confidence today.

'She really does enjoy her jewels now,' says a former lady-in-waiting. Others speak of the enthusiasm with which she showed off the ruby and diamond tiara designed by Garrard and worn for the Canadian tour of 1982. That excitement reverberates all the way back to the girlish gasp of pleasure – heard by the world over a radio microphone – when she celebrated her twenty-first birthday with a gift of 21 unset diamonds.

Princess Elizabeth's childhood had been as sheltered as Princess Victoria's: a quiet domestic life peppered with occasional public appearances. In some ways they were a world, as well as a century, apart. In 1826, seven-year-old Princess Victoria was taken to meet the ageing, dissolute 'bewigged and bedaubed' George IV, who was living with his mistress at Royal Lodge Windsor, that same Royal Lodge where Princess Elizabeth was to watch her father, the King, hacking at the overgrown garden in his old tweeds. Exactly one hundred years after Princess Victoria's uncomfortable encounter with her Uncle King, in the summer of 1926, Princess Elizabeth Alexandra Mary was christened at Buckingham Palace, and was soon 'sitting up by herself in the middle of the huge chesterfield, like a white fluff of thistledown . . . Her fair hair is beginning to curl charmingly,' as the Duchess of York's lady-in-waiting Anne Ring described the baby.

A necklet of coral and pearls made from Mummie's necklaces, for Princess Elizabeth.

Like the future Queen Victoria in her plain cotton dress and simple coloured fichu, Princess Elizabeth and her sister Margaret Rose were dressed as simply as possible. Nanny 'Alah', as Mrs Clara Knight was called, did not approve of the modest flower-printed cotton frocks and cardigans that she was allowed, only occasionally, to exchange for proper princess party dresses, pink organdie frills with coral and real pearl necklaces.

The King seemed to inherit from his father a pathological conservatism. George V had used the same gold collar stud for 50 years, and the same set of hair brushes, periodically rebristled, and insisted that Queen Mary kept her skirts the same ankle length. When Princess Elizabeth was to have her first long frock as bridesmaid to her Uncle Harry of Gloucester, 'Grandpapa England' was concerned to keep the frocks short. Instead of the planned Empire line dress, Norman Hartnell made girlish confections of palest pink satin, the short skirts bordered with bands of ruched pink tulle. The frilly frocks came in useful on the annual family outing to the pantomime, when the princesses, longing to sit in the stalls as much as they begged to ride on a bus, hung over the side of the Royal Box with their father hanging on to their petticoats.

Symbolically the Duke and Duchess of York were hanging on to the girls' childhood. There was no Victorian contact with the darker side of life when their grandfather died in 1936. ('They are so young,' said the Duchess.) The Abdication was washed away in lessons at the swimming pool. The move to Buckingham Palace meant packing up the tack for the toy horses. The Coronation was new silver sandals, and dresses with silver bows and the first regal circlets – coronets made up from silver gilt by a theatrical costumier because the real royal thing – solid gold lined with crimson and velvet and edged with ermine – was far too heavy for slight girls of twelve and seven.

'Yes, the Crown does get rather heavy,' the Queen admitted on the day she was crowned. Cecil Beaton noted even at the age of 26 the 'unspoilt childishness of the smile', and the 'hair curled like a child's for a Christmas party'.

Twelve-year-old Princess Victoria sobbed her heart out as she watched the Coronation procession of her uncle William IV in 1831, because she was forbidden by her mother from taking part in the ceremony. At the same age, Princess Elizabeth could spy from the glass coach clouds and cupids, cherubs and nymphs chasing each other across the painted ceiling of the Coronation coach.

On that sunny spring day in 1937, she had looked out of the Palace window wrapped in an eiderdown and watched her toy coronation peepshow turn into the real-life procession. She saw her mother in a dress embroidered with the Scottish thistle, the English rose and the Welsh leek, as her own Coronation dress would be 16 years later. She saw the Koh-i-noor beaming from her mother's new crown and watched as the Coronation ring stuck on her father's knuckle just like Queen Victoria's in the history books. She stood on the balcony at Buckingham Palace between Mummie and Granny and looked down the Mall at the cheering crowd.

That scene on the balcony captures the three generations of royalty: Queen Mary, come through the trauma of the Abdication a stone lighter but weighed down with her jewels: the crown without its velvet cap on her wiry grey hair; seven diamond necklaces festooned like bunting round her neck; a diamond stomacher and the square Cullinan brooch at her bosom. Queen Elizabeth, Consort to the new King George VI, is in her crown and two rows of pearls and the Crown diamonds. The two Princesses are in their coronets.

At that Coronation of 1937, Princess Elizabeth could draw the distinction between the public and private life of the royal family. It was a line she walked as she took a bunch of violets to Granny on her birthday and then curtsied to her as Queen. However homely the evenings sitting at home with Mummie and Daddy, she knew that the King and Queen also conducted Court presentations in the throne room, where the Princesses would sit by the windows in their dressing-gowns for a 'fly's eye view' of the bejewelled women. The picnics in Scotland and the ponies at Windsor contrasted with the royal garden parties – three thousand people surging across the lawns with the little princesses in hand-smocked tussore silk frocks with matching knickers. Then all of a sudden Princess Elizabeth was grown up enough to be engaged and walked proudly through the crowds showing off her ring.

From the reign of George VI and his wife Elizabeth dates the division between public and private life that is exemplified by the royal jewels. Queen Victoria's domestic bliss with Prince Albert was still immensely grand. Even tea in old age at Osborne meant Victoria's presiding over the family with two turbaned Indian servants standing guard behind her. Edward VII and Queen Alexandra may have teased guests at Sandringham with parlour games and apple-pie beds, but they still dressed for dinner – and a diamond bandeau instead of the formal tiara would not do at all. When George V and Queen

Mary dined alone in the private apartments, 'The King wore a tail coat and the Garter and the Queen always put on a tiara for dinner,' according to their lady-in-waiting. Princess Alice of Gloucester remembers how, even at the relatively informal Balmoral, the ladies were expected to change for tea and again for dinner into high evening dress with gloves and jewellery.

King George VI and his wife changed all that. Lady Elizabeth Bowes Lyon, brought up in a large Scottish family, inevitably softened the stiffness of the royal Court, and she was the first Queen to accept the jewels as part of a stage setting for royalty.

The Abdication had altered the leading actors; the war changed the play. If Princess Elizabeth's adolescence had not been prolonged from 1939 to 1946 at Windsor, she might have come out with more of a flourish into society and been introduced to fine jewellery at an earlier and more impressionable age. As it was, the future Queen of England had her first tiara from Granny for her wedding and her first serious presents of jewellery – a sapphire and a diamond bracelet from her parents – when she was 18. After four years of playing at princesses in Christmas pantomimes, Lilibet, as her family called her, finally broke bud. She was allowed to have her own suite of rooms, her own lady-in-waiting and a new wardrobe from Norman Hartnell – pastel frocks with matching coats like Mummie's and evening dresses with full picture skirts. These replaced the girlish cotton dresses and even her father's tweed plus fours, which had been worn at Balmoral in the make-do-and-mend war years.

As Princess Elizabeth sat at the dressing table in her pink and chintz bedroom looking out towards Big Ben, she had few treasures to contemplate beyond the picture of Prince Philip of Greece (concealed under a blond naval beard) on her mantelshelf. Her jewels were mostly trinkets. The only serious necklace was the triple strand of pearls given to her by her grandfather before he died. Her brooches were all flowers and mostly in sapphires: a diamond leaf brooch with sapphire centre from her parents and another pair of sapphire flower brooches. She had a few other pieces suitable for a young girl, including a pair of aquamarine and diamond clips and pearl flower earrings that were a twentieth-birthday present from Queen Mary.

More flowers began to seed as the Princess started the very first of her public engagements. A diamond chrysanthemum with sapphire stamens – a favourite brooch worn for Princess Anne's christening – came from the owners of the ship *The British Princess* launched by Princess Elizabeth in 1946. ('The most lavish presentations were made by shipping companies when one launched one of their ships,' says Princess Alice of Gloucester. 'They seemed to have a tradition of always giving a piece of jewellery.')

Another flower jewel – an antique diamond brooch – sprouted on Princess Elizabeth's lapel after she launched the HMS *Vanguard*. In it the Family Firm left for South Africa, and three months later sailed back towards home and a waiting Prince Philip, while Princess Elizabeth danced a jig on deck out of 'sheer delight' at travelling home. Fifty-four years before, Princess May of Teck had jigged round her bedroom with the same pleasure on the day she got engaged.

Antique diamond bow brooch: presented to eighteen-year-old Princess Elizabeth by Messrs John Brown when she launched HMS Vanguard *in 1944.*

The tour of South Africa took Princess Elizabeth away from Philip but also away from the 'forlorn and frostbound' winter. 'It's like being stroked,' said Queen Elizabeth, as the *Vanguard* rode out the storms into calm winds and warm sunshine and anchored at Cape Town. There the royal family – and especially the pretty princesses – were fêted with gaudy enthusiasm before they set off in the White Train through the vast Veldt.

From South Africa, the royal family moved across to Rhodesia, where Princess Elizabeth received a twenty-first birthday present – an elongated diamond flower brooch representing the country's flame lily emblem and subscribed to by all the schoolchildren, black and white, of Southern Rhodesia. Princess Elizabeth pinned it proudly on to her crêpe frock; five years later she wore it on her sombre black coat as she flew home from Africa in mourning for her father in February 1952.

But now, in spite of the King's fatigue and concern about the harsh winter back in England, all was sunshine, as the princesses galloped out in the cool of the early morning with the King's equerry Peter Townsend, who was making his first indelible and dashing impression on 16-year-old Princess Margaret. The younger princess received her share of bounty as the royal party trekked through the arid South, through Mafeking, where the South African War had come to its end, to Kimberley, where three million pounds' worth of uncut diamonds were displayed and where Miss Mary Oppenheimer of the de Beers family stepped forward in her white party shoes and frock to make a presentation to the princesses. Inside the blue ground glass caskets, Lilibet's square, and Margaret's round, both decorated with gilded crowns, were uncut diamonds. By the time she was back home at Buckingham Palace, Princess Margaret, always more clothes-conscious than her sister, had made sketches of how her diamonds should be made up and shown them to her governess, Marion Crawford.

The mines of Africa had already poured their tributes into the British royal collection. The mighty Star of Africa and all the diamond Cullinan 'chips' had come from the stone discovered at the premier mine in Pretoria in 1905, and presented to King Edward VII as a peace offering by the people of Transvaal. The diamond lozenge tiara Cartier made up for Queen Elizabeth, the Queen Mother in her daughter's coronation year of 1953, used diamonds presented in 1901 by de Beers.

In the same year, Cartier made up the magnificent flower brooch from the world's most perfect pink diamond, presented to Princess Elizabeth for her wedding six months after the South African tour. The gem was mined in Tanganyika (now Tanzania) and offered by the reclusive Canadian royalist, Dr John T. Williamson, who owned a diamond mine, earned a personal fortune of two million pounds a year from it and found his only happiness in his homage to the British monarchy. Another eccentric millionaire had earlier enriched the Crown by leaving money to Queen Victoria which she used to build Balmoral Castle (Chapter 1).

And now, far from the blustery and rugged Scottish countryside, where Prince Philip had proposed to her when he stayed at Balmoral in the summer of 1946, Princess Elizabeth was 21. She celebrated her coming of age by

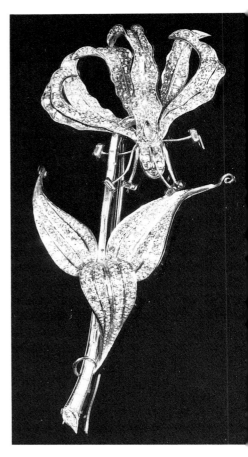

Flame lily brooch: a twenty-first birthday present from the children of Southern Rhodesia during the South African tour in 1947.

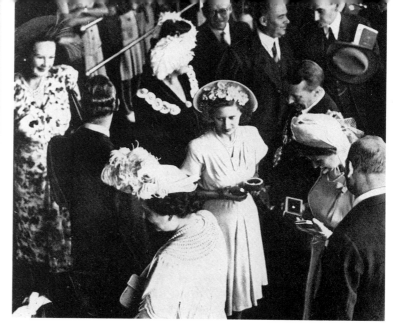

ABOVE Miss Mary Oppenheimer presents Princess Elizabeth with one flawless diamond from de Beers.

ABOVE RIGHT Prince Elizabeth and Princess Margaret Rose with Queen Elizabeth with their gifts.

RIGHT 'My best diamonds' the Queen still calls her twenty-first birthday present from the Government and Union of South Africa in 1947.

BELOW The twenty-one diamonds were made into a necklace and matching bracelet with the de Beers diamond in the bracelet centre.

broadcasting from Cape Town to the Dominions, promising 'that my whole life . . . shall be devoted to your service and the service of our great Imperial Commonwealth to which we all belong'. The speech came out in the same clear, piping voice which had been heard all over the Empire when Princess Elizabeth made her first broadcast in the dark days of the war in October 1940 at the age of fourteen and a half. As a twenty-first birthday present, from the Government and Union of South Africa, the Princess received 21 large diamonds that were made up as a long necklace and later altered to make a short necklace and matching bracelet. From her parents came more personal diamonds – a pair of twin brooches shaped like ivy leaves.

Princess Elizabeth married Lieutenant Philip Mountbatten on 20 November 1947 in a dress designed by Norman Hartnell which had white roses of York embroidered by hand in ten thousand pearls.

The fifteen-yard train embroidered with Boticelli blossoms curved like a horn of plenty across the floor as Princess Elizabeth took her vows in Westminster Abbey and posed for family pictures, flanked by her husband in his naval uniform and her young cousins Prince William of Gloucester and Prince Michael of Kent as pages dressed in tartan kilts. On her head was the diamond fringe tiara. Round her neck, two strands of historic pearls that she decided to wear only at the last moment. They had been on display at St James's Palace with the wedding gifts and the Queen's Private Secretary Sir John Colville had to force his way through the crowds, convince suspicious policemen of his mission and rush the pearls to the Palace.

Gifts from loyal subjects were accepted for the first time at a royal wedding and the nylon stockings, sent in pairs and solemnly displayed among the gorgeous array of wedding presents at St James's Palace, symbolised the end of the war, the loosening of rationing and restrictions and the sense of national celebration following national sacrifice. She possessed more pairs of nylon stockings than most British brides had seen throughout the threadbare war years.

Princess Margaret made a pretty bridesmaid in ivory silk tulle with a 'milky way' of star-shaped blossoms on the full skirt and pearls at her neck. Queen Elizabeth was in warm apricot brocade, Queen Victoria's pearl Jubilee brooch – a favourite for the next four decades – pinned at her garter ribbon. Queen Mary watched her granddaughter wed in grand gold tissue embossed with sea-blue chenille, her famous toque and majestic diamonds.

Queen Mary had at that time just begun to distribute her vast inheritance of jewellery. The centrepiece of the royal wedding present display was the diamond festoon and scroll tiara, with its brilliant upstanding collets, made for Queen Mary for her own wedding in 1893. There was also an eight-inch-long stomacher with its flowers and wreaths and ten lucent diamond drops – too opulent for post-war Britain except when broken into brooches, as Princess Elizabeth was destined to use it. A more approachable brooch was the diamond bow – originally a wedding present to Princess May from the County of Dorset and now passed on to her granddaughter. Other presents that Queen Mary had nurtured since her own marriage were the flowery bracelet with a ruby and diamond rose centre and leaf bands (from the County of Cornwall)

Princess Elizabeth on her wedding day in the Crown pearls and the Hanoverian diamond fringe tiara.

141

and bouton pearl earrings suspended from a dew-drop diamond (from the County of Devon). From the wealth of Indian gifts, Queen Mary chose two narrow Indian bangles studded with diamonds. All these presents – except perhaps the Indian bracelets – were indisputably Queen Mary's personal possessions.

On her marriage Princess Elizabeth received from her parents more presents of fine jewels; and from this point one can date the current confusion between Crown Jewellery, that passes automatically from one monarch to the next, and the private collection. Two superb necklaces of picked and graduated pearls, with a whole pearl as the clasp were a gift to their daughter from the King and Queen, but technically the pearls are Crown property. One of the heirloom necklaces contains 46 pearls, weighs 1,045 gr. and supposedly belonged to Queen Anne; the other is of 50 pearls, weighing 1,429.20 gr., and was originally a necklace of Queen Caroline, the wife of George II. These were the pearls salvaged by Queen Victoria precisely because of their English historic connections when the rest of Queen Charlotte's jewels were returned to Hanover in 1858. They were left to the Crown by Queen Victoria on her death in 1901, and Queen Mary refers to them in her Dress Book specifically as 'Crown Pearls'.

The Crown pearls, given to Princess Elizabeth on her marriage. TOP: *Forty-six pearls with whole pearl snap which belonged to Queen Anne.* BELOW *50 pearls, the inheritance of Queen Caroline, wife of George II. Queen Victoria fought off Hanoverian claims to the jewels because of their English historical connections.*

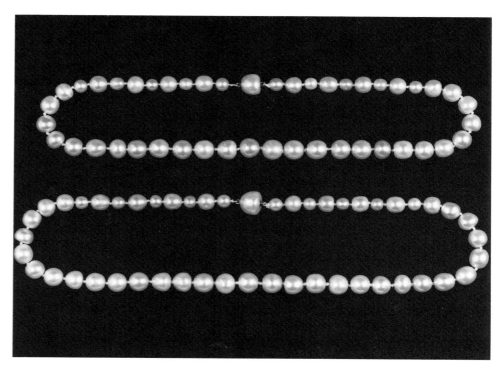

Were the other royal presents also family property, as the wedding presents to Princess Diana have been? The King in his own right gave to his daughter an important sapphire and diamond clusters necklace with a matching pair of earrings that were apparently en suite with the bracelet he had given the Princess on her eighteenth birthday. An elaborate ruby and diamond necklace

Right royal presents to Princess Elizabeth. LEFT: *a ruby and diamond necklace from her parents. The Queen is wearing it with her new ruby tiara in a colour plate with the Queen Mother.* RIGHT: *'Granny's tiara' – Queen Mary's diamond festoon and scroll tiara surmounted with 27 graduated brilliant collets.* FOREGROUND: *chandelier diamond earrings from the King and Queen. The Queen is wearing them in the photograph at the beginning of this chapter.*

from the King and Queen jointly seems to be of Indian workmanship, and the Queen, who very seldom wears it, specifically chose it for the official photographs for the Commonwealth Conference in New Delhi in December 1983. This would be in keeping with her policy of wearing jewellery appropriate to the particular country or foreign visitor – turquoises from Jordan on a State visit to that country; the Dagmar necklace to a gala ballet in Copenhagen; Empress Josephine's necklace when the French President Mitterand came on a State visit to London in 1984.

This 'Indian' necklace could have been a part of the torrent of gifts from India which was still producing a trickle of fine gems in 1947 on the eve of Independence. The Nizam of Hyderabad gave Princess Elizabeth a splendid floral diamond tiara with an English rose set among leafy tendrils. Like its companion diamond necklace, it had been designed by Cartier in Paris. Other Indian maharajahs were less cosmopolitan in their tastes. The Maharajah of Bundi had taken an antique Rajput headdress of gold set with pearls, rubies and diamonds and mounted it as a brooch. The Dominion of India sent two pairs of jewelled anklets set with brilliants and enamel drops mounted as a necklace. Mahatma Gandhi, the new ruler of India, spun a cloth on his own spinning wheel and sent it as an example of Indian craft. Queen Mary considered this native offering most indelicate and Princess Margaret darted ahead to hide the offending object when her grandmother toured the exhibition of gifts.

The presents for this royal marriage at the mid-point of the twentieth century make an interesting study for the state of the nations. Here is the dwindling band of European royalty playing a last reprise of grandeur. Family heirlooms from an earlier and more expansive era were dusted down and offered to the young Princess. There were only a few survivors from the gathering of the royal clans hosted by the Kaiser in Berlin in 1913. Prince and Princess Louis of Hesse, the descendants of Queen Victoria's daughter Alice, gave as their wedding present a Fabergé cigarette case with St George and the dragon picked out in enamel and diamonds. It had been a present to the German family in 1907 from Alicky of Hesse who became the last and ill-fated Russian Empress. An agate snuff box set with a ruby came from one of the last of the Romanovs, the impoverished Grand-Duchess Xenia, whose jewellery had been 'acquired' by Queen Mary 20 years before. Princess Andrew of Greece, the mother of Prince Philip, who described himself mockingly as 'dispossessed Balkan royalty' presented her own diamond tiara, just as she had given her diamond ring to be made into Princess Elizabeth's engagement ring. Prince Philip himself gave his bride a diamond bracelet – a gift repeated by Prince Charles in 1981 when he gave Lady Diana Spencer a diamond and emerald bracelet.

The more lavish presents came from the outposts of Empire or from the new Commonwealth: a necklace of 96 rubies (since broken up) in a carved ivory box from the people of Burma and a ruby and diamond pendant from the All-Burma Women's Freedom League. The South Africans, whose generous gifts of diamonds on the royal tour were displayed alongside the wedding presents, also gave a traditional gift of ostrich feather capes, just as they had to Princess Elizabeth's mother, Lady Elizabeth Bowes Lyon, on her wedding in 1923. The Tanganyikan Government presented an uncut diamond. From the grandly named Canadian Legion of the British Empire Service League came a gold maple leaf brooch set with diamonds. The newly created Earl Mountbatten of Burma, Philip's uncle Dickie, celebrated the fulfilment of his matchmaking dreams by giving the young couple a thoroughly modern cinema.

The last post of the recent war was still echoing through the gifts; the New Zealand disabled servicemen proudly presented Papua shell and gold jewellery they had designed and made themselves; the Disabled Sailors and Soldiers Workshop in Bournemouth made bird brooches. An England emerging from the shadow of the Blitz and still under wartime rationing could not allow its Princess the luxuries denied her future subjects. The only large public present was the Russian pattern diamond necklace (very like the royal tiara) from the City of London. This was a tradition that had started with the diamond necklace given to Princess Alexandra of Denmark on her wedding nearly a century earlier.

There were almost more jewel boxes – and very splendid ones – among the royal gifts than there were jewels to fill them: a tortoiseshell box with jewelled and enamel motifs; an ebony casket set with silver palm trees from the Sultan of Zanzibar and echoed 35 years later by the malachite box decorated with palms given to Princess Diana on her wedding. Norman Hartnell gave the most beautiful jewel casket of all – an antique French Empire box decorated with mother of pearl and ormolu with curving snake handles. It had once belonged to the Empress Josephine, and it would be nice to think that the Queen, with her sense of history, might now keep Empress Josephine's emerald necklace inside her Empire casket.

'Granny's tiara' as Queen Mary originally wore it with upstanding pearl spikes. The Duchess of Gloucester has inherited the pearl choker.

144

The Queen wears Queen Mary's tiara, with the Nizam of Hyderabad's English rose and foliate diamond necklace. The bow brooch was another wedding present from her grandmother – a present to Queen Mary from the County of Dorset on her wedding in 1893.

Princess Elizabeth set off for the Mountbatten family home at Broadlands with her new husband, now created Duke of Edinburgh, and with her best beloved corgi Susan snuggled under a travelling rug. Out of all the wedding presents, which included other brooches and bandeaux as well as smaller pieces of jewellery, what did the new bride actually wear?

The brief five-year span between wedding and Coronation is the clearest guide to the future Queen's taste, before her jewels became invested with the mystique of monarchy and before the myth grew that the abstemious sovereign only ever wears a diamond in the line of duty. Certainly those years belied another legend – that the Queen has never worn black, except for a visit to the Vatican. In that first summer after the wedding, Princess Elizabeth in black lace, with a large comb and a mantilla, danced until dawn at a ball given for the Edinburghs at Coppins, the home of the elegant Princess Marina. 'One can't really dance in a tiara,' Sir Henry 'Chips' Channon heard her complain. She wore a dramatic black dress of finely gathered taffeta with the Nizam of Hyderabad's diamonds. The tiara could be dismantled to make one large and two smaller diamond brooches.

Prince Philip was stationed in Malta just after the birth of their son and heir Prince Charles in 1948. There Princess Elizabeth could wear casual and colourful clothes as she played at being an ordinary wife (although the Maltese shopkeepers noticed that she was slow to count out her money in her first-ever informal shopping expeditions). Her favourite brooch was the diamond Naval crown her husband gave her. That other sailor Prince, later George V, gave Princess May a diamond anchor on her wedding day. By the time of the birth of Princess Anne in August 1950, the Princess's tastes in clothes were becoming more sophisticated. She chose from Norman Hartnell for the tour of Canada and Australia in 1951 an ensemble of olive green velvet, another in slate blue and a third in holly berry red with a black velvet collar. Just before this tour, Princess Elizabeth had her ears pierced and began to wear more dramatic earrings than her basic pearl studs – in particular the superb diamonds, containing every known cut and twinkling like the Palace chandeliers, which had been part of her parents' wedding present to her.

In 1954, just after the Coronation and before the six-month Commonwealth tour, the then Crown Jeweller, Cecil Mann, wrote an article in which he discussed the new Queen's favourite jewels. These included her grandmother's inheritance (for Queen Mary had died on 24 March 1953, leaving incalculable treasures to her grand-daughter).

It is fascinating to see how little this list varies from the jewels that the Queen is wearing 30 years later. First came the tiaras: 'Granny's tiara' with its diamond points and Queen Alexandra's Russian fringe given to her on her silver wedding in 1888 and first worn by the Queen to open Parliament in New Zealand in January 1954. Her other personal tiaras were the Nizam's wedding present; the bow knot tiara given to Princess Diana on her marriage and first worn by the Queen at a State banquet given by the Emperor of Ethiopia, who had presented a gold tiara chased in openwork with symbolic devices on her marriage; the Grand-Duchess Vladimir's interlaced circles of diamonds with 15 pearl drops – interchangeable with the Cambridge emeralds – was seen on

The Williamson pink diamond, given to Princess Elizabeth and made up as a flower brooch in 1953. Princess Anne copies Mummie's pearl necklace.

the Queen at the Royal Film performance in 1953 and has been worn consistently since.

The Crown Jeweller cited the broad band diamond bracelet given by Prince Philip to his bride as her favourite bracelet. Her favourite necklaces were the sapphires from her father, the Cambridge emeralds, the South African diamonds and a suite of square cut aquamarines and diamonds given by the President and people of Brazil for her Coronation. They added a further gift of a matching bracelet in 1958. The Queen removed the pendant on the necklace and had an aquamarine tiara made.

These jewels are all now so familiar to the royal dress designers that they submit sketches with the jewels drawn in. This might be a subtle way of giving advice. When the Queen was in San Francisco in 1983, the shoulder bows on her primrose yellow Hardy Amies dress met the diamond drop earrings, and nudged the ornate Jubilee necklace. Hardy Amies points out in mitigation that the royal yacht *Britannia*, buffeted by storms, had to be unpacked in a hurry. On the next tour, both the earrings and the bows had disappeared.

The Queen's personal jewels at the time of her accession were all representational: the sapphire flower brooches, the flame lily, the Williamson pink diamond flower and the basket filled with jewelled flowers that her parents gave her at the birth of Prince Charles. To them she added two more brooches received as gifts on the Commonwealth tour of 1953/4 – a diamond fern which recalled the embroidery on her mother's Coronation dress was presented by the women of Auckland, New Zealand and a large wattle spray in deep yellow diamonds – the Duchess of Windsor's favourites – given by the Australian Government on the same tour. It took the Queen away from her small children from before Christmas until the following summer. The five-year-old prince Charles was learning to read and showed off his skills to his parents over the telephone.

It is hard to judge at what precise point the young Queen began to see her jewels as part of the accoutrements of sovereignty. If, as a relative suggests, she was overwhelmed, even embarrassed, by her grandmother's inheritance, she may have been equally overawed by the symbolic role played by the Crown Jewels at her Coronation. She was, after all, only 26 when she walked down the nave at Westminster Abbey with her enormous velvet train spreading behind her. She had practised walking round with a sheet pinned to her shoulders just as the young Princess May of Teck had used a chenille tablecloth as a court train.

Cecil Beaton, royal photographer of the day, filled his grey top hat with sustaining sandwiches and Indian ink for his drawings. (When the diplomat Oliver Everett worked for the Prince of Wales, he used his upturned topper to carry Princess Diana's bouquets.) Beaton watched the Queen lead her retinue, 'her hair tightly curled around the Victorian diadem of precious stones' above her sugar-pink cheeks. She wore the diamond diadem to the Abbey, held her small expectant face up towards the Archbishop of Canterbury and the St Edward's Crown and then wore for the homeward Coronation procession the Imperial Crown of State that had been made for her following the pattern of Queen Victoria's crown of 1838: 250 diamonds and precious stones including the historic gems – St Edward's sapphire, the Black Prince's ruby, the pearl earrings of Elizabeth I, the Stuart sapphire and the second Star of Africa.

The most moving moment for the Queen was not the progress through the rain-soaked streets (the crowd no longer identified sunshine as 'Queen's weather' as they had with Queen Victoria). It was not the moment that she advanced to her 'great and lonely station' in her jewel-encrusted dress, its emblems of England and Empire embroidered on the satin skirt. Nor the sight of the peeresses, whom Norman Hartnell described as a delicious feast of 'damson jam of the velvet, bordered with the clotted cream of ermine and sprinkled with the sugar of diamonds'. It was rather the sacred moment of the Anointing, as her elaborate dress was covered with a plain white shroud, 'a funny little shift bordered with lace' Queen Victoria had called it. The Archbishop anointed the oil in the form of a cross and gave her the ring, the symbol of the marriage of sovereign to subjects. Then came the jewelled orb representing the world, and the Royal Sceptre to rule it. From it beams the largest diamond in the world, the Cullinan's Star of Africa.

Queen Alexandra was 57 when she was crowned after a lifetime in the shadow of the throne and she was deeply moved by the religious meaning of the Coronation. Queen Mary had been married for nearly 20 years; Queen Elizabeth for 14. The Queen was still on the threshold of life's experience and especially vulnerable to the symbolism of the Crown Jewels and their association with the most mystical and spiritual part of Kingship.

The Queen's attitude to her jewellery was, inevitably, affected by the Coronation and the extensive tours which followed it. The peoples of the Empire who had fought the war for King and his country expected a show of majesty. The Coronation, viewed round the world by 500 million people, had whetted an appetite for pageantry and suggested a noble and better world expressed in Great Britain by the idea of a 'new Elizabethan age'. The Queen from the beginning of her reign therefore began to divide her jewels into those which gave her personal pleasure – the brooches and family gifts – and those with particular historical associations. The grand gems were worn to suggest sovereignty and to set the Queen apart from her peers.

The collapse of formal society, which was never rebuilt after the war, and the erosion of aristocratic private life by post-war inflation, combined to make the Queen a bejewelled island from whom the rest of society receded. This reinforced in the mind of the Queen – who has little personal vanity – the identification of jewels with majesty. And because she herself makes such a clear distinction between her simple everyday appearance and the regal public display, in her subjects' minds her jewels are identified with the Crown.

The trouble for the jewellery historian is that this division is a matter of feeling, not fact. The jewels which the Queen reserves for state occasions and which seem to spell majesty are not necessarily Crown Jewellery. In fact, the reverse is mostly true. Queen Victoria's sapphire brooch is worn domestically for family occasions but it is actually a Crown brooch; the imposing tiaras are all personal property, except for the Indian regal circlet, which has stayed with the Queen Mother. The very jewels which are most closely identified with Queen Elizabeth II – the interlaced circle tiara with its emerald drops and the

Cambridge emerald necklace that she wears with it, 'Granny's' collet and spike tiara and all the Cullinan diamonds, even Queen Alexandra's Russian fringe tiara, are hers to alter, give away or even sell if she chooses. Probably the only pieces of Crown Jewellery which the public could identify, would be the diamond diadem and the Jubilee necklace with its diamond and pearl trefoils, the first a royal heirloom from the reign of George IV, the necklace left to the Crown by Queen Victoria in 1901.

In the desk drawer in the cubby-hole of an office at Garrard in Regent Street is the Crown Jeweller's bible. It is a slim morocco leather-bound book which contains the inventory of royal jewels in 1901, updated to the present time and giving details of jewellery broken up and altered as well as new pieces made up or received.

William Summers, the Crown Jeweller, is a tall man with upright carriage, sharp eyes more suited to a soldier than a jeweller and the well-polished shoes that are the courtier's trademark. He was an army man before he joined Garrard in 1949, working with the then Crown Jeweller Cecil Mann on the Coronation and particularly on the new crown for the Queen. Today he divides his time (he is a director of the company) between the demands of foreign potentates who hold their own investitures and coronations and are more consistent purchasers than the British royal family, and his work with the Crown and personal royal jewellery. Every spring, along with the first cuckoo, the jewels in the Tower are checked and cleaned and dusted down in conditions of absolute security that contrast with the casual taxi rides across town with a piece of the royal jewellery in a plastic bag, destined for Kensington Palace or the Queen.

Princess Margaret on her wedding day in 1960 in the deep diamond tiara bought for her from Lord Poltimore in a public sale at Sotheby's for £5,500. It can be worn as a full-size tiara, a small circlet or as a necklace.

Part of the royal jewellery is kept underground in the vaults at Garrard, some of it still with faded labels in Queen Mary's handwriting giving the family history or provenance. 'I gave a present from my great-grandfather, to my great-grandson 168 years later,' Queen Mary recorded proudly as she presented a silver cup and cover given by George III when the infant Prince Charles was christened in the Music Room at Buckingham Palace. She was the last sovereign to survey the royal jewel collection. Working from the inventory of jewels taken at the end of Queen Victoria's reign in the morocco-bound book by the man from Garrard, seven separate lists were drawn up, the Crown Jewels in the tower and six others:

1. Jewels left to the Crown by Her Majesty Queen Victoria.
2. Jewels left by Her Majesty the Late Queen Victoria, the property of His Majesty the King (not Crown Jewels although some items have subsequently been given to the Crown).
3. Jewels the property of King George V.
4. Jewels left to 'His Majesty Edward VII by Her Majesty Queen Victoria and hereafter considered as belonging to the Crown and to be worn by all future queens in right of it'.
5. Jewels given to the Crown by Her Majesty Queen Mary 1912.
6. Jewels given to the Crown by His Majesty King George V 1912.

These lists dividing 'Crown' from 'personal' jewellery were made in 1912 at the beginning of the reign of George V. The aim was to save future royal generations from the embarrassment caused by Edward VII's will, which had left his wife all 'his jewels, ornaments, articles of Art of vertu, curiosities and other chattels' for her to select her favourite pieces and hand the rest over to the new king. The jewel that Queen Alexandra was most attached to was the historic diamond diadem, which was finally handed over to Queen Mary in time for the 1911 opening of Parliament.

These lists of jewellery were with the Lord Chamberlain in 1957, at the time that Lord Twining was researching his book *The Crown Jewels of Europe*, published in 1960, and had apparently been kept up to date. According to the Lord Chamberlain's office, they were sent to the Royal Archives at Windsor. They cannot be traced today.

From the information that Lord Twining gleaned, which he published in his book and which appears in his private research papers lodged at Goldsmith's Hall, it is possible to re-create the lists of Crown Jewellery (published in full in Appendix A). This information shows that no major piece designated 'Crown' in 1912 subsequently 'disappeared' from the royal collection at the time of the Abdication; that no presents given to Queen Victoria or Edward VII, from India or elsewhere, were ever listed as Crown property; that the Queen is wearing most of the pieces of Crown Jewellery which were handed down to her; and that the vast part of her collection is personal, unless she has designated it as Crown during her reign, as suggested by the words of the Lord Chamberlain ('In no practical sense does the Queen regard . . . the items as being at her personal disposal' – at the time of the Select Committee in 1971).

The Crown Jewellery that the Queen wears consists of the diamond diadem, the diamond collet necklace, the diamond fringe and other diamonds, the Crown pearls, the Jubilee necklace. There are various brooches, including Queen Victoria's sapphire and the diamond bows. The regal Indian tiara set

New jewels. Princess Margaret in the Poltimore tiara bought for her on her marriage. CENTRE: *Queen Mother in the modern tiara made from South African diamonds. She wears it with Princess Alexandra's necklace and the brooch her husband gave her on their marriage in 1923.* RIGHT: *The Queen wears the new sapphire and diamond tiara she had made to go with the sapphire and diamond clusters necklace and sapphire earrings her father, George VI, gave her as a wedding present.*

with rubies, the crown ruby necklace and the Jubilee brooch have all remained with Queen Elizabeth the Queen Mother.

The only Indian jewellery designated Crown were pieces *taken by conquest* after the annexation of the Punjab from the treasury at Lahore. These are the mighty Koh-i-noor itself, a girdle of carved emeralds originally from the trappings of a horse, the carved Timur ruby, the four-strand pearls with a ruby snap. There is also an enormous cat's eye brooch weighing 313 carats, set in diamonds, taken, again by conquest, from the King of Kandy and presented to Queen Victoria.

A very few of the Indian gems given as presents to members of the royal family were given to the Crown by King George V and Queen Mary. These consisted of two armlets set with spinel rubies, one given to Edward VII at his Coronation, the other to Queen Mary by the Maharajah of Jaipur at the Delhi durbar in 1911. Queen Mary gave them both to the Crown in 1912.

One Indian necklace from among the three chests of trophies presented to the Prince of Wales during his tour of 1875/6 has survived. This was a necklace of 14 lasque diamonds, four pearls, three emeralds and six cabochon rubies, given by Maharajah Scindiah and placed in the Indian collection in 1926. A snap for this necklace made out of a ruby ring given to Queen Victoria by the Maharajah of Mysore in 1862 was given to the India collection by George V at the same time. The date of 1926 is significant, because it was just after the death of Queen Alexandra and suggests that she held these jewels as personal property. Other personal jewels might also have been divided among her other children and grandchildren, including the Prince of Wales who might have given them to Mrs Simpson (Chapter 4).

The real significance of these late bequests of Indian jewels is that they confirm the view that all gifts given from overseas to a member of the royal family are *considered to be private offerings*. This is contrary to some of the statements made on receipt of the jewels. When King Edward VII accepted 'for myself and successors the valuable gift of the Cullinan diamond' as a peace offering from the Transvaal after the end of the South African war, he promised that he would cause 'this great and unique diamond to be kept and preserved among the historic jewels which form the heirlooms of the Crown'. In the event, a deal was done with Asscher of Amsterdam that the jeweller would keep the cleavings of the stone. Therefore, the two large stones were placed in the Crown Jewels in the sceptre and the Imperial State Crown respectively. The 'chips' were purchased by the Union Government of South Africa in 1910 and presented to Queen Mary after Edward VII's death. She considered them her personal property and her granddaughter, the Queen, inherited them on that basis. The Queen wore the Cullinan brooch for a visit to Asscher's in Amsterdam in 1958. The head of the firm, who had fainted when he originally cleaved the mighty stone, saw as a frail old man the flawless pear-shaped diamond dangling from the lapel of the Queen of England.

At the time of the Delhi durbar Queen Mary accepted two emeralds from the Maharanee of Patiala with the words 'your jewels shall pass to future generations as an imperial heirloom' although they were not included in the lists of Crown Jewellery in 1912 or 1926.

In the autumn of 1953, the Queen set off on her grand Commonwealth Coronation tour, landing at Tonga, where the munificent and enormous Queen Salote had laid on a London taxicab ordered in England at the time of the Coronation. The Queen went on to New Zealand and Australia, where she lifted her pearls from her bare neck to prevent sunburn marks as she drove through the crowds in an open car. She learned to give them 'my best bits' – the tiaras and regal necklaces – at the evening receptions. Since that international victory parade, the Queen has made seven more visits to Australia; she has been to Commonwealth Conferences and made State visits in Europe; she has shaken 2,500 hands in Chile and been greeted by Republican Presidents in America, by crowned heads in Holland or Denmark. There have been altogether 103 overseas tours since the Queen came to the throne in 1953, and from them has come an enormous number of gifts, from the baby crocodile in a biscuit tin in Gambia in 1961, to the painting of her horse from President Mitterand in 1984. Among these gifts have been many magnificent jewels.

'Too kind,' the Queen will murmur as she is handed yet another ruby and diamond brooch or one of the more glittering offerings from the last of Empire or the new-rich desert kingdoms. The gift is handed to a lady-in-waiting, filed at home and brought out again on the next tour or a visit from the donor to Buckingham Palace.

Without the most elaborate and painstaking research, it is impossible to assess just how much jewellery the Queen has been given since those first South African diamonds; the Rhodesian flame lily; the wattle diamond brooch and the fine opal and diamonds from Australia in 1954; or the tiny diamond watch the French Government gave in 1958 to replace the one they had given her mother 20 years before, which she had given her daughter and which had been lost in the grounds of Sandringham.

Those early jewels were worn and enjoyed and flashed around with pleasure ('My best diamonds!'). Now the stiff new jewel boxes, with their buff velvet mounts and their white satin interior lids embossed discreetly by Garrard, or by the Arabs' favourite Asprey, are simply absorbed into the royal collection and ignored, occasionally emerging from this vast submerged pool like bubbles rising to the surface. When the Queen suddenly appears in an unfamiliar jewel – turquoises in Jordan, a lampshade fringe of diamonds in Dubai, a different tiara in Riyadh (in fact given by King Faisal on a State visit to Britain in 1967), you can be certain that the Queen is paying her host a gracious compliment by courtesy of the royal filing system. Occasionally the donors themselves may display gifts according to their local customs, as when a suite of magnificent sapphires and a solid gold camel from Sheikh Rashid of Dubai were exhibited alongside the basic royal silver salver. A photograph of the Queen wearing a pink and gold spangled dress, her 'best bits' and a big smile when she was presented with jewels by the Amir of Bahrain, was turned into a postcard and put on sale for tourists at the Gulf airport.

The snuff boxes, cuff links and framed photographs with which the Prince of Wales matched the bounty of the Indian maharajahs a century ago are still standard gifts today, just as they were when an ashen uncrowned Queen

Elizabeth completed the civilities at Sargana lodge in Kenya before flying home
to her father's funeral.

Today, not one single piece of presentation jewellery is *ever* worn except for
reasons of duty. The Queen will complete a tour on which she has been given

*'I get more and more like Granny,'
says the Queen. On her fiftieth
birthday she wore Queen Mary's
pearl and diamond brooch and
Granny's diamond stud and pearl
earrings which were a wedding
present to Queen Mary from the
County of Devon.*

*Queen Mary wears the pearl brooch
at Prince Charles's christening in
1948.*

fine jewels wearing the same familiar pieces – the circle tiara, the Cambridge emeralds, the Jubilee necklace, as though these pieces were all Crown Jewellery and anything else unsuitable. As we have seen, most of the jewellery she wears today is essentially the same as when she was first Queen. The only important new pieces are those she has had made herself, like the ruby and diamond tiara, the diamond necklace with triangular motifs and the four-strand pearls with an elliptical centre which she lent to the Princess of Wales for the Hampton Court Banquet with Queen Beatrix of the Netherlands. The conclusion drawn by her subjects is that the Queen does not have that much jewellery and certainly very few *new* jewels that might draw attention to the royal collection.

The reason for this must flow from the personality of the Queen herself. She is a shy, private, unshowy person, even though her face flares into its smile and her tinkling laugh can surprise people more used to the impenetrable glass wall that slides between sovereign and subjects. 'I get more and more like Granny,' says the Queen, and when you have stepped slightly out of line and she takes a deep, swelling breath and faces you with a still stare, she seems frozen in Queen Mary's image. She is certainly much more like her reserved, dutiful father than her outgoing mother. 'A simple, chattering, sweet-hearted round-faced young woman in pink . . . her wrists twinkling with diamonds,' was how Virginia Woolf described the Queen Mother as a young woman. The Queen may have had that luminous sparkle, but it was switched off by the war, her father's death and her accession, although she can still be funny and indiscreet and rival Princess Margaret's talent for mimicry as she impersonates garden party guests teetering across the lawn in their unaccustomed high heels.

One external influence on her has been Prince Philip, who is also impatient with the outward fuss of fashion. (He is unlikely to find a royal occasion suited to the gold sword with a mother-of-pearl inlaid handle with rubies and diamonds embedded in its scabbard – a gift to him on the Gulf Tour of 1979.) Yet he will give his wife presents like the enamel and gem set necklace in the Queen's perennially favourite flowers, which he bought from a discreet jeweller who also furnishes presents for Princess Diana from Prince Charles. Prince Philip is interested in modern art and design and might have been the moving force for change: the shortening of the South African diamonds to their present length and the new necklace made from gems in store.

On the other side is Bobo MacDonald, who is the keeper of the royal jewels as well as the Queen's dresser and who, right from the earliest days of the royal marriage, was on Her Majesty's side of the interconnecting bedrooms as the young couple chatted through the half-open door. Today the Queen is more likely to be reading a summary of the day's proceedings in Parliament, pinned to her dressing-table mirror, while her hairdresser Charles Martyn threads her hair through the tiara mount. Queen Victoria used hairdressing time equally profitably by reading improving history books.

Miss MacDonald is neat, colourful, conventional in her knife-pleated shirt-waister dresses in bright prints. Dress designers suggest that Bobo, a quarter of a century older than the Queen, has a baleful effect on her appearance, discouraging her royal mistress from sartorial adventures and stopping her from making over some of the jewels, or at least shortening the unfashionably long pearls or following Princess Margaret's lead in patronising modern jewellers.

Another theory, expressed by the ladies-in-waiting, is that the Queen is at heart a countrywoman and simply does not care about clothes and jewels, as opposed to the more cosmopolitan and urbanised Princess Margaret or Queen Mary, who commented on the Badminton estate in the war 'So that's what hay looks like!' This idea is difficult to accept when one considers that the Queen has been exposed to glittering evening galas and state occasions throughout her reign. Lady Elizabeth Bowes Lyon was brought up in the country and in Scotland yet found no difficulty in dressing up in diamonds.

'Mindful of the Church's teaching that Christian marriage is indissoluble, and conscious of my duty to the Commonwealth, I have resolved to put these considerations before any others,' said Princess Margaret on 31 October 1955, as she quenched the fire of gossip that had smouldered since she had first flicked a scrap of fluff off the shoulder of Group Captain Peter Townsend at the Queen's Coronation. She went on to say, in her statement of abdication from the man she loved, 'I have reached this decision entirely alone.' Yet it is hard not to see in her earlier words an echo of her sister's, or to read them as the guiding principles of the Queen's life.

The Queen's genuine and joyful surprise at the welling-up of enthusiasm during the Silver Jubilee celebrations of 1977 suggests that Elizabeth II, like her grandfather George V, could hardly believe that the people loved her 'for herself'. She has brought up her children with firm Christian principles. 'I'm for it,' she said of marriage and the family when she celebrated her Silver Wedding in 1972 and made the guests smile by saying, 'I think everyone will concede that today of all occasions I should begin my speech with "My husband and I".' She put duty above family by waiting a decade before having her 'second' family of Prince Andrew and Prince Edward in 1960 and 1964. She feels more deeply about the unity of the Commonwealth than most of her subjects. She was perplexed at the religious veneration offered to her by her first Prime Minister Winston Churchill – and laughed at his frock coat just as Queen Victoria's mentor, Lord Melbourne, had laughed at his Queen's hairstyles. But she is a religious woman and she has a spiritual belief in the sacred calling of monarchy.

To the Queen, her jewels, the ones she wears to present herself to the people, 'to see and be seen', are as much a part of the special indefinable mystique of sovereignty as are the Crown Jewels themselves. To alter them would be unthinkable, not because the jewels themselves are sacred, but because they have been invested with awe by being worn by and seen on the Queen of England. The gifts from overseas are not touched because it would be rude, hurtful and tactless to do so.

Tact has played a major part in the Queen's make-up since the polite Princess Elizabeth told her sister before a garden party: 'If you do see someone in a funny hat, you must *not* point at it and laugh.' Princess Margaret pranced through the 1960s in beetle-patterned stockings and mini-skirts; she and her design-conscious husband Lord Snowdon eagerly embraced the new. The

'Albert's brooch': the sapphire and diamond brooch given to Queen Victoria by her husband in 1840.

Princess Anne wears one of the copies of Queen Victoria's brooch that Prince Albert had made for his elder daughters. When one came on to the market, the Queen bought it back for her own daughter.

The Queen of diamonds: Her Majesty wears Grand-Duchess Vladimir's tiara and earrings framed by diamonds, both inherited from Queen Mary. The Jubilee diamond and pearl necklace was Queen Victoria's. The brooch is an heirloom from the Queen's great-grandmother, the Duchess of Teck. Queen Mary wears the diamond bracelet in the picture at the beginning of Chapter 3. The diamond watch came from the Swiss Federal Republic. On the pink and blue watered silk ribbons are the Royal Family Orders of George V and VI.

Top left The young mother with husband Philip, Prince Charles, aged two, and his baby sister Anne in 1950. The diamond flower petal brooch with raised sapphire stamens was one of the first official gifts — at the launch of the ship *British Princess* in 1946.

Top centre The Queen's "happy" brooch which she wears for family celebrations. It once belonged to Queen Mary's mother, Princess Mary Adelaide, Duchess of Teck. The pearls were a present from "Granpapa England", King George V.

Top right The Queen inherited from Queen Mary the heart-shaped brooch set with the fifth part of the fabulous Cullinan diamond. It is the centrepiece of an emerald and diamond stomacher.

Left A close-up of the 24-carat Williamson Pink diamond, made up by Cartier as a jonquil brooch in Coronation year. The petals are marquise diamonds; the stem baguettes.

Above The Queen wears the brooch, made up from the gem given by the reclusive millionaire Dr John T. Williamson, a Canadian geologist who owned a diamond mine in Africa.

Above A corgi's ear brushes the most valuable brooch in the world — a square-cut diamond of 62 carats and a pear-shaped 92-carat diamond — the third and fourth parts of the Cullinan. The Queen calls this brooch "Granny's Chips".

Far right Queen Alexandra's Russian fringe tiara, given to her as a silver wedding present in 1888, is worn by the Queen with the triple diamond necklace made up by George VI in 1950 from spare diamonds. The true lovers' knot in diamonds is one of five bow brooches bequeathed by Queen Mary.

Above right The Cambridge Emeralds. The stones were won in a lottery, left to Queen Mary's mother, given by her brother Frank to his mistress and recovered in 1911. The bow-knot brooch was originally a wedding present to Queen Mary from the County of Dorset.

Right A rare glimpse of the Crown amethysts. A suite of jewels which originally belonged to Queen Victoria's mother, the Duchess of Kent.

Top left The diamond fringe necklace of brilliants and baguettes was a gift from King Faisal of Saudi Arabia. With it the Queen wears "Granny's tiara".

Top right Square-cut aquamarines, a Coronation gift from the President and People of Brazil. They added a matching bracelet five years later.

Right The Queen receiving a gift from Sheikh Isa Bin Sulman al Khalifa, Amir of Bahrain. He put this picture on sale as a postcard.

Above Exchange of gifts with Sheikh Rashid of Dubai in 1979: decoration and silver salver *v.* suite of sapphires and diamonds from Asprey and solid gold camel and gold palm tree hung with ruby dates. It is now on the royal yacht *Britannia*.

Queen trod carefully through the new morality in her sensible black shoes and unchanging flesh-coloured stockings. She understood intuitively that the monarchy has a delicate role to play in setting public standards and taste and in maintaining its mystique in a democratic age.

The monarchy also has its critics. The first constitutional crisis of her reign, when the Profumo scandal brought down Harold Macmillan's Government in 1963, followed closely on personal attacks on the Queen and her entourage by Malcolm Muggeridge and, particularly, by Lord Altrincham in 1957. 'When she has lost the bloom of youth,' he wrote, 'the Queen's reputation will depend far more than it does now, upon her personality.' Altrincham, who renounced his title and became plain John Grigg, accused the Queen's Court of being tweedy and stuffy. The Labour MP Willie Hamilton complained of the high cost of royalty and its parasites. Prince Philip's revelations in 1969 that the royal family were almost 'in the red' prompted the inquiry into the Civil List. Periodic rumblings are still heard about the size of the new 'royal mob'.

Perhaps that is why the Queen herself, who was obliged to move the traditional family Christmas from Sandringham to Windsor to accommodate her burgeoning relatives, gives unshowy presents. ('One felt that the donors had always erred, if at all, on the side of economy,' said the royal governess tactfully.) Royal present-giving has come a long way since Fabergé's gee-gaws tumbled out of their crested boxes to Queen Alexandra's childlike cries of delight. The only breath of criticism that the Queen has ever uttered to her mother has been a private moan at her 'extravagance'.

Jewels are so flamboyant a sign of opulence that the Queen has been anxious to damp down their glittering fire. Everybody knows that a royal filly 'The Height of Fashion' from the Queen's personal stud was sold to a Gulf sheikh for over a million pounds and that the Queen bought Gatcombe Park outright as a wedding present for Princess Anne. But it still does not do to be showering her new daughter-in-law with diamonds.

The Queen has resolved for herself the conflict between royal economy and thrift and the need to be seen wearing the royal jewels, by elevating some to quasi-public status – and ignoring the rest. She has not actually made over the jewels to the nation, yet she suggests that they are more than personal, part of some indefinable 'royal heritage'. This paradox between public and private is neatly expressed by a childhood phrase of Princess Margaret's: 'It is yours *and* mine.' That was her reply to the playwright J. M. Barrie when he asked whom the cracker that lay between their plates at Balmoral nursery tea belonged to. Barrie immortalised the line on stage and paid Princess Margaret one penny royalty every time it was used.

The system of keeping the royal jewels public, yet private, of amassing a vast store of jewellery as gifts – yet never wearing them – and of suggesting that the jewels are worn for duty rather than for pleasure, works for the Queen. She will hand on to the next generation a magnificent collection of jewellery, embalmed in the style of an earlier age, untouched for perhaps half a century.

She will also present for a future, more fashion-conscious Queen a dilemma: are the royal jewels a living, changing, personal collection to adore and enjoy? Or should they be preserved for sovereign *and* subjects as a national heritage?

Princess of Jewels

'At the far end of the room sat the King of the Gorms on a huge
throne made from a single amethyst and studded with garnets.'

HRH The Prince of Wales,
The Old Man of Lochnagar

In midsummer 1983, two years after Lady Diana Spencer had become the new
Princess of Wales, Prince Charles was looking for a present for her 22nd
birthday on 1 July. They had just come back from Australia, their first overseas
tour and their first public challenge. Australia already held a special place in
their lives, for it was there that Diana had gone for a last lingering taste of
freedom when their engagement was still a secret and her mother 'was
determined to have what my daughter and I both knew to be our last holiday
together'. Mrs Shand-Kydd was echoing the sentiments of King George VI
when he took the Family Firm, 'us four', off to South Africa just before
Princess Elizabeth's engagement to Prince Philip of Greece was made public.

Prince Charles had set his heart on one particular jewel for his wife – a solid
gold koala bear charm to hang on the bracelet that is her husband's most
personal and private gift to her. For each birthday, or to commemorate some
special moment, he presents her with a significant charm – things that are
never seen in public because the young couple have already drawn a clear line
in jewels as in friends, clothes and the rest of their lives, between the royal and
private worlds.

The koala bear that would have been so easy to pick up in Australia itself
was hard to find among the young jewellers that Prince Charles has started to
patronise. A discreet inquiry from an equerry stirred workshops into a lather
of activity – like the time when the designer Lexi Dick had turned out a white
and yellow gold necklace of sapphire flowers before the wedding. The
commission was completed from sketch pad on 1 July, when Princess Diana
herself decided on a central motif of Prince of Wales feathers instead of the
suggested unicorn, to Buckingham Palace, in just three weeks. The young
jewellery designer felt justifiably proud of her achievement.

But they are all proud and pleased, these young designers, who have been
picked out by Prince Charles to create the private jewels – the necklet of slate
grey and clotted cream baroque pearls, by Leo de Vroomen; Wendy Ram-

*The Princess of Wales's first taste
of the glittering inheritance. She
borrowed the diamond drop
necklace given to the Queen
by an Arab Prince.*

*The Queen wears the drop necklace
with 'Granny's tiara'.*

shaw's pretty, witty gold pin that plays on all the stuffy Prince of Wales motifs, with its tribal tuft of five different coloured feathers; the elegant work of David Thomas; even the solid gold powder compact – a little heavy, perhaps, for those slim evening bags clutched under the Princess's arm, but a present chosen with love and thought by her husband. It seemed symbolic of the sophisticated new face Princess Diana has shown to the world since Prince Charles made his first tentative steps towards marriage in a cabbage patch in the country.

His big present to her, the wedding present, was quite different – an important emerald and diamond antique bracelet bought from a serious jeweller to which he had been introduced by the royal family, and especially recommended by his grandmother, Queen Elizabeth, the Queen Mother.

Prince Charles, to the surprise of anyone who still thinks of him as Action Man Prince, from his days at school at Gordonstoun and his prowess on the polo field, has aesthetic and cultural leanings. He has more than a touch of his great-grandmother Queen Mary and shares a passion for romantic opera with Queen Victoria. He is even weaning his wife away from pop music and towards his own tastes, so that she leapt to her feet at Covent Garden to give an ovation to Luciano Pavarotti, the pearls that edged her dress quivering as she clapped.

Fine feathers: Prince of Wales emblem for an 18-carat yellow and white gold flower necklace set with cabochon sapphires designed by Lexi Dick.

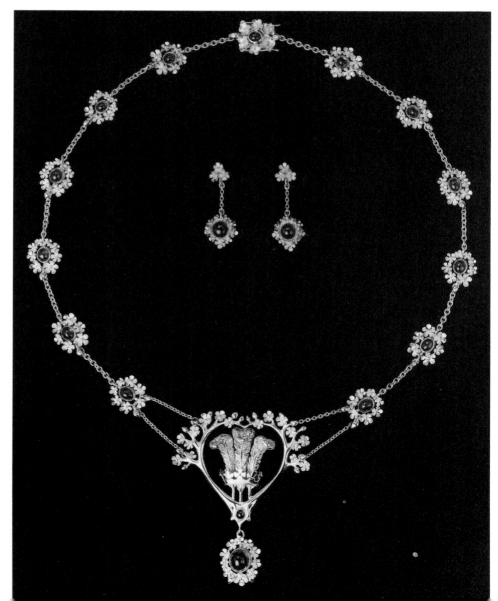

The five-strand choker with its tear drop pendant pearl that bobbed at Diana's throat beneath the jaunty apricot hat of her going-away outfit was popularly assumed to be the Prince's present to his new Princess of Wales. In fact, it was a wedding present to her sister Sarah, and worn by her to the wedding ceremony itself – just as Sarah had worn the Spencer tiara, with its swirls and fleurettes of diamonds, to her own wedding at the Spencer ancestral home at Althorp the previous year. There are other jewels in the family: Diana's stepmother the Countess Spencer is a client of Van Cleef and Arpels; her mother has a bold three-strand pearl necklace with a flower clasp similar to the royal heirloom choker now worn by Princess Anne. Mrs Shand-Kydd lent her youngest daughter the diamond earrings that Diana wore as her only jewellery – apart from the ring – on her wedding day.

But as Lady Diana Spencer she did not have access to any really important jewels, which is why Collingwood's (one of the three jewellers to have the coveted Royal Warrant to the Prince of Wales) lent an impressive diamond necklace with pendant motifs and matching chandelier earrings for the official engagement photographs.

Prince Charles's 'official' jewellers follow the royal pattern set by his mother and grandmother, with the significant exception of Garrard, the Crown Jewellers. Prince Charles patronises Asprey in Bond Street, Wartski, round the corner in Grafton Street, where its owner Kenneth Snowman has a particularly close relationship with the royal family, and Collingwood of Conduit Street.

Lord Snowdon photographed Lady Diana in a sea-green taffeta dress, against a fine tapestry, in an apparent re-creation of Sir Joshua Reynolds's portrait of her famous ancestor Georgiana, Countess Spencer, who also wore Diana's favourite black ribbon velvet choker. But the future Queen Diana's borrowed jewels created the first of two royal jewel fiascos, when they were returned to Collingwood's and subsequently offered for sale in Amsterdam alongside the royal portrait and tagged with the tale that the penurious Spencers were selling up the family diamonds to pay for their daughter's wedding. The second embarrassment was that the sapphire and diamond engagement ring had previously been featured – £28,500 price tag and all – in a Garrard catalogue, just as the Emanuels' closely guarded wedding dress had been displayed in the pages of *Vogue* magazine and Diana's sapphire blue engagement day outfit offered mail order to Harrods' account customers.

Jewel pool: the new Princess of Wales took the choker off her sister Sarah's neck on the royal wedding day.

The 'Miss Diana' who was teaching at the Young England kindergarten in Pimlico had one piece of jewellery which was as familiar then as the bow knot tiara and its tremblant pearls – a present from the Queen – is now. The gold 'D' which she wore on a chain round her neck when the photographers stood her in front of the sun and Prince Charles teased her about her 'spectacular' legs, was a birthday present from her school friends at West Heath. This is the ladylike, academically undemanding school which Diana left in the summer of the Jubilee year of 1977. She wore two other favourite trinkets as a schoolgirl: a gold Russian wedding ring on her little finger and a fine silver bracelet with hearts on it – a forerunner of the charm bracelet and an echo of the chain of crosses that Mrs Simpson wore as a talisman on the day she married the Duke of Windsor.

Lady Diana Spencer may have had little to declare on her marriage but her charm, her youth and her genius for being photographed, but she was quickly steered towards suitable young British dress designers; she was made up and coiffed by experts; and a magic wand was waved over the empty jewel case her father reputedly gave his daughter as her present. There were other boxes too in that heap of gifts from the grand and the humble – a gold decorated box set with diamonds from the Queen of Thailand; a bold heraldic coffer from a Scottish laird and the green slab of malachite with fabulous jewels already inside it from the Crown Prince of Saudi Arabia. Princess Elizabeth had been overwhelmed with decorative boxes on her wedding day, from a domed coffer in old rose velvet decorated with embossed metalwork to a tortoiseshell box with jewelled and enamel motifs.

Princess Diana's first great jewel was the present from her new mother-in-law – the tiara of undulating diamonds curving into lovers' knots of diamonds from which hang 19 perfect drops of milk white pearls. This was another Queen Mary heirloom, a tiara made up for her by Garrard in 1914 using some of her existing jewels, including the three superb rows of pearls originally made by Garrard and given to her on her wedding in 1893 by the Combined Counties – as the name implies, a grouping of various different counties who had all contributed towards a wedding present for Princess May. The original tiara had a row of detachable upstanding pearls, which was how Queen Mary first wore it.

It is intriguing to speculate – for there are no hard historical facts about this tiara – why Queen Mary ordered a new tiara at this moment of political uncertainty in Europe, compounded by unrest in Ireland. 'God grant that this year may be a peaceful one and that the clouds over these dear Islands may disperse,' she wrote in her diary at the start of January 1914.

The fact that Queen Mary used her own jewels to make up the lovers' knot tiara suggests that the design came from her, rather than from Garrard, for whom this tiara is, in any case, quite untypical. Garrard's grandiose, majestic and much more ornate taste is seen in the new crown, with its imposing diamond fleur-de-lis and the central, breathtaking Koh-i-noor diamond, which Queen Mary wore for the Coronation in 1911.

Garrard had also redesigned the sceptre to take that other enormous diamond, the greater 'Star of Africa'. At the same time a group of ladies with the first name Mary had combined to order for their Queen and namesake a set of Garter Insignia as a Coronation gift. The garter badge, star, the diamond encrusted Garter ribbon itself and the shoulder brooch (now worn by the Queen) are all formal, imposing pieces completely different in style from the delicate, airy drop pearl tiara. Even the Chaplet made for the Investiture of the Prince of Wales in the summer of 1911 was a traditional, stately diadem of cross motifs and fleur-de-lis. Under Lord Snowdon's guidance, Prince Charles went to a modern goldsmith for his Investiture coronet in 1969.

The bow knot tiara with its pendant drops is much more typical of the work of Cartier in this period and more particularly of the *kokoshniks* or *tiares russes* made for the Romanov royal family. The interlaced diamond circle tiara owned by the Grand-Duchess Vladimir – the tiara that is now a favourite of the Queen — was temporarily deposited with Cartier and the firm used it in 1911 as the model for three new tiaras with pendant pearls.

The bow knot and ribbon was used in French design in the Belle Époque in a revival of eighteenth-century style (Chapter 2). Bows were also a feature of the Romanov jewels. Pictures of the Russian Crown Jewels, *Les Joyaux du Tresor de Russie* catalogued for the Bolsheviks in Paris in 1924, show 23 different pieces of jewellery with bow motifs, all dating from the eighteenth and nineteenth centuries, including diamond bow earrings, a ribbon and bow knot necklace, bow knot brooches, even a diamond bouquet holder decorated with a bow.

In the corner of a news picture of 1925 there is a tiara which may have been the inspiration for Queen Mary's tiara which Princess Diana has inherited. A Russian diadem with distinctive and apparently identical diamond bows from which hang pearl drops was discovered by the Bolsheviks in 1925. It was in an underground dungeon at the end of a secret passage in the Moscow Palace of Prince Youssoupov — the same Prince who had conspired in the murder of the 'Mad Monk' Rasputin and thus precipitated the Russian Revolution. Princess Zenaïde Youssoupov cut a grand society figure in Paris and in St Petersburg, and in 1914 her son married Princess Irina, niece of the Czar. Irina's grandmother was Queen Alexandra's sister Minnie, the Empress Marie Feodorovna; her mother was the Grand-Duchess Xenia, that same Grand-Duchess who stood with Queen Mary in Buckingham Palace while the Queen sized up her Russian gems (Chapter 3). The Youssoupov wedding in February 1914 was the last Romanov orgy of opulence before the Revolution. Princess Irina wore wedding regalia studded with diamonds and her *kokoshnik* was made of carved rock crystal set with gems. That was found in the Youssoupov treasure, along with the bow knot tiara, 11 other diadems, 255 brooches and superb objects, many of them made by Fabergé who had found a wealthy patron in Princess Youssoupov.

If the Youssoupov diamond bow and drop pearl tiara was the inspiration for Queen Mary, where would she have seen it? In May 1913, Queen Mary and King George V were invited to the wedding of the German Emperor's daughter and they went to Berlin for what was to be the ultimate gathering of the 'royal mob', as Queen Victoria described her network of continental relatives. The German Princess was marrying the son of Princess Thyra, the third Danish sister of Queen Alexandra and the Empress Marie of Russia. Princess Irina (later Youssoupov) was thus intimately connected to the bridegroom's family at the German wedding. The idea that the same tiara could link two royal weddings remains an intriguing speculation.

There was some surprise that Lady Diana Spencer did not choose to wear the bow knot tiara — its provenance is unknown to the royal family — on that July day when the Mall was fluttering with flags and she drove to St Paul's Cathedral to marry her prince. Instead, it was the Spencer tiara that perched on the casual honey gold hair and its sweep of fringe that had already launched a wave of copies — not least in America, where Prince Charles had the embarrassment of being accosted by Diana-look-alikes on the royal tour he made during their engagement.

THE TALE OF A TIARA

Mystery surrounds the elegant bow-knot tiara which the Queen gave to Princess Diana on her marriage in 1981 (2). The tiara (1), with its diamond lovers' knots and 19 drop pearls, was made for Queen Mary (3 and 5) by Garrard in 1914, using pearls she had been given as a wedding present. But the tiara suggests the earlier Belle Epoque jewellery in France and Russia.

An almost identical bow-knot tiara belonging to the Youssoupov family was unearthed in a secret cache in Russia by the Bolsheviks in 1925. Prince Youssoupov was the man who conspired to murder Rasputin. Queen Mary would have seen the distinctive jewels of her Russian relatives. Princess Irina Youssoupov, whose fantastic wedding tiara carved out of solid rock crystal is in the centre of the Bolshevik hoard (4), was the granddaughter of Queen Alexandra's sister Minnie. Queen Mary later acquired her jewels.

The bow-knot tiara originally had a second row of enormous upstanding pearls (5). But it has never been worn like that by the Queen (6) or Princess Diana.

There were no jewels at all around the wedding dress, not even the safe string of plain pearls Diana had worn with her sailor outfit for the engagement pictures with the Queen. Diana wore just her mother's earrings, a bare neck and not even her husband's bracelet on her wrist. Queen Victoria had pinned Albert's sapphire brooch proudly to the Honiton lace flounce of her wedding dress; Princess Alexandra had worn the looped diamond and pearl necklace that was Bertie's present to her when she became Princess of Wales nearly a century before; Wallis Simpson had snapped the sapphire and diamond bracelet the Duke of Windsor gave her round her sky-blue crêpe sleeve on the day they finally wed.

The new Princess of Wales was her own mistress. She had shown that by her choice of two young designers for the wedding dress rather than an establishment couture house. The Emanuels had already lent her a dramatic black strapless gown which had caused a flutter at court and a sensation in the press, although a hundred years before Princess Diana would have had to get a special dispensation from the Lord Chamberlain NOT to wear a low-cut dress, *de rigueur* for court appearances. There may have been another reason why Lady Diana Spencer did not wear any jewellery on her wedding day. She did not – then or now – have so much to choose from.

Given that the royal vaults are overflowing with jewels – including pieces from Queen Alexandra and Queen Mary – which would be eminently suitable

The Spencer diamond tiara and the Saudi sapphire pendant and matching sunburst earrings.

The suite of jewels from the Crown Prince of Saudi Arabia came in a green malachite box decorated with palm tree and crossed swords. Princess Diana wears both the sapphire pendant and the bracelet worn as a choker in the colour plates.

for a young Princess, it seems strange that Princess Diana should have been given so little important jewellery from the palace, to be worn along with her favoured pearl chokers, like the multi-strand with its opal centre and the three-strand with its turquoise flower snap.

The Saudi sapphires were her great wedding gift – a sapphire as large as Queen Victoria's brooch surrounded by an open sunburst and designed as a pendant necklace. Princess Diana wears the pendant also on pearls, on a black velvet choker, and she even had a sapphire blue velvet dress designed specifically for this jewel. The Duchess of Windsor had the same idea when she asked Pierre Balmain to design a midnight blue velvet sheath to go with *her* sapphires.

Sapphire earrings, a second choker necklace, a ring, watch and bracelet make up the rest of Princess Diana's opulent suite from the Crown Prince of Saudi Arabia. It came in a marble green malachite box, embossed in gold with pertinent symbols of the desert kingdom: a palm tree and crossed swords. There was not, as the London gossips claimed, a solid gold camel en suite. That had been presented to the Queen (it is now on the Royal yacht *Britannia*) along with another sapphire necklace by Sheikh Rashid of Dubai on her state visit to the Gulf in 1979.

A life-size picture of the 18-carat yellow gold camel brooch set with six diamonds, made by Jane Sarginson and given to the Princess of Wales in 1984.

There was a gold camel *brooch* – a sculpted camel laden with spices set inside a circle of gold palm trees, the desert sand beneath set with six small diamonds. This was the work of another budding young jewellery designer called Jane Sarginson, who took the camel from the coat of arms of the Grocers' Company, who in turn presented the brooch to the Princess of Wales in January 1984.

Princess Diana's childhood friends who remembered her seventh birthday party permitted themselves a wry smile. Johnny Spencer, trying to make up to Diana for the fact that her mother had left him and the children the year before, hired a camel from the local Dudley zoo for his daughter's birthday in 1968. Photograph albums among the local squirearchy still contain pictures of Lady Diana Spencer grinning as she sat between the humps.

Other foreign kingdoms gave generous presents for the royal wedding: a pearl set of watch, rings and cufflinks from the Emir of Qatar; a glittering watch with diamonds round the face and on its bracelet from Sheikha Fatima Bint Mubarak al-Nayiyan of the United Arab Emirates. More jewellery came from the President of the Seychelles, from General Kenan Evren of the Turkish Republic and from the King and Queen of Tonga. With exquisite, but quite unconscious, irony the Crown Prince and Princess of Jordan presented to the Princess of Wales an antique necklace of Indian origin which recalled the great treasure trove of royal gifts from India over the span of 150 years. It is an elaborately worked gold choker with a pearl fringe, set with multi-coloured gems, including a central emerald, turquoises and diamonds.

The important emerald necklace given to Princess Diana from the royal family on her wedding has never been made public; it simply appeared round her neck on the Welsh tour just after the marriage. With the same sea-green taffeta dress that Princess Diana wore for her engagement pictures (with the borrowed necklace that had caused such right royal embarrassment), there

Queen Mary wears in 1948 the emerald choker that the Queen gave to Princess Diana.

was now Queen Mary's magnificent emerald choker, its green globular centre as impressive as the Cambridge emeralds that the Queen inherited from Queen Mary's family (Chapter 3).

Princess Diana's new emerald necklace excited a great deal of comment from the *cognoscenti*. The diamond set cabochon emeralds are interspersed with geometric plaques of diamonds, with emerald centres, in the Art Deco mode. This was not Queen Mary's style, claims the gossip. These must therefore be the 'Alexandra emeralds', reset for Wallis Simpson in the 1930s, and given back now by the Duchess of Windsor for the new Princess of Wales.

This story is an absolute fabrication, not least because by the summer of 1981 the Duchess of Windsor was in no fit state to donate her emeralds, if she has them, to anyone. In fact the necklace did belong to Queen Mary, and pictures show her wearing it as late as 1948, a decade after the Abdication and two years after the royal family was supposedly involved in an undercover plot to steal the Duchess's jewels in order to get the 'emeralds' back (Chapter 4). The necklace was given to Princess Diana by the Queen, who inherited it from her grandmother, and chose it from a number of pieces in store that she has never herself worn.

Where did Queen Mary get these fine emeralds from? They must have been set in the period between the two world wars, and the most likely source is the India of the Delhi durbar. 'Your jewel shall pass to future generations as an Imperial heirloom,' Queen Mary had told the Maharanee of Patiala when she was presented with a 'necklace and pendant of emeralds set in rosettes of diamonds' on 9 December 1911. Queen Mary's coronation-year Dress Book in the Royal Archives at Windsor proves that she wore the 'new Indian necklace of emeralds' at the Delhi durbar ceremony itself three days later; and again on 4 June 1912 when she described it as an 'Indian emerald necklace'. But the Crown Jeweller cannot identify these gems today. In one version of the Duchess of Windsor story, these are the emeralds that Edward VIII gave to Mrs Simpson.

Queen Mary had two other sources of the limpid green gems: the residue of the Cambridge emeralds she had wrested from her late brother's married lover, Lady Kilmorey, and which cannot all have been used in the present emerald suite. Enough emerald drops were left over to use as an alternative to the drop pearls in the Grand-Duchess Vladimir's circle tiara acquired by Queen Mary in the early 1920s (Chapter 3).

There were also the Romanov jewels and particularly the cabochon emeralds that tumbled out of the sealed box when the Empress Marie's valuables were opened up in Buckingham Palace in the spring of 1929 (Chapter 3). As with so much of Queen Mary's jewellery – including the bow knot tiara discussed above – it remains a mystery where the gems came from and why a queen who was in late middle age, and already had a wealth of jewellery, should have acquired a new emerald choker when she already possessed the Cambridge emeralds, necklace and brooch, an emerald and diamond brooch with cabochon drop and a massive diamond and emerald stomacher.

It is also interesting to enquire why this gift to Princess Diana was not made public at the time of the wedding. The battery of flash bulbs exploding in the face of the 20-year-old Lady Diana Spencer seemed to drive the beleaguered royal family behind a barricade of silence. Information that was freely given – and published – right up to the present royal generation, is now withheld. Official portraits of Queen Mary give details of the jewellery she was wearing and this was true, to a more limited extent, for the Queen.

The royal family has now become coy about giving so-called 'personal' information. Princess Diana's drop pearl tiara and the emerald choker are not Crown Jewellery nor are they considered to be state pieces (Chapter 6). But neither are the sapphire and diamond clusters necklace given by King George VI to Princess Elizabeth on her marriage or the ruby and diamond Indian necklace given by both her parents. Yet these were made public and put on display with the other wedding presents – including Queen Mary's generous gift of jewels – at St James's Palace in 1947.

In the same way, the shutters have come down on the royal wardrobe. Previous royal brides had the details of their trousseaux revealed to the world; every last hat feather and fur wrap ordered by Lady Elizabeth Bowes Lyon was lovingly listed; at that wedding, the designer of each outfit was given with the details of the carriage procession. The monarchy today has become both more accessible and more secretive.

More than half a century later, the young bride who had left her parents' home as Elizabeth Bowes Lyon to marry a royal prince in 1923, looked at Lady Diana Spencer as she stood in her ivory silk crinoline wedding gown in the dressing room at Clarence House. 'My dear, you look simply enchanting,' said the Queen Mother, according to royal hairdresser Kevin Shanley. Diana stepped into the glass coach and left behind her for ever the Cinderella world of flat-sharing and mucking out the chalet on a skiing holiday, of buying her sweets from a local shop and driving where she pleased in her own car.

She had swapped all that for all this: the pair of bays trotting beside the mounted police through the delirious crowd as the glass coach – built by George V in 1910 for his Coronation – carried her towards St Paul's Cathedral. The tiny figure in white, engulfed by the majestic building, stood before the altar, her train spreading in a white pool across the red carpet as she promised 'to have and to hold . . . for richer for poorer . . . to love and to cherish'. They sealed it with a kiss on the balcony at Buckingham Palace and sailed away in the royal yacht together.

Did Princess Diana find in her new jewels the romance and excitement expressed by Princess May of Teck when she sailed for the Isle of Wight and Cowes in another royal yacht, the *Alberta*, in 1893? 'The 1st evening at dinner I wore my white broché satin low with the Iveagh's tiara, Gdmama's necklace, the Kensington bow on the front of the bodice, and the Warwick's sun on the side. I wish you had seen me,' wrote the new bride to her mother. A century and a world away, the new Princess of Wales went sightseeing on her honeymoon in Bermuda shorts and a cotton blouse. The nearest she got to dressing up was the flowered silk dress – in patriotic red, white, and blue – for embarkation at Gibraltar, with her pearl and turquoise choker at her throat.

The truth is that there was not much in Princess Diana's new jewels that was really to her taste. Or, to put it another way, her taste in jewellery is unformed

The emerald choker with its enormous cabochon centre and plaques of diamonds. Selected by the Queen from store and given to Princess Diana on her marriage.

and most of her new presents were grand, classic and not particularly suitable for a young girl with short and casual hair. Her experiments with different hairstyles have been precisely because of the problem of putting a regal tiara on a fringe. The young Duchess of Gloucester wrestled for some years with the same problem, and has only just come to terms with short hair worked round the tiara. Princess Michael of Kent has kept long hair to sweep into a chignon. On the day of a 'big dressing' you could call round at Kensington Palace and find all the royal ladies (and even their ladies-in-waiting) sitting at nursery tea in a kilt skirt or simple sweater, a tiara planted incongruously on each head. Princess Margaret claims that only her sister can put on a tiara while walking downstairs.

What jewels will Princess Diana have to play with, even before she inherits the Crown Jewellery and the more important royal pieces? Theoretically, she and the Prince of Wales should already have access to the vaults and be able to borrow heirloom jewellery. The Queen brought out of store part of her Queen Mary inheritance when she selected the emerald and diamond choker for the Princess of Wales, and there are many more jewels which the Queen herself has never worn. The quantity and variety of Queen Mary's jewels in the last decade of her life makes her inheritance truly breathtaking – even allowing for bequests to all her children (Parisians claim that she even left a string of pearls to the Duke of Windsor). Added to that are the other jewels bought and received over the years, and the loose gemstones, like the opals removed from Queen Victoria's tiara and the 124 diamond collets in a brown box from the Crown Jewels.

The Queen has received many jewels as presents throughout her reign, and Princess Diana, as wife to the heir to the throne, is just starting out along that diamond-strewn path. When Prince Charles visited Botswana in southern Africa in 1984 he received a flawless diamond which has been set as a ring. But when a jeweller presented Princess Diana publicly with a diamond ring she was obliged to give it to charity.

But a gift of unset gemstones is unusual. Most presents and most of the jewels in store are items of jewellery, and the business of breaking them up is costly (not necessarily a problem for an extremely wealthy royal couple) and delicate. The Queen has reset one major wedding gift (30 years after it was given) to make a new tiara, and Queen Mary traded in her own wedding presents to make the diamond and pearl tiara Diana is wearing. But jewels presented to the royal family are normally catalogued, stored and brought out when donor meets recipient. This is one of the jobs (along with storing and organizing the royal Orders) undertaken by the ladies-in-waiting and is meticulously observed by the Queen, who considers it a mark of favour (and also perhaps a *jeu d'esprit*) to match jewels to the occasion.

Daughters-in-law traditionally see their mother-in-law's or grandmother's jewels as something to be reset in their own tastes, says Shirley Bury, ex-keeper of jewellery and metalwork at the Victoria and Albert Museum in London. But for the Princess of Wales, gifts to the Queen must be out of bounds and the inheritance of Queen Alexandra and Queen Mary, because it has lain dormant for at least one generation, is now assuming an historical importance.

Princess Diana borrowed a necklace from her royal mother-in-law for the Netherlands banquet in November 1982. She wears it with her wedding present bow-knot tiara and pins the Queen's personal gift of the royal family order on her dress. The huge sapphire brooch was Diana's wedding gift from the Queen Mother.

The elliptical diamond motif to the four-strand pearl choker is a modern design made for the Queen.

170

Queen Alexandra, during her long apprenticeship to the Crown, had the great good fortune to have a generous (even profligate) husband and an enormous number of gems and jewels which nobody felt protective towards, flowing in from India and Empire. Queen Mary herself started her reign with the cleavings of the Cullinan diamond which she could set to her taste, quite apart from the offerings at her Coronation and at the Delhi durbar.

Princess Diana will find it much harder to ravage the existing royal collection in order to create beautiful jewels in her own image. The fact that the Queen has had almost nothing remade during her own reign and has treated the jewels as part of history and tradition makes the position of the Prince and Princess of Wales even more difficult.

Princess Margaret, brought up within the royal circle, interested in design and with a husband who actively disliked the effect of a heavy, old, outdated tiara on his young wife, had a great deal of her jewellery remade by designers like John Donald and Andrew Grima. 'Is that Grima?' Prince Charles asked a young jewellery designer, who was, of course, wearing her own creation at a craft exhibition.

Prince Charles must be his wife's best hope of support and encouragement if she wants to remodel, even slightly, the royal jewel heritage. The Prince of Wales has pushed his mother to be more adventurous with jewels, asking her why she never wears Queen Alexandra's amethysts, which he apparently admires. The Queen wore amethysts at the time of the Duke of Windsor's death when she specifically asked Bobo to get them out in preparation for mourning and she was also seen in them on the tour of Portugal in 1985.

The future King of England had his first draught of royal pageantry at his investiture at Caernarfon Castle at the age of 21. On a grey July day in 1969 – the ninth birthday of the future Princess of Wales – Prince Charles sat on a throne of Welsh slate in a ceremony master-minded by his design-conscious (and Welsh-born) uncle Lord Snowdon, who wanted to avoid at all costs the pantomime appearance in white hose and principal boy doublet that had so mortified the future Edward VIII at his investiture in 1911.

Lord Snowdon's proposal for his nephew's new crown had been a simple gold circlet. In the end Prince Charles wore a more traditional crown, a medieval-looking coronet with spanning arches and the familiar flecked ermine trim and purple velvet cap. It was designed by the modern goldsmith Louis Osman – not by the Crown Jeweller – and was studded with 75 diamonds and 12 emeralds. In it, 'our most dear son Charles Philip Arthur George' (Lady Diana Spencer was to get those names in the wrong order on her wedding day) knelt before his mother the Queen, as this 'Prince of the United Kingdom of Great Britain and Northern Ireland, Duke of Cornwall and Rothesay, Earl of Carrick, Baron Renfrew, Lord of the Isles and Great Steward of Scotland, Prince of Wales and Earl of Chester' fulfilled the ancient ritual before his Sovereign and a television audience.

Prince Charles has been brought up in a world where home is a palace, his mother is the Queen, and where jewels are a part of that life. In his Scottish fairy tale *The Old Man of Lochnagar*, originally related to his two younger brothers, the 'hero' finds himself 'in a vast hall with a shining wooden floor

The Princess of Wales wears with pride the Queen's wedding present to her — Queen Mary's diamond bow-knot and drop pearl tiara. The Queen's Royal Family Order on a chartreuse ribbon exactly matches her dress. The diamond heart was a present for Prince William's arrival.

Far left Princess Diana's most private jewel is her charm bracelet. Prince Charles gave her the koala bear charm for her twenty-second birthday on their return from Australia in the summer of 1983.

Left "William" reads the inscription in Prince Charles's hand-writing on Diana's medallion — a royal trinket of which Queen Victoria would have approved.

Below Princess Diana's £28,500 sapphire and diamond engagement ring was bought from Garrard, chosen from eight taken down to Windsor by the Crown Jeweller.

Right Queen Mary's cabochon emerald and diamond choker was a wedding present from the Queen. It was selected from jewellery in store. Prince Charles bought her an Art Deco emerald and diamond bracelet to match.

Top Princess Diana set a fashion for chokers. The multi-strand pearls with an opal and diamond centre echoes the style of the earlier Princess of Wales, Alexandra.

Above A choker necklace from the generous suite given by the Crown Prince of Saudi Arabia and worn over a black velvet ribbon.

Far left The Saudi sapphire pendant worn with a specially designed midnight blue velvet dress trimmed with Queen Victoria's antique lace from Balmoral. Matching earrings, a ring, watch and bracelet complete the suite.

Left The Spencer tiara: Princess Diana's family heirloom. The Prince of Wales feather pendant was a wedding present.

Below The Princess of Wales prefers pearls to diamonds and wears them for grand evening occasions with drop pearl and diamond earrings.

Royal trinkets: Princess Diana's diamond heart, given to her as a baby present for Prince William, echoes Queen Victoria's family keepsakes. Prince Charles wears his signet ring engraved with Prince of Wales feathers.

Queen Victoria as a young wife and mother in the Garter ribbon and a locket round her neck. Painted by Robert Thorburn in 1844 as a gift for Prince Albert.

and the fabulous cairngorm and amethyst chandelier he had heard so much about. At the far end of the room sat the King of the Gorms on a huge throne made from a single amethyst and studded with garnets.' The King appears as a shimmering vision with six heads and six legs, 'such was the reflecting quality of the amethyst'. The baby prince, who had peered at his own image mirrored in the Cullinan diamonds at his great-grandmother's breastbone, was writing from his own experience.

One day, Prince Charles himself will become not 'King of the Gorms', but Sovereign of Great Britain and its Commonwealth. He will sit in St Edward's throne chair at Westminster Abbey to receive the Imperial State Crown with its historic stones – the blood-red Black Prince's ruby and the fiery white Cullinan diamond. On the top of the Crown, in the centre of the Cross that gives the Coronation ceremony its religious significance, is the oldest stone of all, the St Edward's sapphire that is the British monarchy's closest link with its roots. The awesome and legendary Koh-i-noor diamond will shimmer in the crown of the Queen Consort, and enhance the mystique of monarchy expressed in the Crown Jewels.

At the present moment, one of the future Queen Diana's treasured possessions is the gold medallion Prince Charles gave her, engraved with the name of her first-born son in her husband's own handwriting. Queen Victoria, who stirred into the royal jewel collection such a mix of majestic gems and private trinkets, great diadems with initialled lockets, superb diamonds with Scottish pebbles, would most certainly have been amused.

The new royal bride's taste in jewellery is a mirror image of her 'very good friend', the Princess of Wales.

Sarah Ferguson before her marriage collected the trinkets that are Sloane Ranger style. Like Diana, whose first jewel was a necklace with the letter D (which she still wears today), Sarah hung a gold 'S' on a chain at her throat, as well as a more cheeky gold 'G.B.'. Sarah also wore on her little finger the same kind of triple-band Russian wedding ring that Diana received as an early birthday present. When Sarah was first invited to Ascot by the Queen, she chose a pearl choker that was the signature of the young Princess of Wales. For her engagement day, she chose Diana's favourite heart earrings.

Sarah, like Diana, also favours sapphires and, given a free choice, would probably have picked a sapphire engagement ring, or perhaps a turquoise which is one of her favourite colours. That stone would not be considered important enough for a gem-set royal ring.

The fine oval ruby, set cluster-style with ten drop diamonds and mounted in 18 carat yellow and white gold, was designed by Prince Andrew. He went to William Summers, the Crown Jeweller, who brought to him a selection of rings from Garrard from which the shape of the royal engagement ring was adapted and refined.

Andrew amused his future bride by describing his initial design as 'diamond rugby balls', and calling the expert craftsmen at Garrard 'engineers'.

In fact, the jewellers worked night and day to make up the ring, after the Queen had given her consent to the royal engagement, just four days before the announcement. The city was scoured for ten perfectly matched diamonds to surround the Burmese ruby from the royal collection.

Although Sarah approved the idea of a ruby, she was not involved in the design of the ring. Princess Margaret also chose a ruby engagement ring, so it is in the royal tradition. Emeralds might have been considered an attractive foil for Sarah's mane of red hair.

She learned to sweep that hair up under a tiara and to wear imposing necklaces, rather than her earlier chokers. The off-the-shoulder dress that she chose for the Queen's 60th birthday celebrations and her first grand royal outing, was designed to show off the festoon necklace of diamonds and ink-blue sapphires, on loan from a jeweller.

The diamond hair clips which the Queen wore in her youth would be a glamorous gift for her new daughter-in-law. Sarah has received her first taste of jewellery in the royal wedding presents, but she will never inherit the vast reserves of crown and royal jewellery that will one day belong to the Princess of Wales.

As a navy wife, Sarah will continue to enjoy her smaller personal pieces of jewellery, and to wear her bold sports watch – a taste that Prince Andrew and his vivacious bride both share.

APPENDIX A

The Crown Jewellery

(Excluding jewels in the Tower of London)

Jewels Left to the Crown by Her Majesty Queen Victoria

THE DIAMOND DIADEM
Made for the coronation of George IV with hired jewels
Reset with permanent jewels by Queen Victoria
Band remounted 1902 by Queen Alexandra
Row of cultured pearls added 1937

BRILLIANT REGAL TIARA
Made for Queen Victoria on 1 April 1853 for the Koh-i-noor diamond
Diamonds remounted by Garrard in 1937 for the crown of Queen Elizabeth,
 the Queen Mother

REGAL INDIAN TIARA
Diamond tiara of oriental design set with opals made for Queen Victoria in
 1853
Remounted for Queen Alexandra 1902: opals replaced with 11 rubies from
 Indian necklace given by Sir Jung Bahadore in 1876

JEWELLED ORDERS
Including brilliant Star and Garter in diamonds and badges set with gems

TWO SWORDS
Set with gems

A COCKADE
Cockade set with brilliants altered for Queen Alexandra as 3-part cloak clasp

AN EMERALD GIRDLE
From the horse trappings of Maharajah Ranjit Singh, given to Queen Victoria
 by the Honourable East India Company in 1851

THE TIMUR RUBY
Enormous spinel ruby weighing 352½ carats, carved with Arabic inscriptions
 giving dates and owners, set in a necklace flanked by two other uncut rubies
 and diamond clusters

THE DIAMOND COLLET
Necklace of 28 brilliant collets made from diamonds taken from the Garter
 Badge and Sword for Queen Victoria

Detachable pendant also used in the Crown of Queen Elizabeth, the Queen
  Mother
Necklace reduced and drop diamond earrings made 1937

Two Diamond Collet Necklaces
A diamond collet necklace of 45 collets
A diamond collet necklace of 42 collets. Spare 154 collets

Diamond Fringe
Fringe pattern necklace set in 1830 with brilliants from George III

Queen Anne/Queen Caroline Pearls
Two pearl necklaces supposedly inherited from Queen Anne and from Queen
  Caroline, wife of George II

Indian Pearls
Four strand pearls from treasury at Lahore, presented to Queen Victoria by
  the Honourable East India Company in 1851 with ruby snap
Reset 1941

Amethysts
A suite of amethysts formerly belonging to the Duchess of Kent, mother of
  Queen Victoria

Twenty-one Rings
A brilliant half hoop
A ruby half hoop
A turquoise half hoop
A portrait ring
A double diamond ring containing hair
An engraved ring with diamond border
A ring set with hair and *'Toujours chère'*
A ring with diamond border and cypher
A locket ring with diamond border
A diamond ring engraved 'Queen Charlotte'
A diamond birds ring enamelled with *'Toujours chère'*
An oval mourning ring
A black enamelled and diamond ring
A ring with oblong diamond
An old portrait ring set with paste
A slide set with brilliants
A portrait ring engraved 'George II'
A portrait ring engraved 'George III'
A lasque ring
A diamond ring engraved 'Frederick, Duke of York'
An opal and diamond ring. (Opal removed and reset with pink tourmaline
  1936)

Four Historic Bracelets
Four rows of graduated pearls, mounted 1838
Four rows of brilliants, mounted 1838

Five square foliage tablets set with brilliants
Blue enamel and gold bracelet containing hair and inscription

DIAMOND BOW BROOCHES
Two large and one small bow brooches set with diamonds made by Garrard
   for Queen Victoria

QUEEN VICTORIA'S SAPPHIRE BROOCH
Large sapphire surrounded by 12 large diamonds, given to Queen Victoria by
   Prince Albert on their marriage, 1840

BROOCHES
Diamonds and pearls with three pendant pearls
Circular brooch set with brilliants. Stones formerly property of George III
Six brooches with wheat leaf design. Stones from George III
Oval brooch with diamond border
Ruby pendant set in brilliants with diamond pendant and drop

CAT'S EYE BROOCH
Enormous cat's eye weighing 313¼ carats set in diamonds taken in conquest
   from King of Kandy and presented to Queen Victoria

EARRINGS
Large brilliant ear-tops and drops, taken from setting of Koh-i-noor
Diamond tops with emerald drops and diamond fringes
Pearl tops and drop pearls, given to Queen Victoria by Prince Albert 1847
Two diamond collets taken from collet necklace
Ruby and diamond earrings given by King George V to Queen Mary for her
   birthday 1926

ORDERS AND MEMENTOES
Enamelled portrait of George IV set in diamonds
Queen Charlotte's guard ring
Miniature of Queen Charlotte set in diamonds
Stars of order of Garter, Thistle, Bath, St Patrick

QUEEN VICTORIA'S EMERALD BRACELET
An emerald and diamond bracelet. Wedding present to Queen Victoria

QUEEN VICTORIA'S OPALS
Suite of opal brooch and earrings designed by Prince Consort
Opals in earrings replaced by rubies 1902
Opals in brooch replaced by rubies 1926
Necklace of opals and brilliants, replaced by rubies 1902
Opal and brilliant drop brooch, opal replaced by ruby
Opal slide, original opal replaced by ruby

EMPRESS EUGENIE'S FLOWER HOLDER
Ruby, diamond and pearl flower holder presented by Empress Eugénie to
   Queen Victoria on state visit to Paris 1855

JUBILEE NECKLACE
Diamond and pearl trefoil necklace with pearl drop detachable as brooch, given to Queen Victoria by The Daughters of Empire 1887
Earrings to match

OTHER JUBILEE JEWELS
Pearl and diamond brooch with pearl centre and pearl drop. Present to Queen Victoria from The Ladies and Gentlemen of Her Majesty's Household on her Diamond Jubilee 1897
Commemorative bracelet set with diamonds, rubies and sapphires presented to Queen Victoria from her servants in 1897
Diamond and pearl drop pendant with George and dragon on a Garter, present to Queen Victoria from the Household of the Prince and Princess of Wales in 1887

MEMENTO OF PRINCE CONSORT
Silver cross with crown of thorns, photograph of Prince Consort and lock of his hair given to Queen Victoria by her daughter Vicky, the Crown Princess and Crown Prince of Prussia after Albert's death, 1862

JEWELS BELONGING TO HRH THE PRINCE CONSORT
Various jewelled orders and badges, including foreign orders

PRESENTS FROM THE PRINCE CONSORT
These items all left to Edward VII by Queen Victoria in her will, to be considered 'as belonging to the Crown and to be worn by all future Queens in right of it'.
Bracelet with enamel portrait of Prince Consort given to Queen Victoria by Prince Albert Christmas 1840
Blue enamel on gold bracelet containing six portraits of Queen Victoria's children, 1845
Similar bracelet containing portraits of Queen Victoria's younger sons, 1854
Shawl pin modelled on antique Irish brooch given Christmas 1848
Scottish pebble set as Celtic brooch, 1848
Turkish crescent in diamonds, rubies and sapphires with Crimean ribbon
Prince of Wales feather and gold coronet brooch, 1842

Historic and Family Jewels

Bracelet portrait of Princess Augusta
Bracelet with miniature of Princess Charlotte
Bracelet with portraits of George III
Bracelet containing miniatures of King and Queen of Portugal
Bracelet left to Queen Victoria by Queen of the Belgians
Bracelet with gold chain and blue enamel heart, containing first lock of Prince of Wales's hair
Lockets with hair of other royal children
Bracelet containing hair of George III, Queen Charlotte and their children

Five rings containing locks of hair, bequeathed by Princess Sophia Mathilda of
　　Gloucester
Necklace of pearls from River Tay
Four pictures of royal Princes to be placed in diamond and emerald settings on
　　velvet bands
Vinaigrette, watch seal and key and ancient Indian enamel ring given by family
　　as presents to Queen Victoria

Indian Jewels given to Crown by Queen Mary

Indian armlet of spinel ruby and two pearls, presented by Maharajah of
　　Jeypore (sic) in December of the Delhi durbar, 1911. Given to Crown, 1912
Second Indian armlet of spinel ruby and pearls from Jeypore
　　Armlet with spinel ruby engraved with names of three Mogul emperors
　　given to Edward VII at his Coronation by Maharajah Sir Hira Singh. Given
　　to Queen Mary by George V in 1912 and put in Crown India Collection
Indian necklace of 14 lasque diamonds, 4 pearls, 3 emeralds and 6 cabochon
　　rubies, given to Prince of Wales in 1876 by Maharajah Scindiah given to
　　India Collection in 1926
Snap of this necklace made out of ruby ring given to Queen Victoria by
　　Maharajah of Mysore 1862 given by King George V to India Collection

Jewellery Sent to Windsor Castle by Queen Mary, 1910

Seventeen out of 21 historic rings listed above
Five rings containing locks of hair, as above

Regalia Ring Sent to Tower by Queen Mary

Sapphire ring with ruby cross and diamonds given to Queen Victoria by her
　　mother the Duchess of Kent in 1838
Later given by Queen Alexandra to Queen Mary
Added to regalia in Tower of London, 1919

Source:
Twining Papers, Goldsmith's Hall Library
Royal Library, Windsor

APPENDIX B

The Royal Family Orders

The family orders of miniatures of each sovereign are the most personal mark of royal favour. They date back to 1820 and George IV, and from the moment that her 'Uncle King' pinned his order on Princess Victoria, the badges have been considered as royal rites of passage. The family orders are not given automatically to female members of the royal family, as the list of current holders shows. With the exception of Edward VIII, the orders have been renewed each reign. The Queen normally wears the Orders of King George V and King George VI. The badges are all made by Garrard.

The Royal Family Order of George V

Obverse: A miniature of His Majesty in the uniform of the Admiral of the Fleet with decorations, inset within an oval band of large diamonds surmounted by an Imperial Crown with a crimson-enamelled cap.
Reverse: The Royal Cypher in gold on a radiating background. The whole is set in silver and gold.
Riband: Light sky blue. This riband was chosen as similar to the Royal Guelphic Order of Hanover instituted by King George IV, but which became obsolete in 1837.

The Royal Family Order of George VI

Obverse: The miniature of His Majesty in the uniform of Admiral of the Fleet, complete with decorations, set within an oval diamond border composed of pairs of brilliant diamonds separated by baguette diamonds, the whole surmounted by the Imperial Crown in diamonds and enamel.
Reverse: The Cypher of the King in gold, the cushion of the Crown inset with red enamel, on a radiating engraved background.
The badge is set in platinum and gold.
Riband: Rose pink.

The Royal Family Order of Queen Elizabeth II

Obverse: Miniature portrait of the Queen set within a diamond border composed of brilliant diamonds set in threes separated by rows of baguette diamonds, surmounted by the Imperial Crown with red enamel cushion.

The miniature is based on the famous Dorothy Wilding portrait of the Queen wearing evening dress with the Riband and Star of the Order of the Garter. She is wearing the diamond necklace that was part of her wedding present from the Nizam of Hyderabad.

Reverse: The Cypher of the Queen in gold with red enamel cushion.

Riband: watered silk (in a bow) two inches wide in chartreuse yellow.

The badges of these Orders are worn on the left shoulder suspended from bows of the ribands to which are fitted, behind the bows, platinum brooch pins attached to the diamond Imperial crowns.

Distribution

The present holders of the Queen's Family Order are:

Queen Elizabeth, the Queen Mother; The Princess of Wales; The Princess Anne, Mrs Mark Phillips; The Princess Margaret; Princess Alice, Duchess of Gloucester; The Duchess of Gloucester; The Duchess of Kent; Princess Alexandra, Mrs Angus Ogilvy.

APPENDIX C

List of the Personal Jewels Worn by HM the Queen on State and Semi-State Occasions

Orders

FAMILY ORDERS: worn on the left shoulder on State occasions. (Appendix B) When these are worn, the Queen keeps her Garter ribbon in place with

A DOUBLE BAR BROOCH: left to her by Queen Mary. Otherwise she pins her Garter ribbon with

A DIAMOND BOW BROOCH: given to her by Queen Mary, and originally a present to the latter as Princess May on her marriage in 1893. The Garter ribbon is also pinned with

DIAMOND BROOCH: central part of a stomacher given to Princess Elizabeth on her marriage in 1947 by her grandmother Queen Mary

Tiaras

DIAMOND DIADEM: completely circular head ornament with emblems of rose, thistle and shamrock alternating with cross motifs. Designed by George IV, frequently worn by Queen Victoria. Worn by the Queen at the Opening of Parliament (Crown)

SCROLL AND COLLET SPIKE TIARA: wedding gift, originally given to the future Queen Mary by the girls of Great Britain and Ireland on her marriage; known as 'Granny's tiara'

TIARA OF INTERLACED CIRCLES: hung interchangeably with drop pearls or cabochon emeralds. Originally made for the Grand-Duchess Vladimir of Russia with pearls. Emeralds originally belonged to Queen Mary's grandmother Augusta, Duchess of Cambridge, daughter-in-law of George III (see Cambridge Emeralds)

RUSSIAN FRINGE TIARA: given to Queen Alexandra on the occasion of her silver wedding in 1888 by subscription from Ladies in Society

RUBY AND DIAMOND FLOWER MOTIF TIARA: made for the Queen, circa 1973

SAPPHIRE AND DIAMOND TIARA: made for the Queen, circa 1964

AQUAMARINE AND DIAMOND TIARA: made for the Queen to complete aquamarine suite (see Brazilian Aquamarines)

BANDEAU TIARA: English rose and foliage design. Wedding gift from Nizam of Hyderabad (see English Rose Necklace)

Necklaces

JUBILEE NECKLACE: diamond trefoils set with pearls. Pearl drop suspended from centrepiece surmounted by a crown. Presented to Queen Victoria in 1887 from residue of money subscribed for building Albert Memorial (Crown)

DIAMOND FRINGE NECKLACE (also worn as tiara): made in 1830 from brilliants formerly property of George III (Crown)

DIAMOND COLLET: made for Queen Victoria. Detachable diamond drop from original setting of Koh-i-Noor diamond presented to Queen Victoria in 1851 (Crown)

CROWN PEARLS: two strings of historic pearls, wedding present from George VI and Queen Elizabeth (Crown)

TRIPLE STRING OF PEARLS: gift from George V, the Queen's grandfather, when she was a child

CAMBRIDGE EMERALDS: necklace of emeralds and diamonds with large emerald drop. Marquise diamond drop is the fifth part of the Cullinan diamond. Suite consists of matching necklace, brooch, stomacher, earrings and two bracelets, plus drops for tiara. Emeralds won in a lottery in Frankfurt in 19th century, inherited from Augusta, Duchess of Cambridge, grandmother to Queen Mary

RUBY AND DIAMOND NECKLACE: wedding gift from George VI and Queen Elizabeth

SAPPHIRE AND DIAMOND CLUSTERS NECKLACE (and earrings): wedding gift from George VI

TRIPLE-ROW DIAMOND FESTOON NECKLACE: made up in 1950 from spare collets

TWENTY-ONE DIAMOND NECKLACE (and bracelet); stones presented by the Government of the Union of South Africa to Princess Elizabeth on the occasion of her twenty-first birthday in 1947. One diamond a gift from de Beers ('my best diamonds')

FRINGE DIAMOND NECKLACE: wedding gift from Lord Mayor and City of London interests

ENGLISH ROSE DIAMOND AND FOLIAGE DESIGN NECKLACE: wedding gift from Nizam of Hyderabad (seldom worn)

DAGMAR NECKLACE: elaborate looped necklace of diamonds and pearls with detachable enamel cross. Dowry from Danish King to Princess Alexandra of Denmark on her marriage to the future Edward VII in 1863 (seldom worn)

BRAZILIAN AQUAMARINES: large, square-cut with matching earrings, presented by the President of Brazil in Coronation Year, 1953. Matching bracelet presented in 1958

FRINGED NECKLACE: drop diamonds and baguettes, presented by King Faisal of Saudi Arabia during his State visit of 1967

Brooches

QUEEN VICTORIA'S SAPPHIRE BROOCH: large sapphire set in diamonds. Originally given by Prince Albert to Queen Victoria on their marriage in 1840 (Crown)

DIAMOND FLOWER: large central diamond surrounded by seven others; inheritance of Queen Alexandra

CULLINAN DIAMOND BROOCH: made up of square cushion-shaped 62-carat diamond and pendant pear-drop 92-carat diamond, third and fourth parts of Cullinan diamond; known as 'Granny's chips' (seldom worn)

CULLINAN HEART BROOCH: contains large heart-shaped central diamond, fifth part of Cullinan diamond; inheritance of Queen Mary

CULLINAN MARQUISE BROOCH: pendant marquise diamond (Cullinan VII) on a brooch with central oblong stone (Cullinan VIII)

WILLIAMSON PINK: world's finest rose-pink diamond weighing 54 carats, presented to Princess Elizabeth on her marriage by Dr John T. Williamson, owner of a diamond mine in Tanganyika (now Tanzania). Made up as flower brooch by Cartier in 1953

CAMBRIDGE EMERALDS BROOCH: diamond scroll brooch with cabochon emerald centre and cabochon emerald drop; part of Cambridge suite

TWIN IVY-LEAF DIAMOND CLIPS: a twenty-first birthday present from George VI during the South African tour of 1947

DIAMOND BOWS: made for Queen Victoria in 1858 as set of three; (Crown)

DIAMOND BOW WITH PEARL DROP: originally a wedding present to Queen Mary in 1893 from the inhabitants of Kensington

DIAMOND LOVERS' KNOT BROOCH: inherited from Queen Mary

HEAVY DIAMOND BOW: brooch originally presented to the future Queen Mary on her marriage by the County of Dorset

CABOCHON EMERALD DROP BROOCH: surrounded by two circles of diamonds with large cabochon emerald drop; inheritance of Queen Mary

CABOCHON SAPPHIRE AND PEARL DROP BROOCH: sapphire set in double circle of diamonds. Originally a wedding present to Empress Marie Feodorovna from her sister Queen Alexandra and Edward VII

CABOCHON SAPPHIRE AND DIAMOND BROOCH: originally a wedding present from Empress Marie Feodorovna to the future Queen Mary

PEARL AND DIAMOND FESTOON BROOCH: pearl surrounded by triple diamond circle of plaited diamonds with hanging half-circle and pearl drops inherited by Queen Mary from her mother, Princess Mary Adelaide, Duchess of Teck and granddaughter of George III

DIAMOND AND PEARL DROP BROOCH: originally a wedding present to the future Queen Mary from the women of Hampshire

DIAMOND STOMACHER: intersecting circles and semi-circles, separating into three brooches. Wedding present from Queen Mary

FLAME LILY BROOCH: diamond and platinum brooch presented to Princess Elizabeth on her twenty-first birthday in 1947 from the children of Southern Rhodesia (now Zimbabwe)

DIAMOND FERN BROOCH: presented by the women of Auckland, New Zealand, in 1953

DIAMOND WATTLE BROOCH: in 150 yellow and white diamonds. Presented by the Commonwealth of Australia in 1954

BASKET OF FLOWERS: multi-coloured stones. Given to Princess Elizabeth by her parents

SAPPHIRE AND DIAMOND FLOWER: with raised centre. Presented to Princess Elizabeth on launch of the ship *British Princess* in 1946

ANTIQUE DIAMOND FLOWER: with bow at base of stem. Presented on launch of battleship HMS *Vanguard*

Earrings

DIAMOND COLLET TOP AND DROP: made up in 1937 by removing two collets from diamond collet necklace (Crown)

DIAMOND FRAME DROP PEARL: inheritance of Queen Mary

DIAMOND FLORETS: central diamond surrounded by seven others; inheritance of Queen Mary

PEARL FLORETS: central pearl with ten surrounding diamonds; inheritance of Queen Alexandra

PEARL FLOWERS: twentieth birthday present from Queen Mary

DIAMOND STUD AND PEARL: larger pearl below stud. Wedding present from Queen Mary in 1947. Originally wedding present to her from County of Devon in 1893

LARGE DIAMOND STUD: with central stone; inheritance of Queen Mary

DIAMOND STUD: in smaller cluster; inheritance of Queen Mary

DIAMOND CHANDELIERS: containing diamonds with every known modern cut. A wedding gift from George VI and Queen Elizabeth

DIAMOND FLOWERS: present from diplomatic corps in 1947

DIAMOND DROP EARRINGS: wedding present from Sheikh of Bahrain

EMERALD AND DIAMOND: part of Cambridge suite

RUBY AND DIAMOND: matching necklace

SAPPHIRE AND DIAMOND: matching necklace

AQUAMARINE AND DIAMOND: matching Brazilian necklace

PEARL STUDS: made in 1951

Bracelets

BROAD DIAMOND BRACELET: a present from Prince Philip on their marriage in 1947

DIAMOND DOUBLE INDIAN BANGLES: wedding present from Queen Mary

RUBY AND DIAMOND FLOWER: wedding present from Queen Mary; originally a present to her from County of Cornwall

DIAMOND LINK AND CHAIN: inheritance of Queen Mary

PEARL STRAND WITH SAPPHIRE CLASP: four strand; inheritance of Queen Alexandra

PEARL STRAND WITH DIAMOND CLASP: five strands; inheritance of Queen Mary

SQUARE-CUT EMERALDS AND DIAMOND: inheritance of Queen Mary

CABOCHON EMERALD BRACELET: part of Cambridge suite

SAPPHIRE AND DIAMOND BRACELET: eighteenth birthday present from George VI

BLACK AND WHITE PEARL AND DIAMOND BRACELET: alternate black and white pearl centres to diamond flowers

SAPPHIRE AND DIAMOND BRACELET: acquired circa 1960

DIAMOND BRACELET: made up from twenty-first birthday presents from the Government of the Union of South Africa and de Beers Corporation

Watches

NARROW PLATINUM AND DIAMOND WATCH: gift from the President of the French Republic during the Queen's visit to France in 1957. Replaced similar watch presented to Queen Elizabeth by the French Government in 1938, given to Princess Elizabeth and lost at Sandringham in 1955

DIAMOND ENCIRCLED WATCH: part of the wedding gift of the Swiss Federal Republic

GOLD DAY WATCH

Rings

ENGAGEMENT RING: solitaire diamond supported by diamond shoulders. Heirloom stones from Prince Philip's mother, Princess Andrew of Greece

WEDDING RING: narrow band of Welsh gold

CULLINAN DIAMOND: pear-shaped diamond, part IX of Cullinan stone mounted by Queen Mary in claw setting (seldom worn)

Sources:

'A List of Personal Jewels often worn by HM The Queen on State and Semi-State Occasions', Lord Chamberlain's Office

The Queen's Jewellery by Sheila Young, Ebury Press, 1968

Private information to the author

APPENDIX D

Jewellers Holding Royal Warrants

HM The Queen

Royal Warrants of Appointment to Her Majesty Queen Elizabeth II
Department of Her Majesty's Privy Purse

Asprey and Co., PLC	Goldsmiths, Silversmiths and Jewellers
Carrington and Company Ltd	Silversmiths and Jewellers
Cartier Ltd	Jewellers and Goldsmiths
Collingwood of Conduit Street Ltd	Jewellers and Silversmiths
Cox, Harold and Sons (Jewellers) Ltd	Jeweller, Windsor
Devlin Stuart Ltd	Goldsmith and Jeweller
Grima, Andrew Ltd	Jewellers
Longmire, Paul Ltd	Supplier of Jewellery and Leather goods
Wartski Ltd	Jewellers

Royal Warrants of Appointment to Her Majesty Queen Elizabeth II
Lord Chamberlain's Office

Garrard and Co., Ltd	Goldsmiths and Crown Jewellers

HM Queen Elizabeth the Queen Mother

Royal Warrants of Appointment to Her Majesty Queen Elizabeth the Queen
Mother

Asprey and Co., PLC	Goldsmiths, Silversmiths and Jewellers
Carrington and Company Ltd	Silversmiths and Jewellers
Cartier Ltd	Jewellers and Goldsmiths
Collingwood of Conduit Street Ltd	Jewellers and Silversmiths
Garrard and Co.; Ltd	Jewellers and Silversmiths
Wartski Ltd	Jewellers

187

HRH the Prince of Wales

Royal Warrants of Appointment to His Royal Highness the Prince of Wales

Asprey and Co., PLC	Goldsmiths, Silversmiths and Jewellers
Collingwood of Conduit Street Ltd	Jewellers and Silversmiths
Wartski Ltd	Jewellers

Fourteenth Supplement to
The London Gazette
of Friday, 28 December 1984

Glossary of
Jewellery Terms

AIGRETTE Jewelled plume

BAGUETTE Diamond cut to suit requirements of design, usually in square or oblong with straight edge. See also CALIBRE

BRILLIANT Type of cut favoured for diamonds, multi-faceted on a circular stone

BRIOLETTE Type of gem-cutting, adaptation of rose cut: sphere covered with triangular reflecting facets

CABOCHON Dome-shaped, cut with no facets. Top of stone rounded. Used in Indian settings for emeralds and rubies

CALIBRE Straight-sided stone used in pattern. Term applied only to coloured gem-stones. For diamonds see BAGUETTE

CARAT Term used for measurement of gem-stones by weight or as measure of purity of gold

CHOKER Throat necklace usually consisting of rows of pearls. Also known as dog-collar. Popularised by Queen Alexandra

COLLET Method of setting stones, usually diamonds. Gem-stone enclosed in metal band

CUT Different methods of giving natural gem-stones brilliance and sparkle, e.g. brilliant, rose-cut, marquise

FACET Flat surface cut into gem-stone

JACYNTH Gem-stone red/orange in colour

MARQUISE Type of cut in tapered boat shape. Also known as Navette

PARURE Suite of matching jewels, e.g. necklace, earrings, bracelet

PEAR-SHAPE Type of cut, especially for diamonds. Also known as teardrop

PERIDOT Gem-stone, watery green in colour

REVIVALIST Jewellery design reviving styles of previous eras, especially historical or archaeological. Well-known exponents: Carlo and Arthur Giuliano and Castellani

ROSE-CUT Type of cut, often for diamond, with multi-faceted top and triangular base

SAUTOIR Originally a muff chain. Continuous chain used according to taste of wearer. Often with tasselled ends

SPINEL Generic gem-stone name for ruby

STOMACHER Jewelled ornament fixed to bodice of dress from bosom to waist. Also known as 'bijoux bien placé'

THE FAMILY OF QUEEN VICTORIA

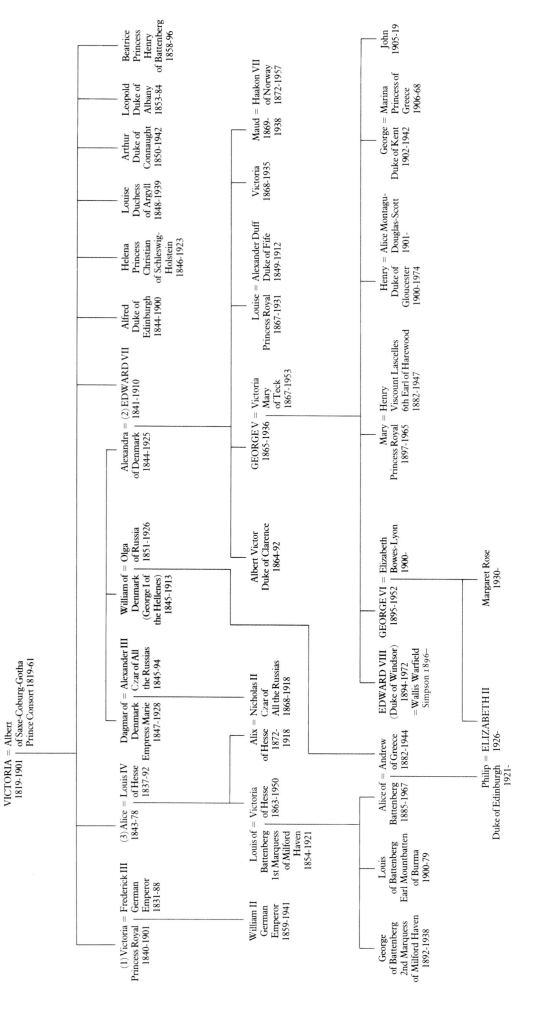

THE FAMILY OF THE QUEEN

EDWARD VIII = Wallis Warfield Simpson
(Duke of Windsor)   1896-
1894-1972
1936

GEORGE VI = Elizabeth Bowes-Lyon
(b. 1895)   1900-
1936-1952

Mary = Henry Viscount Lascelles
Princess Royal   6th Earl of Harewood
1897-1965   1882-1947

and issue

Henry = Alice Montagu-Douglas-Scott
Duke of Gloucester   1901-
1900-74

William   Richard = Birgitte van Deurs
1941-72   Duke of Gloucester   1946-
             1944-

Alexander   Davina   Rose
Earl of Ulster   1977-   1980-
1974-

George = Marina Princess of Greece
Duke of Kent   1906-68
1902-42

Edward = Katharine Worsley
Duke of Kent   1933-
1935-

Alexandra = Angus Ogilvy
1936-   1928-

Michael = Marie Christine von Reibnitz
1942-   1945-

George   Helen   Nicholas
Earl of   1964-   1970-
St Andrews
1962-

James   Marina
1964-   1966-

Frederick   Gabriella
1979-   1981-

Philip = **ELIZABETH II**
Duke of Edinburgh   (b. 1926)
1921-   **1952-**

Margaret Rose = Antony Armstrong-Jones
1930-   1st Earl of Snowdon
         1930-
         (div.)

Charles = Lady Diana Spencer
Prince of Wales   1961-
1948-

Anne = Mark Phillips
1950-   1948-

Andrew   Edward
1960-   1964-

David   Sarah
Viscount Linley   1964-
1961-

William   Henry
1982-   1984-

Peter   Zara
1977-   1981-

Bibliography

Queen Victoria

ARGYLL, His Grace the Duke of: *VRI, Her Life and Empire*, Eyre & Spottiswoode, 1901

BAPST, Germain: *Le Maréchal Canrobert*, Librairie Plon (Paris), 1902

BENNETT, Daphne: *King without a Crown: Albert, Prince Consort of England*, William Heinemann, 1977

BENSON, Arthur Christopher and Viscount Esher, eds.: *The Letters of Queen Victoria, a Selection of Her Majesty's Correspondence between the Years 1837 and 1861*, John Murray, 1908

BROOKE, John: *King George III*, Constable, 1972

DAWE, Rev. C. S.: *Queen Victoria and Her People*, The Educational Supply Association, 1897

ESHER, Viscount: *The Girlhood of Queen Victoria, a Selection of Her Majesty's Diaries between the Years 1832 and 1840*, Vols I and II, John Murray, 1912

FULFORD, Roger, ed.: *Dearest Child, Letters between Queen Victoria and the Princess Royal, 1858–1861*, Evans, 1964

FULFORD, Roger: *The Prince Consort*, Macmillan, 1949

GREVILLE, Charles: *The Greville Memoirs, 1875–1887*, ed. Lytton Strachey and Roger Fulford, Macmillan, 1938

HARDY, Alan: *Queen Victoria Was Amused*, John Murray, 1976

HIBBERT, Christopher: *Victoria, a Biography*, Park Lane Press, 1979

LONGFORD, Elizabeth: *Victoria RI*, Weidenfeld & Nicolson, 1964

LYTTON, Lady: *Court Diary, 1895–1899*, Rupert Hart-Davis, 1961

MACAULAY, Dr: *Victoria R, Her Life and Reign*, The Religious Tract Society, 1887

MALLET, Victor, ed.: *Life with Queen Victoria – Marie Mallet's Letters from Court, 1887–1901*, John Murray, 1968

MAXWELL, Sir Herbert: *Sixty Years a Queen*, Eyre & Spottiswoode, 1897

PONSONBY, Sir Frederick: *Recollections of Three Reigns*, Eyre & Spottiswoode, 1951

PONSONBY, Sir Frederick: *Sidelights on Queen Victoria*, Macmillan, 1930

RAYMOND, John, ed.: *Queen Victoria's Early Letters*, Batsford, 1907

RHODES JAMES, Robert: *Albert, Prince Consort*, Hamish Hamilton, 1983

STRACHEY, Lytton: *Queen Victoria*, Chatto & Windus, 1921

TOOLEY, Sarah: *The Personal Life of Queen Victoria*, Hodder & Stoughton, 1896
WATSON, Vera: *A Queen at Home*, W. H. Allen, 1952
WOODHAM-SMITH, Cecil: *Queen Victoria*, Hamish Hamilton, 1971

Queen Alexandra

ALEXANDER, Michael and Shushila Arnaud: *Queen Victoria's Maharajah, Dhuleep Singh, 1838–1893*, Weidenfeld & Nicolson, 1980
ALLEN, Charles and Sharada Dwivedi: *Lives of the Indian Princes*, Century Publishing, 1984
ALLINGHAM, J. W.: 'Five Months with the Prince in India'. *Daily Telegraph*, 1876, India Office Library ref. T.12361
ARMSTRONG, L. H.: *Letters to a Bride (including Letters to a Débutante)*, London, 1896. Court Dress Collection, Kensington
BATTISCOMBE, Georgina: *Queen Alexandra*, Constable, 1969
BROADLEY, A. M.: *The Boyhood of a Great King, 1841–1858*, Harper, 1906
CUST, Sir Lionel: *Edward VII and His Court*, John Murray, 1930
DUFF, David: *Alexandra, Princess and Queen*, Collins, 1980
FISHER, Graham and Heather: *Bertie and Alix*, Robert Hale, 1974
GAY, J. Drew: *From Pall Mall to the Punjab, or, with the Prince in India*, Chatto, 1876. India Office Library ref. T.35828
HIBBERT, Christopher: 'The Prince of Wales in India', *History Today*, Vol. 25, No. 9, Sept. 1975
HIBBERT, Christopher: *Edward VII*, Allen Lane, 1976
LANGTRY, Lillie: *The Days I Knew*, Hutchinson, 1925
MAGNUS, Philip: *King Edward VII*, John Murray, 1964
RUSSELL, H. W. H.: *Memorial of the Marriage of HRH Prince of Wales and HRH Princess Alexandra of Denmark*, Events and Gifts illustrated by Robert Dudley, Chelsea Library ref. 942.08 f Rus.
SIMPSON, W.: *Shikare and Tomasha: a souvenir of the visit of HRH the Prince of Wales to India*, London, 1876. India Office Library ref. W.2199
STONE, Julia, A.: *Illustrated India*, Hartford (Conn.), 1877. India Office Library ref. T.36105
VANDERBILT, Consuela: *The Glitter and the Gold*, New York, 1952

Queen Mary

AIRLIE, Mabell, Countess of: *Thatched with Gold*, Hutchinson, 1962
GRAHAM, Evelyn: *Princess Mary, Viscountess Lascelles*, Hutchinson, N.D.
Historical Record of the Imperial Visit to India 1911: Compiled from the Official Records, John Murray, 1914. India Office Library ref. W.3808
JOHNSTONE, J. W. D.: *Gwalior, Visit of the Prince and Princess of Wales*, Bumpus, 1907. India Office Library ref. W.3440

MACKENZIE, F. A.: *King George V in His Own Words*, Ernest Benn, 1929

MAKIN, J. W.: *The Life of King George the Fifth*, George Newnes, 1936

MARIE LOUISE, Her Royal Highness Princess: *My Memories of Six Reigns*, Evans, 1956

MARY, Princess: *Gift Book*, Hodder & Stoughton, N.D.

NICOLSON, Harold: *King George the Fifth*, Constable, 1952

POPE-HENNESSY, James: *Queen Mary, 1867–1953*, Allen & Unwin, 1959

REED, Sir Stanley: *The King and Queen in India*, Bennett, Coleman (Bombay), 1912. India Office Library ref. W.1981

ROSE, Kenneth: *King George V*, Weidenfeld & Nicolson, 1983

VORRES, Ian: *The Last Grand-Duchess*, Hutchinson, 1964

WOODWARD, Kathleen: *Queen Mary, a Life and Intimate Study*, Hutchinson, N.D.

Duchess of Windsor

BALMAIN, Pierre: *My Years and Seasons*, Cassell, 1964

BLOCH, Michael: *The Duke of Windsor's War*, Weidenfeld & Nicolson, 1982

BLOCH, Michael: *Operation Willi*, Weidenfeld & Nicolson, 1984

BOLITHO, Hector: *King Edward VIII*, Eyre & Spottiswoode, 1937

BROAD, Lewis: *The Abdication Twenty-five Years After*, Frederick Muller, 1961

BRYAN III, Joe and Charles Murphy: *The Windsor Story*, Granada, 1979

CHANNON, Sir Henry: *Chips: The Diaries of Sir Henry Channon* (ed. Robert Rhodes James), Weidenfeld & Nicolson, 1967

COOPER, Diana: *The Light of Common Day*, Rupert Hart-Davis, 1959

COWARD, Noël: *The Noël Coward Diaries* (ed. Graham Payn and Sheridan Morley), Weidenfeld & Nicolson, 1982

DONALDSON, Frances: *Edward VIII*, Weidenfeld & Nicolson, 1974

LAHIRI, V. C.: *The Prince of Wales's Complete Tour of India and Burma*, Ratan Press (Delhi) 1922. India Office Library ref. T.37227

LAWFORD, Valentine: *Vogue's Book of Houses, Gardens, People*, Condé Nast Publications, 1963

LOWNDES, Mary Belloc: *Diaries and Letters*, Chatto & Windus, 1977

MACKENZIE, Compton: *The Windsor Tapestry*, Rich & Cowan, 1938

MOSLEY, Diana: *The Duchess of Windsor*, Sidgwick & Jackson, 1980

NICOLSON, Harold: *Diaries and Letters, 1930–1939*, Collins, 1966

SHAH, L. D.: *The Prince of Wales and the Princes of India*, Vols I and II, Rajkot, 1923. India Office Library ref. W.3048

TIMES OF INDIA: *The Prince in India, 1921–1922*, Bombay, 1922. India Office Library ref. W.5811

TOWNSEND, W. and L.: *The Biography of HRH The Prince of Wales*, Albert E. Marriott & Son, 1929

VREELAND, Diana: *D.V.*, Weidenfeld & Nicolson, 1984

WINDSOR, The Duchess of: *The Heart Has its Reasons*, Michael Joseph, 1956

WINDSOR, The Duke of: *A King's Story, The Memoirs of the Duke of Windsor*, Putnam, New York, 1947

ZIEGLER, Philip: *Diana Cooper*, Hamish Hamilton, 1981

Queen Elizabeth the Queen Mother

ASQUITH, Lady Cynthia: *The Family Life of Queen Elizabeth*, Hutchinson, 1938

ASQUITH, Lady Cynthia: *Queen Elizabeth*, Hutchinson, 1937

BEATON, Cecil: *Self-Portrait with Friends* (ed. Richard Buckle), Weidenfeld & Nicolson, 1979

BOLITHO, Hector: *King George VI*, Eyre & Spottiswoode, 1937

CRAWFORD, Marion: *The Little Princesses*, Cassell, 1950

DUFF, DAVID: *Mother of the Queen*, Frederick Muller, 1965

King George and Queen Elizabeth Coronation Souvenir book, Allied Newspapers, 1937

LAIRD, Dorothy: *Queen Elizabeth the Queen Mother*, Hodder & Stoughton, 1966

LONGFORD, Elizabeth: *The Queen Mother, a Biography*, Weidenfeld & Nicolson, 1981

MORROW, Ann: *The Queen Mother*, Granada, 1984

Queen's Book of the Red Cross, The, Hodder & Stoughton, 1939

Royal Family in Wartime, The, Odhams Press, 1945

STUART, Dorothy: *King George the Sixth*, Harrap, 1937

WHEELER-BENNETT, John W.: *King George VI, His Life and Reign*, Macmillan, 1958

The Queen

AMIES, Hardy: *Still Here, An Autobiography*, Weidenfeld & Nicolson, 1984

CATHCART, Helen: *The Married Life of the Queen*, W. H. Allen, 1970

CRAWFORD, Marion: *Happy and Glorious!*, George Newnes, 1953

CRAWFORD, Marion: *Queen Elizabeth II*, George Newnes, 1952

DEAN, John: *HRH Prince Philip, A Portrait by His Valet*, Robert Hale, N.D.

HARTNELL, Norman: *Silver and Gold*, Evans, 1953

LACEY, Robert: *Majesty, Elizabeth II and the House of Windsor*, Hutchinson, 1977

LAIRD, Dorothy: *How the Queen Reigns*, Hodder & Stoughton, 1959

LONGFORD, Elizabeth: *Elizabeth R*, Weidenfeld & Nicolson, 1983

MORROW, Ann: *The Queen*, Granada, 1983

Queen Elizabeth Coronation Souvenir, 1953

TOWNSEND, Peter: *Time and Chance*, Collins, 1978

Diana, Princess of Wales

BATTISCOMBE, Georgina: *The Spencers of Althorp*, Constable, 1984

HOLDEN, Anthony: *Charles, Prince of Wales*, Weidenfeld & Nicolson, 1979

JUNOR, Penny: *Diana, Princess of Wales*, Sidgwick & Jackson, 1982
LACEY, Robert: *Princess*, Hutchinson, 1982
WALES, HRH The Prince of: *The Old Man of Lochnagar*, Hamish Hamilton, N.D.

Jewellery Books

Garrard, 1721–1911, Crown Jewellers and Goldsmiths during Six Reigns and in Three Centuries, Stanley Paul, 1912
GAUTIER, Gilberte: *Cartier, The Legend*, Arlington Books, 1983
HINKS, Peter: *Nineteenth-Century Jewellery*, Faber & Faber, 1975
HINKS, Peter: *Twentieth-Century British Jewellery, 1900–1980*, Faber & Faber, 1983
MICHAEL, Prince of Greece: *Crown Jewels of Britain and Europe*, J. M. Dent, 1983
MUNN, Geoffrey: *Castellani and Giuliano: Revivalist Jewellers of the Nineteenth Century*, Trefoil 1984
NADELHOFFER, Hans: *Cartier, Jewellers Extraordinary*, Thames & Hudson, 1984
SNOWMAN, A. Kenneth: *The Art of Carl Fabergé*, Faber & Faber, 1953
SCARISBRICK, Diana: *Jewellery*, Batsford, 1984
TAYLOR, Lou: *Mourning Dress, a Costume and Social History*, Allen & Unwin, 1983
TWINING, Lord: *History of the Crown Jewels of Europe*, Batsford, 1960
YOUNG, Sheila: *The Queen's Jewellery*, Ebury Press, 1968

General/Royal/Social/Biographical

ALICE, HRH Princess, Countess of Athlone: *For My Grandchildren*, Evans, 1966
BARWICK, Sandra: *A Century of Style*, Allen & Unwin, 1984
BENTLEY, Nicholas: *Golden Sovereigns*, Mitchell Beazley, 1970
DAY, J. Wentworth: *HRH Princess Marina, Duchess of Kent*, Robert Hale, 1962
EDGAR, Donald: *Palace*, W. H. Allen, 1983
FINESTONE, Jeffrey: *The Last Courts of Europe*, J. M. Dent, 1981
HICHENS, Phoebe: *All About the Royal Family*, Macmillan, N.D.
HOBSBAWM, Eric and Terence Ranger, eds.: *The Invention of Tradition*, Cambridge University Press, 1983
MORRIS, Constance Lily: *On Tour with Queen Marie*. Privately published, circa 1926
PRINGLE, Margaret: *Dance Little Ladies, The Days of the Débutante*, Orbis Publishing, 1977
SEEBOHM, Caroline: *The Man Who Was Vogue, The Life and Times of Condé Nast*, Weidenfeld & Nicolson, 1982
SOMERSET, Anne: *Ladies-in-Waiting, from the Tudors to the Present Day*, Weidenfeld & Nicolson, 1984

Source Notes

Chapter 1 Victoria: Private and Public

This chapter draws on unpublished information about Queen Victoria's purchases of jewellery, including details of stones, settings and prices, found in the Garrard ledger at the Victoria and Albert Museum, London. It covers the period of her reign from 1842 to 1901. Material from the Royal Archives (RA) is by gracious permission of Her Majesty The Queen.

Page 1
Quotation: Germain Bapst, *Le Maréchal Canrobert*, Part II, p. 517.
Para 1: ART OF LOCAL WIG-MAKER: Ibid., p. 510.
Para 2: ENGULFED BY A LARGE WHITE SILK HAT: Ibid, p. 513.
   LORD MELBOURNE: Viscount Esher. *The Girlhood of Queen Victoria*, Vol. II, p. 127.
Para 3: EMERALD SERPENT ENGAGEMENT RING: Sarah Tooley, *The Personal Life of Queen Victoria*, p. 105.
Para 4: WHITE DRESS ... EMBROIDERED GERANIUMS: Bapst, *Le Maréchal Canrobert*, p. 511 and following.

Page 2
Para 4: FRENCH CROWN JEWELS RESET: Hans Nadelhoffer, *Cartier, Jewellers Extraordinary*, p. 45.

Page 3
Para 3: BIRTHDAY PRESENT FROM 'UNCLE KING': Tooley, *Personal Life*, p. 21.
Para 4: PRINCESS VICTORIA OWED HER EXISTENCE ...: Elizabeth Longford, *Victoria RI*, pp. 17–40.

Page 4
Para 3: TOY CRIB WITH A CROWN: In State apartments, Kensington Palace.
   'MY OWN DEAREST, KINDEST FATHER: A. C. Benson and Viscount Esher (eds.), *Letters of Queen Victoria*, Vol. III, p. 473.
Para 4: 'OUR LITTLE PRINCESS': Longford, *Victoria RI*, p. 34.
Para 5: 'THE BREAKFAST ROOM IS MAGNIFICENT': Esher, *The Girlhood of Queen Victoria*, Vol. I, pp. 50–1.

Page 5
Para 2: SOLID GOLD EGG CUP: Sir Frederick Ponsonby, *Recollections of Three Reigns*, p. 74.
Para 3: 'FROM DEAR MAMMA ...': Esher, *The Girlhood of Queen Victoria*, Vol. I, p. 17.
Para 4: OUR ROYAL FAMILY CELEBRATE ...: Peter Townsend, *Time and Chance*, p. 162.
Para 5: RECORDED HER CHRISTMAS GIFTS: Esher, *The Girlhood of Queen Victoria*, Vol. I, p. 179.
Para 6: BRACELET MADE OF HER OWN HAIR: *Catalogue of Exhibition of Royal and Historic Treasures at 145 Piccadilly*, 1939, p. 75.
Para 7–Page 6, para 1: 'HARDLY BE TRUSTED TO CHOOSE A BONNET': Longford, *Victoria RI*, p. 104.

Page 6
Para 2: LUCRATIVE TRADE IN CROWNS: Vera Watson, *A Queen at Home*, p. 27.
Para 3: 'I HAD THE GREATEST DIFFICULTY ...': Esher, *The Girlhood of Queen Victoria*, Vol. I, p. 360.
Para 4: 'THE LOVELIEST MOMENT OF ALL': Sir Henry Channon, *Chips: Diaries*, p. 125.

Page 7
Para 1: 'AS THOU DOST THIS DAY ...': *The Times*, 29 June 1838.
Para 2: THE CORONATION DECORATIONS: Ibid.
Para 3: 'RESETTING THE DIAMONDS ...': Watson, *A Queen at Home*, p. 27.
Para 4 and following: SUMS WHICH QUEEN VICTORIA STARTED TO SPEND: Garrard ledger, Victoria and Albert Museum, London.

Page 9
Para 1: 'LOVED BY SUCH AN ANGEL': Christopher Hibbert, *Victoria, a Biography*, p. 55.
Para 3: GAVE ALBERT A DIAMOND STAR: Esher, *The Girlhood of Queen Victoria*, Vol. II, p. 317.
Para 5: PINK AND WHITE INVITATION CARDS: *The Times*, 11 February 1840.
Para 7: SHE LEFT IT TO ARTHUR, DUKE OF CONNAUGHT: Esher, *The Girlhood of Queen Victoria*, Vol. II, p. 318, note.

Page 10
Para 3: THE CROWN WAS AGAIN THE SYMBOL: *The Times*, 11 February 1840.
Para 4: PREDATORY EAGLE BROOCH: shown to author, June 1984.
Para 5: MODEL OF HER DEAD FATHER'S EYE: *Catalogue of Exhibition of Royal and Historic Treasures*, 1939, p. 75.

Page 11
Para 2: 'NO CHANCE OF TWO FOR SOME TIME': Roger Fulford (ed.), *Dearest Child, Letters between Queen Victoria and the Princess Royal, 1858–1861*, p. 147.
Para 5: 'AN UNCERTAINTY IN EVERYTHING EXISTING': Benson and Esher (eds.), *Selected Letters*, Vol. II, p. 183.
   INVESTING £1,400 ON A SUITE OF DIAMONDS: Garrard ledger, 16 August 1848.
Para 6: THE OLD DUKE OF WELLINGTON: *Garrard, 1721–1911, Crown Jewellers*, p. 103.

Page 13
Para 2: THE KOH-I-NOOR WAS SET LIKE A GIANT BLOOM: Garrard ledger, 1 April 1853.
Para 4: BETWEEN APRIL AND NOVEMBER: Garrard ledger.

Page 14
Para 2: TARTAN SPLENDOUR ... GERANIUM-EMBROIDERED DRESS: Daphne Bennett, *King without a Crown*, pp. 208, 281.

Para 4: WHO SENT A CASTELLANI BROOCH: In Victoria and Albert Museum.

BOTH THE QUEEN AND PRINCESS MARGARET: Geoffrey Munn, at Wartski Ltd, Castellani and Giuliano Exhibition, March 1984.

Para 5: 'MY BELOVED ONE GAVE ME . . .': RA, Queen Victoria's Journal, 10 February 1846.

Para 6: DISPUTE OVER JEWELLERY: RA, c.58/24.

Page 15
Para 2: THE CUMBERLAND DIAMOND: Lord Twining, *History of the Crown Jewels of Europe*, p. 371.

Para 4: 'I HEAR THE QUEEN OF HANOVER WEARS THE JEWELS': Fulford (ed.), *Dearest Child*, p. 200.

Para 7: A SERIES OF 'SCOTCH' TROPHIES: Garrard ledger.

Page 16
Para 2: QUEEN VICTORIA LEFT ALL THESE PIECES: Twining, *Crown Jewels of Europe*, p. 195.

Para 4: 'TO THE MEDICAL GENTLEMEN AT BERLIN': Garrard ledger.

Para 6: THE BIRTHDAY BOOK: Ponsonby, *Recollections of Three Reigns*, pp. 36–9.

Page 17
Para 2: ALL HER JEWELS WERE NOW IN ONYX: Garrard ledger.

Para 3: FIRST AND SECONDARY MOURNING: Lou Taylor, *Mourning Dress*, p. 224.

Page 20
Para 6: THE COURT JOURNAL REGISTER: Court Dress Collection Archives, Kensington Palace, London.

Page 21
Para 1: 'PRESENT A HEARSE-LIKE APPEARANCE': Victor Mallet (ed.), *Life with Queen Victoria – Marie Mallet's Letters*, extracted from Court Dress Collection Archives.

Para 2: THE COURT DRESS: Court Dress Collection Archives.

Para 5: GOLD HORSESHOE COLLAR STUDS: Garrard ledger.

Para 6: DECKED HERSELF OUT IN THESE INDIAN JEWELS: Longford, *Victoria RI*, p. 109.

Page 22
Para 1: 'LIST OF ARTICLES SENT . . .': John Raymond (ed.): *Queen Victoria's Early Letters*, p. 77.

Para 4: 'HAVE YOU SEEN THE SHAH?': Sir Frederick Ponsonby, *Sidelights on Queen Victoria*, pp. 118–28.

Page 23
Para 4: FLORENCE NIGHTINGALE . . . CRIMEAN BROOCH: *Garrard, 1721–1911*, p. 109.

Para 7: THE DEATH OF JOHN BROWN: Ponsonby, *Recollections of Three Reigns*, p. 96.

Page 24
Para 5: CZARINA ALEXANDRA . . . LADY LONDONDERRY: Diana Scarisbrick, 'Blazing Like the Sun', *Country Life*, 14 June 1984.

Page 25
Para 2: A SENSE OF REVERENCE: Ponsonby, *Recollections of Three Reigns*, p. 13.

Para 3: 'THE LOFTY VIEW OF HER OWN POSITION': Lytton Strachey, *Queen Victoria*, pp. 258–69.

CHAPTER 2: Imperial Alexandra

Georgina Battiscombe's *Queen Alexandra* provided an essential background. The vivid, detailed and lengthy reports in *The Times* brought the Prince of Wales's trip to India alive. The *Times of India* provided a fascinating counterpoint. The Archives of the Court

Dress Collection at Kensington Palace place Queen Alexandra in the social context of her era.

Page 27
Quotation: Fulford (ed.), *Dearest Child*, pp. 323, 342.

Para 2: 'RULED BY A SCEPTRE': Longford, *Victoria RI*, p. 627.
'GILDING FOR THEIR MONEY': Ibid.

Page 28
Para 1: 'THE SEA KING'S DAUGHTER': Battiscombe, *Queen Alexandra*, pp. 31–45.

Para 2: 'INDESCRIBABLE CHARMING': Fulford (ed.), *Dearest Child*, 4 June 1861, p. 313.

Para 5: 'THE MOTHER'S FAMILY ARE BAD . . .': Ibid., 25 February 1861.

Page 29
Para 1: WHITE SILK BONNET . . . MADE AT HOME: Philip Magnus, *King Edward VII*, pp. 42–59.

Para 4: 'I SHALL WEAR EXACTLY WHAT I LIKE': David Duff, *Alexandra Princess and Queen*, p. 215.

Page 30
Para 2: 'GRACIOUS WITHOUT SMILING': Battiscombe, *Queen Alexandra*, p. 54.

Para 3: '. . . HORRID RUSSIANS . . . SUCH A JEWEL': Fulford (ed.), *Dearest Child*, pp. 323, 342.

Para 4: BERTIE SPELLED THE GEMS: Sheila Young, *The Queen's Jewellery*, p. 52.

Para 5: PARURE OF DIAMONDS AND PEARLS: H. W. H. Russell, *Memorial of the Marriage of HRH Prince of Wales and HRH Princess Alexandra of Denmark*.

Page 31
Para 3: 'TAPERING WAIST . . .': *The Times*, 18 March 1863.

Para 5: CORNUCOPIA OF JEWELS . . .: Russell, *Memorial of the Marriage*.

Page 33
Para 6: 'TROUBLE TO WEAR . . .': Consuela Vanderbilt, *The Glitter and the Gold*, p. 152.

Page 34
Para 4: 'EVERYONE POINTS TO MY SIMPLICITY': Magnus, *Edward VII*, p. 152.

Pages 34–40
Summary of Indian tour
The Times, October 1875–March 1876, daily news reports.
The *Times of India*, ditto.
J. W. Allingham: 'Five Months with the Prince in India'.
J. Drew Gay: *From Pall Mall to the Punjab*.
W. Simpson: *Shikare and Tomasha*.
Julia A. Stone: *Illustrated India*.

Page 40
Para 5: PIERRE CARTIER . . . WAS SUMMONED: Nadelhoffer, *Cartier*, p. 157.

Page 41
Para 1: COLLIER RÉSILLE: Cartier Archives, Paris, 22 August 1904.

Para 4: 'BLACK MOUSSELINE DE SOIE': Diana Scarisbrick, *Jewellery*, p. 72.

MAHARAJAH OF PATIALA: Charles Allen and Sharada Dwivedi, *Lives of the Indian Princes*, p. 216.

Para 5: SERPENT BRACELET . . . THE QUEEN . . .' Private information to the author.

Page 42
Para 2: 'GARLAND' STYLE: Nadelhoffer, *Cartier*, pp. 45–65.
Para 4: VENETIAN FANCY-DRESS BALL: *The Times*, 23 July 1874.

Page 43
Para 3: HIGH COURT DRESS: *Lord Chamberlain's Regulations*, Archives, Court Dress Collection, Kensington.
Para 4: LADY VIOLET GREVILLE: extract from *The Gentlewoman in Society*, Archives, Court Dress Collection, Kensington.

Page 45
Para 3: 'WHEN WE ATTEND A DRAWING-ROOM. . .': I. F. Austin, 'Our Notebook', *Illustrated London News*, p. 186.
'A LITTLE OVERBORNE': James Pope-Hennessy, *Queen Mary*, p. 429.

Page 47
Para 2: 'DICKENS IN A CARTIER SETTING': Duke of Windsor, *A King's Story*, p. 52.

Page 48
Para 3: FRITZ PONSONBY . . . SILVER CIGARETTE CASE: Ponsonby, *Three Reigns*, pp. 219–20.
Para 7: SIDE BY SIDE IN THE LEDGER: Cartier Archives, 23 July 1901.

Page 49
Para 3: NEW CROWN MADE FOR QUEEN ALEXANDRA: Now in Museum of London.
Para 4: 'SELECTION OF FALSE JEWELLERY': Cecil Beaton, *Self-Portrait with Friends*, p. 266.

CHAPTER 3: Majestic Mary

James Pope-Hennessy's *Queen Mary* provided the background to this chapter. I am grateful to HM The Queen for graciously permitting me to study Queen Mary's Dress Book preserved in the Royal Archives at Windsor. My thanks also to a relative of Queen Mary's for information about the sale of Empress Marie's valuables and the story of Prince Frank of Teck and the Cambridge emeralds: both stories were confirmed from other sources.

Page 51
Quotation: Channon, *Chips: Diaries*, p. 177.
Para 1: PRINCESS LILIBET . . . SANDCASTLES: Pope-Hennessy, *Queen Mary*, p. 546.
Para 2: FABLED ROMANOV ROYAL COLLECTION: Ponsonby, *Recollections of Three Reigns*, pp. 336–40.
Para 5: STUNNED LONDON SOCIETY: Battiscombe, *Queen Alexandra*, p. 128.

Page 52
Para 2: MATCHLESS PEARLS TO A PAIR OF CHEAP CROOKS: *The Times*, 18 April 1923.
Para 6: RAY'S BARBERSHOP: Ian Vorres, *The Last Grand-Duchess*, illustration on p. 145.

Page 53
Para 2: 'ANYTHING THAT WAS NOT PAID WAS COMPENSATED FOR': Tikhon Koulikovsky to the author, 10 December 1984.
Paras 3–4: GURI KOULIKOVSKY . . . QUEEN SETTLED the debt: Private information to author, Paris, June 1984; Canada, December 1984; confirmed London, January 1985, primary source.
Para 6: GLITTERING DIAMOND TIARA: *List of Gifts on Marriage of HRH the Princess Elizabeth and Lt Philip Mountbatten*, November 1947.
Para 8: PRINCESS MARY ADELAIDE: Pope-Hennessy, *Queen Mary*, pp. 30–6.

Page 54
Para 2: SEVENTEEN HISTORIC ROYAL RINGS: Twining, *Crown Jewels of Europe*, p. 192.
Para 3: QUEEN MARY'S PRECISE WRITING: Crown Jeweller to author, 6 February 1984.
Para 4: DUCHESS OF CAMBRIDGE: Kenneth Rose, *King George V*, p. 30.
'I LIKE TO FEEL YOUR BIRTHDAY . . .': Pope-Hennessy, *Queen Mary*, p. 25.

Page 55
Para 2: 'NOW SHE HAS DRAWN THE FIRST PRIZE': Ibid., p. 215.

Page 56
Para 1: TWO JET TIARAS AND A BANDEAU: Viewed by author, Museum of London, December 1984.
Para 3: CLOCKWORK RITUAL OF THE GRAND-DUCAL COURTS: HRH Princess Marie Louise, *My Memories of Six Reigns*, p. 64.

Page 57
Para 3: MAY WAS A BRIDESMAID TO HER COUSIN: Pope-Hennessy, *Queen Mary*, p. 181.

Page 58
Para 6: THE DUKE OF YORK'S BRIDE: *Illustrated London News*, 15 July 1893.
LADY GERALDINE SOMERSET: Pope-Hennessy, *Queen Mary*, p. 270.

Page 60
Para 5: THE MAJOR ROYAL PRESENTS: *The Times*, 5 July 1893; *Illustrated London News*, 10 July 1893.

Page 62
Para 4: '. . . LADY YOUNGER THAN THEMSELVES': Queen Victoria to Duchess of Teck, Pope-Hennessy, *Queen Mary*, p. 292.

Page 63
Para 2: 'COMBINED COUNTIES PEARLS': Duchess of York to Duchess of Teck, Ibid., p. 287.
Para 3: 'NATTIER BLUE BROCADE . . .': Queen Mary's Dress Book, 'The Queen at Principal Functions, RA, GV CC 58.
Para 6: 'I AM DELIGHTED THAT THEY HAVE GOT THEIR KING GUARDED': Prince Frank of Teck, 21 December 1895, Pope-Hennessy, *Queen Mary*, p. 317.

Page 64
Para 1: . . . CENTRAL STONE . . . PLAIT OF DIAMONDS: Young, *The Queen's Jewellery*, p. 86.
Para 5: A SUMMONS TO 'THE LIBRARY': Duke of Windsor, *A King's Story*, p. 29.

Page 65
Para 3: GAVE THIS NECKLACE TO PRINCE HARRY'S WIFE: Duchess of Gloucester to the author, 13 November 1984.

Page 66
Para 2: 'SOUTIEN-GEORGES': Rose, *King George V*, p. 79.
Para 3: THREE THOUSAND AND TWENTY-FIVE CARATS: Twining, *Crown Jewels of Europe*, p. 184.
Para 7: 'RECHRISTENED AT THE AGE OF 43 . . . ALIX RETAINING . . . CROWN': Pope-Hennessy, *Queen Mary*, pp. 421–3.

Page 67
Para 6: Lady Kilmorey and Frank of Teck: Private information to author, December 1984; Ireland, 14 March 1985; Surrey, 21 March 1985.

Page 69
Para 4: PRINCE FRANK'S WILL WAS THEREFORE 'SEALED': Michael Nash, 'The Strange History of Royal Wills', unpublished paper, Cambridge 1984.
Para 6: QUEEN MARY STARTED TO KEEP A BOOK: Queen Mary's Dress Book, 22 June 1911, RA, GV CC 58.

Page 70
Para 1: THE LISTINGS CONTINUE IN LOVING DETAIL: Ibid., 30 June 1911; Ibid., 24 June 1911; Ibid., 8 September 1911.
Para 2: THE NEW IMPERIAL CROWN OF INDIA: Twining, *Crown Jewels of Europe*, p. 169; Rose, *King George V*, p. 133.
Para 3: ORIENTAL MAGNIFICENCE OF THE TENT CITY: *The Times*, 8 December 1911.

Page 71
Para 1: 'FIRST WAS THE NIZAM . . . VERY PUT OUT': Allen and Dwivedi, *Lives of the Indian Princes*, p. 210.
Para 3: WILLIAM BELL OF GARRARD: Crown Jeweller to author, 13 July 1984.
Para 4: MAHARAJAH OF PATIALA: Nadelhoffer, *Cartier*, p. 180.
Para 5: '. . . THE JEWEL YOU HAVE GIVEN ME . . .': *The Times*, 11 December 1911.

Page 72
Para 2: 'DIAMOND COLLAR . . .': Dress Book, 12 December 1911, RA, GV CC 58.
Para 3: 'SHE ALSO WORE MATCHING CLOTHES . . .': Diana Vreeland, *D.V.*, p. 65.

Page 73
Para 2: THIS OSSIFICATION OF STYLE: Rose, *King George V*, p. 301.
'IS IT RAINING IN HERE?': Duke of Windsor, *A King's Story*, p. 83.
Para 4: LISTED HER JEWELS: Dress Book, 24 May 1913, RA, GV CC 58.
Para 6: THE CZAR WHO LOOKED LIKE GEORGIE'S TWIN: Rose, *King George V*, p. 209.

Page 74
Para 1: 'DOWAGERS AND DEBUTANTES HAD TO FACE . . .': *The Queen*, 7 June 1919; Court Dress Collection Archives, Kensington Palace.
Para 2: SHE WORE SKY BLUE CRÊPE-DE-CHINE: 5 July 1919, Court Dress Collection Archives, Kensington Palace.
Para 3: 'MY COUSIN MAY . . .': Channon, *Chips: Diaries*, p. 429.
Para 5: 'SCOTS IN THEIR TARTANS . . .': Vreeland, *D.V.*, p. 61.
Para 7: LADY CYNTHIA COLVILLE: Colville, *A Crowded Life*, p. 40, extracted in Court Dress Collection Archives.

Page 75
Para 5: THE GREAT HOUSES OF LONDON: Duke of Windsor, *A King's Story*, p. 165.
THE MARCHIONESS OF CAMBRIDGE: To the author, 12 December 1984.

Page 76
Para 3: 'SHE WAS GENEROUS IN SPIRIT . . .': Private information to the author, December 1984.
Para 4: A MINIATURE FABERGÉ ELEPHANT: Kenneth Snowman, *The Art of Carl Fabergé*, p. 148.
Para 5: QUEEN MARY'S DOLL'S HOUSE: HRH Princess Marie Louise, *My Memories of Six Reigns*, pp. 199–203.

Page 77
Para 1: PINK TOPAZ AND DIAMOND PENDANT: Pope-Hennessy, *Queen Mary*, p. 545.
Para 2: GRAND-DUCHESS VLADIMIR: Nadelhoffer, *Cartier*, pp. 117–20.

Page 79
Para 4: 'CAN I HAVE ONE TOO?': J. Wentworth Day, *HRH Princess Marina, Duchess of Kent*, p. 41.
Para 6: BERTIE STOPFORD: Ibid., pp. 54–5.

Page 80
Para 2: VLADIMIR EMERALDS . . .: Nadelhoffer, *Cartier*, p. 123.
Para 3: PRINCE YOUSSOUPOV: Ibid., p. 286.
Para 4: DAGMAR NECKLACE . . .: Crown Jeweller to the author, July 1984.

Page 81
Para 2: '. . . FELT VERY SAD AT PARTING': Pope-Hennessy, *Queen Mary*, p. 566.
Para 3: JET DIADEMS: Amanda Herries, Museum of London, to the author, 18 December 1984.

CHAPTER 4: The Wallis Collection

I am grateful to Michael Bloch for his help and encouragement and to Cartier, Paris, for the opportunity to study the archives.

Page 83
Quotation: Joe Bryan III and Charles Murphy, *The Windsor Story*, p. 577.
Paras 1–4: THEFT OF JEWELS: *The Times*, 18 October 1946.
Para 3: FEROCIOUS PANTHER RAMPANT: Nadelhoffer, *Cartier*, p. 331.

Page 84
Para 1: LAWYER THEODORE GODDARD: Frances Donaldson, *Edward VIII*, p. 287.
Para 2: DIANA COOPER HAD DINED . . . EMERALD CUNARD . . .: Channon, *Chips: Diaries*, pp. 43, 77.
DRESSMAKER'S EMERALDS: Marie Belloc Lowndes, *Diaries and Letters*, p. 144.
Para 3: THE DIARIES OF THE WITTY . . .: Channon, *Chips: Diaries*, p. 84.
Para 5: STOLEN JEWELLERY LIST: *The Times*, 19 October 1946.

Page 85
Para 1: 'WALLIS COLLECTION': Beaton, *Selected Diaries*, pp. 48–9.
Para 3: FLAMINGO BROOCH: Cartier Archives, Paris, 4 March 1940.
IMPORTANT JEWELLED BIRD: Ibid., 25 February 1946.
Para 4: CHOKER OF AMETHYSTS AND TURQUOISE: Joe Bryan III to author, 12 March 1984.
Para 5: DIAMOND BALL EARRINGS: Cartier Archives, Paris, March 1940.

Page 87
Para 1: AQUAMARINE FLOWER CLIPS: Ibid., 31 December 1936.
Para 2: FIRST SHOWED HER LOVE OF AQUAMARINES: Popperfoto Archive.

Page 88
Para 2: BLUE-GREEN FEATHER: Bryan and Murphy, *The Windsor Story*, p. 9.

Page 89
Para 2: HER HEIRLOOM GIFT FROM THE KING OF DENMARK: Russell, *Memorial to the Marriage of HRH Prince of Wales and HRH Princess Alexandra of Denmark*.
Para 3: FAVOURITE DISH WAS SALMON . . .: Chef James Viane to author, March 1984.
Para 6: MASSIVE PENDANT EMERALDS: *Times of India*, 1875–6. See Chapter 2.

Page 90
Para 1: COLLIER RÉSILLE . . . EMERALD AND DIAMOND CHOKER: Cartier Archives, Paris, 22 August 1904; 30 November 1907.

Para 2: EARLIER MISTRESS . . . SELLING BACK: Bond Street jeweller to author, November 1984.

Para 4: EMERALD AND DIAMOND CHARM: Bryan and Murphy, *The Windsor Story*, p. 94.

Para 5: 'CRESCENDO OF GORGEOUSNESS': *Times of India*, 24–8 November, 5 December 1921.

Page 91

Para 2: 'I FEEL I AM DOING NO GOOD . . .': Duke of Windsor, *A King's Story*, p. 173.

Para 3: HEAVY GOLD CHAIN: *Statesman* (India), 24 November 1921.

Para 5: SAPPHIRE BLUE DEEP PILE VELVET BOOK: L. D. Shah, *The Prince of Wales and the Princes of India*, p. 75.

Page 94

Para 2: LADY DIANA COOPER: To author, 8 February 1984.

Para 5: 'HE GIVES MRS SIMPSON . . .': Mabell, Countess of Airlie, *Thatched with Gold*, p. 198.

Para 7: SCRAPBOOK IN THE BILLIARD ROOM: Viewed by author, Polesden Lacey, January 1985.
'COVERED WITH JEWELS': Channon, *Chips: Diaries*, p. 328.

Para 2: Bennett's letter: Polesden Lacey scrapbook.

Para 4: BILLS FROM CARTIER . . . MAÎTRE SUZANNE BLUM TODAY: Private information to author, November 1984.

Para 5: 'SOMETHING MUST BE DONE . . .': Donaldson, *Edward VIII*, p. 253.

Page 96

Para 1: 'ROOM SEEMED TO SWAY WITH JEWELS': Channon, *Chips: Diaries*, p. 83.

Para 3: CRUISE ON THE NÄHLIN: Private information to the author, written proof, November 1984.
MADAME TUSSAUD'S: Bryan and Murphy, *The Windsor Story*, p. 299.

Para 4: FOUR REGAL DINNER SERVICES: Valentine Lawford, *Vogue's Book of Houses, Gardens, People*, p. 184.
FORTNUM AND MASON: Ginette Spanier to the author, 2 January 1985.

Para 5: 'BLAZING WITH RINGS . . .': Bryan and Murphy, *The Windsor Story*, p. 498.
LINGERIE . . . FORT BELVEDERE: Vreeland, *D.V.*, p. 69.

Para 6: PHONE CALL FROM THE PRINCE: Marchioness of Cambridge to the author, 12 December 1984.

Page 97

Para 2: 'DAMNABLE WEDDING PRESENT': Bryan and Murphy, *The Windsor Story*, p. 341.
'THREE STONES INTO A POOL': Harold Nicolson, *Diaries and Letters*, p. 352.

Para 3: 'I JUST LOVE YOUR PANSIES': Comment to author, Paris, January 1985.

Para 4: 'NEVER QUITE ENOUGH': Lady Diana Cooper to author, 8 February 1984.
'LIKE OPERA BOXES': Diana Vreeland to author, 10 January 1985.

Para 5: WEARING HER PARURE OF SAPPHIRES: Ibid.
MRS SIMPSON TO QUEEN OLGA: Channon, *Chips: Diaries*, p. 81.

Page 98

Para 2: LADY DIANA COOPER REMEMBERS: To author, 8 February 1984.

Para 3: DID NOT CONTAIN HUGE GEMS: Close associate of the Duchess of Windsor, to the author, Paris, November 1984.
'WALLIS WEARING COSTUME JEWELLERY': Diana Vreeland to the author, January 1985.

Para 5: JEANNE TOUSSAINT'S FLAT: Gilberte Gautier, *Cartier, The Legend*, p. 210.

Page 99

Para 1: FIRST OF THE GREAT TOUSSAINT PANTHERS: Cartier Archives, Paris, 29 October 1948; 28 January 1949.

Para 2: 'DICKENS IN A CARTIER SETTING': Duke of Windsor, *A King's Story*, p. 52.
'WHAT DOES CHRISTMAS MEAN TO YOU NOW?': Bryan and Murphy, *The Windsor Story*, p. 528.

Para 3: SENSUAL SERPENT . . . STYLISED STRAWBERRIES: Gilberte Gautier to author, 27 March 1984.

Page 100

Para 2: 'TO HAVE HAD THE CURIOSITY': Maître Lecuyer to author, March 1985.

Para 4: LADY MONCKTON PROMISED . . .: Bryan and Murphy, *The Windsor Story*, p. 568.

Para 5: LADY PAMELA BERRY: Hardy Amies to the author, 16 October 1984.

Para 6: DEATH OF THE PRINCESS ROYAL: Christie's Catalogue, 29 June 1966.

Page 101

Para 2: JEWELLERY . . . SOLD IN ENGLAND: Bond Street jeweller to author, December 1984.

Para 3: 'JOLLY GOOD THING . . .': Lady Cambridge to author, 12 December 1984.

Page 102

Para 2: LORD TWINING: Twining Papers, Goldsmith's Hall Library, London.

CHAPTER 5: The Pearly Queen

Page 105

Quotation: Beaton, *Selected Diaries*, p. 69.

Para 2: VISION OF VICTORIANA: Norman Hartnell: *Silver and Gold*, pp. 95–100.

Para 3: ALL THE GREAT DRESSES: Shown to author at Clarence House, 15 February 1985.

Page 106

Para 2: 'MUMMIE WILL GIVE IT BACK': Private information to author, 7 December 1984.

Para 3: HER FAVOURITE BROOCH: Dorothy Laird, *Queen Elizabeth the Queen Mother*, photograph facing p. 208.

Page 107

Para 6: 'BIG DRESSING': Member of the royal family to author, Kensington Palace, 21 March 1984.

Page 108

Para 1: DEW-DROP DIAMONDS: Hartnell, *Silver and Gold*, pp. 90–1.

Para 2 and following: WEDDING PRESENTS: *The Times*, 13/14/21 April 1923.

Para 6: 'FOR LADY ELIZABETH . . .': Ann Morrow, *The Queen Mother*, p. 38.

Page 109

Para 3: THE WEDDING WAS . . . A FEAST OF SPLENDOUR: *The Times*, 26 April 1923.

Page 112

Para 1: WHITE SILK BAG: Clarence House, 15 February 1985.

Para 2: MRS RONALD GREVILLE: Information from Polesden Lacey, 7 March 1985.

Para 3: 'WONDERFUL DIAMONDS': *Sunday Times*, 16 April 1937.

Para 5: SHE HAD RECEIVED SOME SPLENDID GIFTS: *The Times*, 17 April 1923.

Page 113
Para 2: THE ROYAL TROUSSEAU: Ibid., 14 April 1923.
Para 6: ROMP WITH THEIR LITTLE GIRLS: Marion Crawford, *The Little Princesses*, p. 25.

Page 114
Para 2: '... KNOW WHEN NOT TO SMILE': Beaton, *Selected Diaries*, p. 69.
Para 4: 'OUR ... INDUSTRIOUS PRINCE': *The Times*, 26 April 1923.
Para 5: NEW-FANGLED AMERICAN STATION WAGON: Duchess of Windsor, *The Heart has its Reasons*, p. 225.

Page 115
Para 2: CHINTZY CHAIRS ...: Lady Cynthia Asquith: *The Family Life of Queen Elizabeth*, pp. 32–8.
Para 5: '... DRESS LIKE AUNT MARINA': Crawford, *The Little Princesses*, p. 54.
Para 6: TO PERCH A TIARA DIRECTLY ON THE CROWN: Member of royal family to author, Kensington Palace, March 1984.

Page 116
Para 3: 'TO GARRARD'S TO SEE ...': Pope-Hennessy, *Queen Mary*, p. 585.
Para 4: THE KOH-I-NOOR WAS ALSO PUT INTO THE NEW CROWN: Twining, *Crown Jewels of Europe*, p. 169.

Page 117
Para 1: 'THAT WAS AN OPERETTA': Channon, *Chips: Diaries*, p. 119.
Para 2: 'FLASH OF LIGHT': Duke of Windsor, *A King's Story*, p. 269.
Para 3: 'FELT VERY SAD AT PARTING': Pope-Hennessy, *Queen Mary*, p. 566.
Para 4: IN 1937 SHE REMOVED TWO STONES: Twining, *Crown Jewels of Europe*, p. 191.
Para 5: THE REGAL TIARA IN AN INDIAN DESIGN: Garrard ledger, Victoria and Albert Museum, 1 April 1853.

Page 119
Para 1: 'THE CHOICE ISN'T VERY GREAT': Beaton, *Selected Diaries*, p. 69.
Para 2: QUEEN VICTORIA'S LIST ...: Twining Papers, Goldsmith's Hall.
Para 6: STUFFED INTO LEATHER HATBOXES: Crawford, *The Little Princesses*, p. 72.

Page 121
Para 1: '... SIDEWAYS, LILTING WALK': Channon, Chips: Diaries, p. 438.
'SHAPED AS A PLAYING CARD': *The Tatler*, 18 December 1940.
Para 2: BY THE NEXT ASCOT: Channon, *Chips: Diaries*, p. 446.
Para 4: AN IMPRESSIVE UNSET MARQUISE DIAMOND: *Marriage of Princess Elizabeth Catalogue of Gifts*, November 1947.

Page 122
Para 3: QUEEN MARY'S MAGNIFICENT PRESENTS ...: Ibid.
Para 4: 'THE BABY WAS SO SWEET ...': Elizabeth Longford, *The Queen Mother*, p. 36.

Page 123
Para 4: THE CARTIER TIARA: Nadelhoffer, *Cartier*, pp. 68, 241.
Para 6: INTERNATIONAL EXHIBITION OF MODERN JEWELLERY: David Duff, *Mother of the Queen*, p. 279.

Page 125
Para 1: TINY WATCH GIVEN ... BY THE FRENCH: Laird, *Queen Elizabeth*, p. 304.
Para 2: CASTLE OF MEY: Morrow, *The Queen Mother*, p. 147; Longford, *The Queen Mother*, p. 122.

ROYAL LODGE AT WINDSOR: Duff, *Mother of the Queen*, p. 275.
Para 3: 'A GREAT CLEAR OUT': Courtier to the author, 11 December 1984.
Para 4: THAT YEAR OF THE BABIES: Duff, *Mother of the Queen*, p. 293.

Page 126
Para 1: MABELL, COUNTESS OF AIRLIE: Airlie, *Thatched with Gold*, p. 236.
Para 3: GREEK FAMILY TRADITION: Hardy Amies to author, 14 December 1984.
Para 4: 'PRINCESS ALEXANDRA AND THE DUCHESS OF KENT ...': Bryan and Murphy, *The Windsor Story*, p. 566.
Para 5: DUCHESS OF GLOUCESTER IS HEIR: Duchess of Gloucester to author, 13 November 1984.

Page 127
Para 2: LASCELLES BOYS: Evelyn Graham, *Princess Mary, Viscountess Lascelles*, p. 234.
Para 3: THE SALE OF THE PRINCESS ROYAL'S JEWELS: Christie's Catalogue, 29 June 1966.
Para 6: '... SUCH A GIFT FOR GIVING PLEASURE': Private information to the author, December 1984.

CHAPTER 6: The Queen of Diamonds

Page 131
Quotation: Crawford, *The Little Princesses*, p. 26.
Paras 1–3: HOW MANY CROWNS: Twining, *Crown Jewels of Europe*; Twining Papers, Goldsmith's Hall; Young, *The Queen's Jewellery*; The Lord Chamberlain's Office, 'A List of Personal Jewels'; A. C. Mann, 'Her Majesty's Personal Jewels', *The Queen*, 17 November 1954; 'The Queen's Jewels', *Housewife*, February 1961; Private information to the author.

Page 132
Para 3: 'IN NO PRACTICAL SENSE ...': Select Committee 1971, quoted in Robert Lacey, *Majesty*, p. 387.
'HEAVEN AND BOBO MACDONALD': Member of Lord Chamberlain's Office to author, March 1984.
Para 4: 'LOOKED LIKE A VIKING': Crawford, *The Little Princesses*, p. 108.
PHILIP ANTROBUS: Young, *The Queen's Jewellery*, p. 34.
Para 8: 'IF ONLY I HAD THE TIME': Marchioness of Cambridge to the author, 12 December 1984.
Para 9: FAVOURITE NECKLACE ... JUBILEE: Twining, *Crown Jewels of Europe*, p. 194.

Page 133
Para 2: 'I GAVE THEM MY BEST BITS': Private information, October 1984.
Para 5: 'IT IS A FASCINATING NECKLACE': *The Royal Family*, BBC TV, 1969.
Para 7: 'THAT WILL GO WITH THE CAMBRIDGE EMERALDS': Royal dressmaker to author, October 1984.
Para 8: LADYBIRD BROOCH: Crawford, *The Little Princesses*, p. 26.

Page 136
Para 2: 'SHE REALLY DOES ENJOY HER JEWELS NOW': To author, January 1985.
TIARA DESIGNED BY GARRARD: Crown Jeweller to author, March 1984.
Para 3: 'FLUFF OF THISTLEDOWN': Anne Ring, *The Story of Princess Elizabeth*, quoted in Lacey, *Majesty*, p. 60.
Para 4: PROPER PRINCESS PARTY DRESSES: Crawford, *The Little Princesses*, p. 18.

Para 5: SAME GOLD COLLAR STUD: Lacey, *Majesty*, p. 42.
NORMAN HARTNELL MADE GIRLISH CONFECTIONS: Hartnell, *Silver and Gold*, p. 90,
HANGING ON TO THEIR PETTICOATS: Crawford, *The Little Princesses*, p. 24.
Para 6: 'THEY ARE SO YOUNG': Crawford, *The Little Princesses*, pp. 40–4.

Page 137
Para 2: 'UNSPOILT CHILDISHNESS OF THE SMILE': Beaton, *Selected Diaries*, pp. 253–9.
Para 3: TWELVE-YEAR-OLD-PRINCESS VICTORIA: Longford, *Victoria RI*, p. 51.
Para 4: ON THAT SUNNY SPRING DAY: Marion Crawford, *Happy and Glorious!*, pp. 28–33.

Page 138
Para 1: PUT ON A TIARA: Colville, *A Crowded Life*, p. 123, extracted in Court Dress Collection Archives, Kensington.
Para 4: HER BROOCHES WERE ALL FLOWERS: Young, *The Queen's Jewellery*, p. 25.

Page 139
Para 1: THE TOUR OF SOUTH AFRICA: Townsend, *Time and Chance*, p. 175.
Para 3: MISS MARY OPPENHEIMER: Photographic archives of de Beers.
Para 5: DR JOHN T. WILLIAMSON: Young, *The Queen's Jewellery*, p. 47.

Page 141
Para 1: 'DEVOTED TO YOUR SERVICE': Lacey, *Majesty*, pp. 177, 194, 198.
Para 3: SIR JOHN COLVILLE: Elizabeth Longford, *Elizabeth R*, p. 119.
Para 5: 'MILKY WAY': Hartnell, *Silver and Gold*, p. 113.
Para 6: THE ROYAL WEDDING PRESENT DISPLAY: *Catalogue of Wedding Gifts, November 1947*.

Page 142
Para 2: TWO SUPERB NECKLACES: Twining, *Crown Jewels of Europe*, p. 191.

Page 143
Para 2: THE NIZAM OF HYDERABAD: Nadelhoffer, *Cartier*, p. 77.
Para 3: THE PRESENTS FOR THIS ROYAL MARRIAGE: *Catalogue of Wedding Gifts*, November 1947.

Page 145
Para 2: PRINCESS ELIZABETH DANCED: Channon, *Chips: Diaries*, p. 425.

Page 146
Para 2: CROWN JEWELLER, CECIL MANN: 'Her Majesty's Personal Jewels', *The Queen*, 17 November 1954.

Page 147
Para 3: HARDY AMIES POINTS OUT IN MITIGATION: Amies to author, December 1984.
Para 6: CECIL BEATON ... SUSTAINING SANDWICHES: Beaton, *Selected Diaries*, p. 256.

Page 148
Para 2: 'DAMSON JAM OF THE VELVET': Hartnell, *Silver and Gold*, p. 132.

Page 149
Para 4: FADED LABELS IN QUEEN MARY'S HANDWRITING: Crown Jeweller to author, February 1984.

'I GAVE A PRESENT . . .': Pope-Hennessy, *Queen Mary*, p. 616.
INVENTORY OF JEWELS: Twining, *Crown Jewels of Europe*, pp. 189–96; Twining Papers, Goldsmith's Hall.

Page 151
Para 5: KING EDWARD VII ACCEPTED: Ibid., p. 185.

Page 152
Para 1: LANDING AT TONGA: Lacey, *Majesty*, p. 260.
LIFTED HER PEARLS FROM HER BARE NECK: Longford, *Elizabeth R*, p. 169.
Para 2: 'TOO KIND': Morrow, *The Queen*, p. 176.
Para 4: AMIR OF BAHRAIN: Postcard seen by author, December 1984.

Page 154
Para 3: GOLD SWORD: Morrow, *The Queen*, p. 182.

Page 155
Para 2: 'SO THAT'S WHAT HAY LOOKS LIKE': Pope-Hennessy, *Queen Mary*, p. 598.
Para 3: 'MINDFUL OF THE CHURCH'S TEACHING': Lacey, *Majesty*, p. 291.
Para 4: 'I'M FOR IT': Longford, *Elizabeth R*, p. 290.

Page 157
Para 2: 'WHEN SHE HAS LOST THE BLOOM OF YOUTH': Lacey, *Majesty*, p. 318.
Para 5: 'IT IS YOURS AND MINE': Crawford, *The Little Princesses*, p. 26.

CHAPTER 7: Princess of Jewels

I am grateful to all those people who helped me with this chapter. I quote no source which betrays a confidence or indiscretion.

Page 159
Quotation: HRH The Prince of Wales, *The Old Man of Lochnagar*.
Para 1: LOOKING FOR A PRESENT: Private information to the author.
Para 3: THE COMMISSION WAS COMPLETED: Lexi Dick to author, December 1982.
Para 4: THESE YOUNG DESIGNERS: Leo de Vroomen to author, 13 February 1985; Wendy Ramshaw to author, January 1985; David Thomas to author, November 1984.

Page 161
Para 3: PRINCE CHARLES'S 'OFFICIAL' JEWELLERS: Fourteenth Supplement to *The London Gazette*, 28 December 1984. See Appendix D.

Page 162
Para 2: ANOTHER QUEEN MARY HEIRLOOM: Crown Jeweller to author, 28 November 1984.
COMBINED COUNTIES: *Garrard, 1721–1911*, p. 114.
Para 3: 'GOD GRANT THAT THIS YEAR . . .': Pope-Hennessy, *Queen Mary*, p. 482.
Para 5: A SET OF GARTER INSIGNIA: *Garrard, 1721–1911*, pp. 117–48.
Para 6: GRAND-DUCHESS VLADIMIR: Nadelhoffer, *Cartier*, p. 78.

Page 163
Para 2: LES JOYAUX DU TRESOR DE RUSSIE: Viewed by author at Wartski Ltd.
Para 3: CORNER OF A NEWS PICTURE: See photograph, 'The Tale of a Tiara', pp. 164–5.

Page 167
Para 4: GOLD CAMEL BROOCH: Jane Sarginson to author, January 1985.

Para 5: SEVENTH BIRTHDAY PARTY: Georgina Battiscombe, *The Spencers of Althorp*, p. 259.
Para 6: CROWN PRINCE AND PRINCESS OF JORDAN: Embassy of Hashemite Kingdom to the author, 12 January 1983.

Page 168
Para 3: THE NECKLACE WAS GIVEN TO PRINCESS DIANA BY THE QUEEN: Private information to author, July 1984.

Page 169
Para 3: PREVIOUS ROYAL BRIDES HAD THE DETAILS . . .: *The Times*, 17 April 1923.
Para 4: ROYAL HAIRDRESSER KEVIN SHANLEY: *Sunday Mirror*, 3 February 1985.
Para 6: 'THE 1ST EVENING AT DINNER . . .': Pope-Hennessy, *Queen Mary*, p. 287.

Page 170
Para 2: THE LOOSE GEMSTONES: Twining Papers, Goldsmith's Hall.
Para 3: PRINCE CHARLES VISITED BOTSWANA: Diplomat to author, November 1984.
Para 5: DAUGHTERS-IN-LAW . . . RESET TO THEIR OWN TASTES: Shirley Bury to author, December 1982.

Page 172
Para 3: PRINCESS MARGARET . . . OUTDATED TIARA: Lord Snowdon to author, 26 July 1984.
Para 5: FIRST DRAUGHT OF ROYAL PAGEANTRY: Anthony Holden, *Charles, Prince of Wales*, p. 161.

Page 173
Para 1: 'THE FABULOUS CAIRNGORM AND AMETHYST CHANDELIER': HRH The Prince of Wales, *The Old Man of Lochnagar*.

Illustration Credits

Colour Pictures

Princess Alexandra wearing the drop pearl brooch, painted by Winterhalter. HM The Queen
Queen Victoria's wedding present to Princess Alexandra. W. H. Russell, 'Memorial'
The Dagmar necklace from the King of Denmark. W. H. Russell, 'Memorial' Courtesy of the Royal Borough of Kensington and Chelsea Libraries and Arts Service
The Queen wearing the Dagmar necklace in Denmark in 1957. Photo Source
Fabulous Indian emerald girdle. HM The Queen
Maharajah Dhuleep Singh's bouquet holder. W. H. Russell, 'Memorial'
Princess Alexandra, painted by Sir Luke Fildes in 1889. National Portrait Gallery
The Fabergé cigarette case given to Edward VII by Mrs Keppel. HM The Queen
Queen Mary wearing the diamond circle tiara, painted by Elwes. HM The Queen
Queen Mary's Dress Book. HM The Queen
Queen Mary on Coronation Day 1911 painted by Henry Macbeth Raeburn in 1918, after Sir William Llewellyn PRA. By kind permission of the House of Lords
Queen Mary wearing the bow-knot tiara, painted by Arthur G. Nowell. Courtesy of The Royal Pavilion, Art Gallery and Museums, Brighton
The Duchess of Windsor wearing the flamingo brooch given to her by the Duke. Popperfoto
The ledger sheet showing the jewels used in the flamingo brooch. Courtesy of Cartier, Paris

The Duchess of Windsor wearing her panther's head brooch. Rex Features
The ledger sheet showing the price of the cabochon sapphire for the Duchess's panther brooch. Courtesy of Cartier, Paris
The Duchess of Windsor wearing the panther brooch. Rex Features
The panther set. Courtesy of Cartier, Paris

The Queen Mother wearing Princess Alexandra's diamond and pearl necklace, photographed by Norman Parkinson. Camera Press
Princess Alexandra's necklace. W. H. Russell 'Memorial'
Lady Elizabeth Bowes Lyon painted by Savely Sorine. Reproduced by gracious permission of Her Majesty Queen Elizabeth The Queen Mother
Queen Elizabeth painted by Sir Gerald Kelly in 1938. National Portrait Gallery
The Queen and the Queen Mother wearing tiaras at the Hampton Court Banquet in 1982. Syndication International
The Queen Mother wearing the three strand pearl necklace, photographed by Norman Parkinson. Camera Press

The Queen Mother wearing the Jubilee brooch. Tim Graham
Princess Michael of Kent wearing Princess Marina's diamond tiara, photographed by Anthony Crickmay. Camera Press
Princess Marina of Greece wearing the diamond tiara, photographed by Dorothy Wilding. Camera Press
The Duchess of Gloucester wearing the diamond and turquoise suite, photographed by John Swannell. Camera Press
Princess Margaret photographed by Lord Snowdon. Camera Press
Princess Anne photographed by Norman Parkinson. Camera Press

The Queen glittering with diamonds. Camera Press
The young Queen wearing the diamond flower petal brooch. Camera Press
The Queen wearing her 'happy brooch'. Photographers International
The Queen wearing Queen Mary's heart-shaped brooch. Tim Graham
The Williamson pink diamond brooch. Courtesy of Cartier, Paris
A corgi brushing past the Cullinan brooch, photographed by Karsh of Ottawa. Camera Press
The Queen wearing the Russian fringe tiara in Finland 1976. Anwar Hussein
The Queen wearing the Cambridge Emeralds, photographed by Les Wilson. Camera Press
The Crown amethysts. Anwar Hussein
The Queen wearing the fringe necklace given by King Faisal. Tim Graham
The Coronation aquamarines given by the President of Brazil. Anwar Hussein
The Queen receiving a gift from Sheikh Isa Bin Sulman al Khalifa, Amir of Bahrain. Tim Graham
Exchanging gifts with Sheikh Rashid of Dubai in 1979. Tim Graham

The Princess of Wales wearing the Queen's wedding present to her. Tim Graham
Princess Diana wearing her koala charm bracelet. Anwar Hussein
Princess Diana wearing the 'William' medallion. Anwar Hussein
The Princess's engagement ring. Tim Graham
The Princess of Wales wearing Queen Mary's cabochon emerald choker. Courtesy of the GLC Photographic Unit/Festival Hall
The Princess wearing the multi-strand pearl choker. Tim Graham
The choker from the Crown Prince of Saudi Arabia's suite. Anwar Hussein
The Saudi sapphire pendant worn with a specially designed dress. Tim Graham
The Princess wearing the Spencer tiara. Tim Graham
The Princess's drop pearl and diamond earrings. Photographers International

Index